Queering Mennonite Literature

Queering
Mennonite Literature

Archives, Activism, and the Search for Community

Daniel Shank Cruz

The Pennsylvania State University Press
University Park, Pennsylvania

Library of Congress Cataloging-in-
Publication Data

Names: Cruz, Daniel Shank, 1980– author.
Title: Queering Mennonite literature :
archives, activism, and the search for
community / Daniel Shank Cruz.
Description: University Park, Pennsylvania :
The Pennsylvania State University Press,
[2019] | Includes bibliographical references
and index.
Summary: "Examines the ways queer theory
and Mennonite literature have intersected
over the past decade and how these two
traditions hold fundamental commitments
to social justice in common"—Provided by
publisher.
Identifiers: LCCN 2018045234 | ISBN
9780271082455 (cloth : alk. paper)
Subjects: LCSH: Canadian
literature—Mennonite authors—History and
criticism. | American literature—Mennonite
authors—History and criticism. | Queer
theory.
Classification: LCC PR9188.2.M45 C78 2019 |
DDC 810.9/382897—dc23
LC record available at
https://lccn.loc.gov/2018045234

The Pennsylvania State University Press is
a member of the Association of University
Presses.

It is the policy of The Pennsylvania State
University Press to use acid-free paper.
Publications on uncoated stock satisfy
the minimum requirements of American
National Standard for Information
Sciences—Permanence of Paper for Printed
Library Material, ANSI Z39.48-1992.

This book is dedicated to my parents with love.

Contents

Acknowledgments

Many people have helped make *Queering Mennonite Literature: Archives, Activism, and the Search for Community* a reality. As the book argues, healthy community is both a queer and a Mennonite ideal. I have experienced this kind of community throughout the duration of my project.

First, huge thanks are due to Ervin Beck, Jeff Gundy, Ann Hostetler, Julia Spicher Kasdorf, Royden Loewen, Jesse Nathan, Magdalene Redekop, Hildi Froese Tiessen, Paul Tiessen, and Robert Zacharias from the After Identity: Mennonite/s Writing in North America symposium at Penn State University in May 2013, where the seeds of this project were first planted. You all have been a wonderful, nurturing community of scholars in which to work.

In addition to the After Identity folks, major thanks to those of you who read and commented on part or all of the manuscript through the years of its gestation: Stephen Beachy, Jan Guenther Braun, Rachel Epp Buller, Christopher Castiglia, Sean Desilets, Matt Kruback, Corey Redekop, Natasha Sajé, Athena Thiessen, Jake Yoder, an anonymous peer reviewer, and especially Suzanne Richardson and Stephanie Selvick—thanks for helping me survive.

Thanks to my students who have discussed some of the books I investigate with me in various courses, especially Alison Brown, Sam Drake, James Gulick, Tatyana Lyubezhanina, Lauren Merritt, and Brooke Rando.

I am lucky to know many of the writers whose work I examine here. Thanks to all of you for your words, your support, and your friendship. Big-time thanks to Casey Plett for letting me read *Little Fish* in manuscript. I can't wait to write more about it!

To my Menno House peeps, thanks always for the best two years of my life. Chapter 2 is for you.

For various other kinds of support, thanks to Kelsie Baab, Bella the cat, the late Scott Cameron, Christina Cruz, Jesus Cruz, Miriam Cruz, Tony DiSanto, Kandis Friesen, Ibis Gomez-Vega, Andy Harnish, Rachel Holtz, Jim Giles, Wanda Giles, Joe Kotva, Christina Marrocco, Nan the cat, Elsie Neufeld, the NIU Book Coalition!, Hannah Ruszala, and Sofia Samatar.

Thanks to M. L. DeLaFleur and the rest of the Utica College Interlibrary Loan Department for fulfilling my many research requests with speed and congeniality, and thanks to the Utica College Copy Center staff for their professionalism and hard work.

Thanks to Kathryn Yahner, Hannah Hebert, Bradley Cox, and the rest of the team at Penn State University Press for believing in this project and helping it come to fruition.

Parts of this manuscript have been published in somewhat different form. The introduction and chapters 2 and 6 draw from "Queering Mennonite Literature," in *After Identity: Mennonite Writing in North America*, edited by Robert Zacharias (University Park: Pennsylvania State University Press, 2015), 143–58. Chapter 1 draws from "Archiving Queer Space in *Widows of Hamilton House*," in *11 Encounters with Mennonite Fiction*, edited by Hildi Froese Tiessen (Winnipeg: Mennonite Literary Society, 2017), 103–18; and "The Queer Call of Wes Funk," in the *Journal of Mennonite Studies* 36 (2018): 101–15. Chapter 4 draws from "Stephen Beachy's *boneyard*, the *Martyrs Mirror*, and Anabaptist Activism," in *Mennonite Life* 70 (2016): https://ml.bethelks .edu/issue/vol-70/article/stephen-beachys-boneyard-the-martyrs-mirror-and -an/. Thanks to the editors of these publications for both their feedback on these pieces and their willingness to let them be reproduced here. Major thanks to Rob for suggesting that there might be a book to be made out of them and to Ann H. for the conversation that helped me see how the book might come into being.

Miki, note 17 of chapter 5 is for you. Mwah!

x

Introduction

Queering Mennonite Literature

In Jan Guenther Braun's 2008 novel *Somewhere Else*, the protagonist, Jess, laments that "the words 'queer Mennonite' are an oxymoron."[1] While *Somewhere Else* offers a model for how these two seemingly opposed identities can coexist, and while this modeling is also present in an increasing number of other pieces of Mennonite literature, little has been done in the realm of Mennonite literary criticism to explore the tension between these two identities.[2] This lack is dangerous because, as the history of literary criticism on various minority literatures shows, focusing on a single aspect of a person's identity is ultimately an oppressive dead end for both academic theory and lived practice.[3] One may be a Mennonite—itself a term that glosses over numerous variations—but one is also female, or Canadian, or Latinx, or middle class, or, yes, queer, and it is necessary to examine these intersections. Drawing in part on the work of the godmother of Mennonite literary criticism, Hildi Froese Tiessen, Mennonite historian Felipe Hinojosa argues for a "relational approach" to Mennonite studies that examines how Mennonitism intersects with issues of class, race, sex, and place.[4] In light of Hinojosa's call, literary critics must therefore wrestle with questions such as how hybrid identities manifest themselves in Mennonite literature. How should we as critics write about these identities? And perhaps more basically, why should we care?

One immediate answer to this last question is that if Mennonite literary criticism is going to have something to say to the field of literary studies in general, it must figure out how to make the socially activist messages found in much of Mennonite literature accessible to those readers who otherwise have no connection to the Mennonite community. The work of Mennonite writers is often radical compared to mainstream societal standards, not just traditional Mennonite theological values. It is important to recognize that Mennonite literature does not just critique the Mennonite community (when it does at all). It frequently critiques society in general, but it often happens to involve Mennonite subject matter to do so. For instance, Casey Plett's short story "Other Women" is about Sophie's struggle against North American society's transphobia, which is shared by her Mennonite community as a learned behavior from its broader context.[5] If, however, the Mennonite elements were removed from the story, its primary political import would remain the same.

It is time for critics to acknowledge this wider focus and to examine what Mennonite literature says to an extended audience. As Hinojosa writes, it is necessary "to look at Mennonite studies from the outside-in."[6] Mennonites like myself writing about Mennonite topics must try to investigate our subject from the perspective of someone outside the boundaries of the community, not just as insiders. Put another way, it is time for Mennonite literary criticism to be in the world *and* of it in order to help non-Mennonite readers and critics see why Mennonite literature is worth reading.

In light of this necessity, *Queering Mennonite Literature: Archives, Activism, and the Search for Community* examines the intersection of queer and Mennonite elements in recent Mennonite literature as an example of how Mennonite literary criticism can dialogue with other areas within literary criticism and theory in the relational manner advocated by Hinojosa. The contribution the book makes is to present an investigation of how the queer theoretical project of the past thirty or so years has manifested itself within a Mennonite literary context. Queer theory's lifespan has coincided with the rise of Mennonite literature as a field of academic study, and as will become clear, the two fields also share many thematic similarities that manifest themselves in queer Mennonite literature despite seeming like the "oxymoron" that Jess suggests them to be. *Queering Mennonite Literature* serves as an archive of these manifestations in order to illustrate how queer theory, which is concerned with the marginal in terms of both fighting oppression and investigating elements of culture that the mainstream ignores, helps illuminate a field on the literary margins. Queer theorist Elizabeth Grosz argues that while members of oppressed groups are denied access to certain societal privileges, their position on the margins "also produces certain skills and modes of resourcefulness, the capacity precisely for self-sustenance and creativity that are lost for the dominator."[7] Things on the margins are difficult, but they can also be vibrant and fun and full of transformative potential. Anything can happen because on the margins there is a certain invisibility that makes space for a generative artistic freedom. Queer Mennonite literature uses this position of "creative" possibilities as a base for social activism on a host of issues, including gender, violence, disability, race, and of course, sexuality. *Queering Mennonite Literature* celebrates this activism.

Defining the "Queer" in Queer Theory

The term *queer theory*, which was first coined by Teresa de Lauretis at a conference on queer sexualities in 1990,[8] has a slippery definition because *queer* as a reclaimed term gets used in different ways. Most commonly in general public discourse, it is used as a synonym for nonheterosexual sexuality, as in the abbreviation "LGBTQ" (lesbian, gay, bisexual, trans, queer).[9] All the main characters in the books discussed here fall somewhere on this sexual spectrum. However, queer theorists insist that the term is not necessarily tied to sexuality but is political, with a radical vision for a transformed, non-oppressive, intersectional society and thus that queer theory is inherently political.[10] From this perspective, it is possible to be LGBT without being queer. For instance, one might be a gay man who is sexist or racist or transphobic. In other words, the queer in "queer theory" is not just about sexual orientation; it is about how one views the world, using the act of queering to question basic assumptions, such as the male/female binary in service of an antihegemonic worldview. As I show below, this political definition of queer could also be applied to aspects of the Mennonite tradition. One must be activist to be queer regardless of one's sexuality, and one way the texts *Queering Mennonite Literature* analyzes are queer is in their activist nature. It is in this broader political sense that I use the term, though this sense is also entwined with the sexual in queer Mennonite literature in that the books' activism stems from their characters' LGBT identities.

In naming its political aspect, queer theory's definition is an open, contested one. Queer writer and critic Maggie Nelson observes that words such as *queer* that have been used oppressively in the past "retain [. . .] a sense of the fugitive."[11] In the process of these terms' revision, they are difficult to define and thus liberatingly transgressive because of their refusal to be pinned down. Their contested nature offers room for dialogue and, in the case of an academic term such as *queer theory*, room for revisions when they become necessary. Thus Eli Clare asserts that "queer celebrates [. . .] difference," and Alison Kafer claims that "queerness is something always to be queered," to be questioned in service of creating a better world. In its advocacy for change, for the queering of society, queer theory offers "a critique of the normal" according to Ann Cvetkovich; it "embraces, even celebrates, transgression" according to Richard Thompson Ford; and it is "a site of struggle" according to Rosemary Hennessy.[12] Queer theory causes a sense of uneasiness, of discomfort, as it works from the margins to cause change. As *Queering Mennonite Literature* shows throughout, queer Mennonite literature often works to make readers uncomfortable in order to make its antioppressive messages clear.

Some question queer theory's continuing usefulness. Janet Halley and Andrew Parker write in the introduction to their essay anthology *After Sex? On Writing Since Queer Theory* that there are scholars who feel queer theory is "approaching its expiration date," as they question its initial emphasis on sexual identity (the "sex" of the title) and look to other approaches, such as affect theory.[13] However, I write from the position that it still has something to offer, and much of the queer theory that I cite has been published after *After Sex?* showing that the field remains vibrant. The question mark in Halley and Parker's title affords space to consider whether queer theory's relevance is truly waning, and they note that the "after" in their title can mean to pursue the queer.[14] *Queering Mennonite Literature* pursues the relationships between queer theory and Mennonite literature, especially as these relationships suggest a practical philosophy for how to live one's life as manifested in the messages of the books considered here. Halley and Parker do acknowledge "that queer theory's powers are practical and political."[15] This is why I am attracted to it as a critical outlook. Frankly, the North American Mennonite community is behind the times with regard to issues of sexuality, and queer theory still has relevance for it.

A Brief History of Mennonite Literary Criticism

Mennonite literature as a field rather than as one or two scattered texts here and there began to become visible in the late 1980s and early 1990s with the publication of several collections of creative work.[16] Phyllis Pellman Good's mini anthology *Three Mennonite Poets*, Hildi Froese Tiessen's short story anthology *Liars and Rascals*, and special issues of *The New Quarterly* and *Prairie Fire*, also edited by Tiessen, helped establish an archive of Mennonite writing.[17] In Canada, the government's emphasis on multiculturalism beginning in the 1960s and the subsequent funding of multiculturalism in the arts led to Mennonites being seen in Canada's literary public as an ethnic group rather than just a theological sect and thus to Mennonite literature being seen as an ethnic literature.[18] This view is evident in the fact that Tiessen's two special issues were published by non-Mennonite secular periodicals. The increasing visibility of Mennonite writers in Canada led to the first

Mennonite/s [*sic*] Writing conference in Waterloo, Ontario, in 1990.[19] This conference helped bring the field to the attention of U.S. writers and critics,[20] and there has been a steady stream of Mennonite literary criticism written on both sides of the border since then.

Aside from occasional articles in Mennonite journals such as *Conrad Grebel Review*, the *Journal of Mennonite Studies*,[21] the *Journal of Mennonite Writing* (formerly the *Journal of the Center for Mennonite Writing* until mid-2017), *Mennonite Life*, *Mennonite Quarterly Review*, and *Rhubarb* (which unfortunately became defunct at the end of 2017) and, infrequently, in non-Mennonite publications, there are eight books of Mennonite literary criticism that have played a germinal role in the theorization of the field. Hildi Froese Tiessen and Peter Hinchcliffe's *Acts of Concealment* and John D. Roth and Ervin Beck's *Migrant Muses* collected essays from the first two Mennonite/s Writing conferences and were instrumental in helping make the conferences' construction of the field and its canon visible to a broader audience.[22] Al Reimer's *Mennonite Literary Voices*, Julia Spicher Kasdorf's *The Body and the Book*, Douglas Reimer's *Surplus at the Border*, Jeff Gundy's *Walker in the Fog* and *Songs from an Empty Cage*, and Robert Zacharias's critical anthology *After Identity* all examined the field as a whole and wrestled in one way or another with the question of what it means to be a Mennonite in general and a Mennonite writer in particular and thus what Mennonite literature is and how it has (or whether it has) value when considered as its own field.

Just as *After Sex* raises questions about queer theory's future, *After Identity* asks where the field of Mennonite literature is heading. The field has spent much time debating what "Mennonite literature" entails, wrestling with questions such as, Does it have to be by an author theologically affiliated with Mennonites? Does it have to include Mennonite characters? Can it be by an author who grew up Mennonite but has repudiated all aspects of their Mennonite upbringing? One consistent tension in the field has been the question of how to respond to the reality that many Mennonite writers are no longer theologically Mennonite. Is it fair for literary critics to still speak of these writers and their work as Mennonite? These questions were first raised in the ur-text of Mennonite literary criticism, John L. Ruth's *Mennonite Identity and Literary Art*, which argues that Mennonite literature should serve the theological Mennonite community, and Reimer's *Mennonite Literary Voices*, which argues that Mennonite writers' first loyalty should be to their art.[23] A number of subsequent pieces of Mennonite literary criticism comment on this debate.[24] I will not rehash it here other than to say that the general consensus now is that "Mennonite literature" is literature by an author who is a theological or ethnic Mennonite whether it includes explicitly Mennonite subject matter or not. It follows that the field defines "Mennonite" more broadly than Mennonite theology does. Just like the "after" in Halley and Parker's title, the "after" in Zacharias's title in some cases signifies the desire to be finished with this worn question of what makes a work a piece of Mennonite literature, but it also sometimes signifies a way to meld Mennonite identities with other identities, such as the identity "queer Mennonite" that is the subject of this book. The field's inclusion of secular Mennonite writers has helped broaden the idea of what being a Mennonite can mean for me and other younger Mennonite writers and critics in ways that make our Mennonite identity usable even when we find Mennonite theology to no longer be so.[25] As I discuss throughout, this influence is an important one for queer Mennonite literature and helps it offer its own expanded conceptions of what it means to be Mennonite.

A Word on "Identity" and Mennonite Ethnicity

While theoretical dismissal of the concept of "identity," which can be used as a tool to divide people, has its merits, on a practical level in society, one is still seen as one's identity, and in the case of marginalized groups, one is oppressed as a result, so the formation and acknowledgment of an identity can still be a powerful political act of resistance. Christopher Castiglia and Christopher Reed argue that queer theory, in its rush to reject identity, has tended to forget the positive aspects of LGBT community, including its "integration of activism and scholarship."[26] Queer theory can still benefit from its practitioners' claiming of their identities, sexual and otherwise.

Recent queer work on religion and ethnicity illustrates this principle. In its rush to reject the notion of identity, queer theory has at times marginalized certain segments of the queer community. For instance, regarding religion, queer theologian Patrick S. Cheng observes that "it is difficult to be [. . .] out" as religious in many queer settings. Similarly, Ann Pellegrini argues that queer theory is built around a "religious/secular divide," which assumes that the religious has nothing to offer the queer.[27] Regarding ethnicity, Kaila Adia Story contends that white queer theorists' rejection of identity is unintentionally racist because it fails to acknowledge how people of color have used their ethnicities as rallying points for antiracist organizing but believes that queer theory and the claiming of an ethnic or sexual identity can coexist in powerful ways.[28] *Queering Mennonite Literature* operates from this belief. As Kafer writes, it is necessary to name one's identities—which are never completely fixed in the first place—in order to make sure that one's theorizing is grounded in practical applications toward ending oppression even as one works toward a postidentity intersectionality.[29] Nelson looks toward this postidentity reality, contending that "the binary of normal/ transgressive [. . . is] unsustainable" because eventually North American society will accept queer lives.[30] I hope for this reality, but obviously we are not yet there, and thus queer Mennonite literature (and queer literature in general) remains transgressive in powerful ways as it envisions new relationships both within and outside of Mennonite contexts. *Queering Mennonite Literature* therefore explores how the choice to be politically queer is influenced in many cases by the characters' Mennonite context, which gives them an identity that is in some ways chosen and in other ways not.

The field of Mennonite literature has always treated being Mennonite as an ethnic identity in both Canada and the United States and thus has always treated Mennonite literature as an ethnic literature even though the field does include authors such as Todd Davis and David Wright, who are theological Mennonites, not ethnic Mennonites.[31] Of course, Mennonites' theological distinctiveness has helped create Mennonite ethnicity. Mennonites' emphasis on ethics, and especially on helping the poor and oppressed through agencies such as Mennonite Central Committee and Mennonite Disaster Service, which offer material aid without being explicitly evangelical, is taught from an early age and is so ingrained in Mennonite identity that Mennonite theologian Paul G. Doerksen muses "that much of Anabaptist work would carry on even if you took Jesus out of the mix."[32] However, other nontheological elements of Mennonite life also play a part in Mennonite ethnicity's construction. Folklorist Ervin Beck writes that North American Mennonites' shared "history of immigration, [. . .] distinctive foods," and the existence of Mennonite jokes told both by themselves and by others show that it is proper to define Mennonites as an ethnic group.[33] This ethnicity gives many Mennonites a sense of community even though our shared identity often goes unremarked by outsiders because most ethnic Mennonites are white and thus can pass as something else while benefitting from white privilege.

Some Mennonites dislike the idea of a "Mennonite ethnicity." Rudy Wiebe writes against it in an essay from all the way back in 1964, and more recently historian Benjamin W. Goossen argues that "the language of 'Mennonite ethnicity' [. . .] frequently undergirds white supremacy" because it implies that ethnic Mennonites in North America are somehow "more special" than nonethnic Mennonites, whether in North America or elsewhere.[34] However, they and others who have made a similar argument throughout the years examine the concept from a theological perspective rather than a sociological one, whereas the field of Mennonite literature uses the latter view. From the field's standpoint, Mennonite ethnicity exists as a secular element of Mennonite identity whether it is a helpful construction or not. In cases such as Jess's in *Somewhere Else*, sometimes Mennonite ethnicity is the only remaining connection to other Mennonites, and this tenuous attachment is valuable because it keeps the possibility of staying within the Mennonite community alive. I find the concept useful in this project because of my explorations of how Mennonite sensibilities, in which ethnicity has an important part for many ethnic Mennonites, play off of queer sensibilities. When one claims both of these identities, it is a powerful act.

There are actually two prominent North American Mennonite ethnicities that manifest themselves in Mennonite literature. The group known as "Swiss Mennonites" began coming from Switzerland and Germany to Pennsylvania in the late 1600s and slowly moved west, south, and north, creating significant communities in Ohio, Indiana, Illinois, Iowa, Virginia, and Ontario. The group known as "Russian Mennonites" originated in Germany, the Netherlands, and what is now Poland, moved to what is now Ukraine in the late 1700s, and then fled religious persecution to North America in two waves, one in the 1870s and another in the aftermath of the Russian Revolution in the 1920s, settling primarily in Manitoba, Saskatchewan, and Kansas. A third wave in the 1940s settled primarily in South America. While Russian Mennonites wrote the first North American literary texts, since the 1990s numerous Swiss Mennonites have also published work and become important as critics. The field has treated these two ethnicities side by side since at least Tiessen's anthology *Liars and Rascals*.

National identity also plays a role in Mennonite literature, albeit a unique one in that it tends to be deemphasized unlike in other literary fields. Although it received its initial impetus from Canadian literature's multicultural landscape, Mennonite literature has been a transnational field since its early days, with *Three Mennonite Poets* including a Canadian writer, a Canadian living and working in the United States whom the field now considers an American writer, and a Japanese writer. This trend has continued to the present.[35] National divisions thereby play less of a role in Mennonite literature than in North American Mennonitism in general. Nationality is even less important when discussing queer Mennonite literature because institutional Mennonite homophobia has functioned the same way on both sides of the border, so queer Mennonites from Canada and the United States have much in common, and binational connections in the queer Mennonite literary community are strong. Therefore, while Mennonite literature has always had a robust sense of place, and while this sense is evident in the books discussed here, the national contexts of these places are less important than their local ones.

Mennonite literature's inclusion of multiple Mennonite ethnicities along with its transnational nature are rarities in literary studies and show a willingness to cross boundaries that resonates with queer ideas of openness and transgressiveness. Thus while using the language of identity, which some may find divisive or passé, *Queering Mennonite Literature* insists on the inclusion of all identities, investigating texts by Canadians, Americans, Swiss Mennonites, Russian Mennonites, trans authors, cis authors, and authors across the LGBT spectrum. All the texts it examines have sexually queer characters and are queer in the sense that, as I describe below, Mennonitism in general is queer. But not all the authors are sexually queer, and the texts are queer because they are politically active, not just because they have sexually queer characters.

The Queer/Mennonite Intersection

Queering Mennonite Literature's stance is not a dogmatic one but one that embraces leisurely perambulations through its subject matter as one implement in its antihegemonic toolbox. The book is influenced by several works of queer theory that in many ways offer resonances with Mennonite thought, though there is not one overarching theoretical framework for the book other than queer theory in general. The book quotes from a number of queer theorists without attempting to be systematic. This is a process that is itself queer, as various queer theorists explain. For instance, Kafer acknowledges that her writing includes "contradictions," and J. Jack Halberstam argues that we should "resist mastery" academically.[36] These assertions are important moves to show that queer writing should be a dialogue because one does not have all the answers oneself. Queer theory's openness is one of its most powerful aspects, and this openness requires that one write with a light touch in order to make space for others to enter the conversation.

My writing approach is inspired not only by queer theorists but also by Gundy's "Manifesto of Anabaptist Surrealism."[37] Gundy's intentionally playful document, which lauds a number of Mennonite and non-Mennonite figures as writing models, insists on an attitude of humility and wonder in explorations of literature and how it can lead us to truth. Gundy argues that while we can never fully grasp enlightenment, seeking after it is an essential journey. *Queering Mennonite Literature* is an example of this seeking. Gundy's use of the term *Anabaptist* in his title hearkens back to Mennonitism's radical roots in the sixteenth century. The early Anabaptists' theology was inherently politically queer because disagreeing with the doctrines of the state church was a treasonous act. Their refusal to baptize their babies struck at the foundations of the state because it meant that their children were not entered into the tax rolls. Their employment of theatrically dissident acts, such as eating sausage together during Lent or interrupting worship services to dispute with state church ministers, calls to mind more recent queer activist strategies, such as ACT UP's confrontational style. The memory of early Anabaptist radicalism still resonates with Mennonites today. As a result, aside from acknowledging our historical roots, Mennonites' current use of "Anabaptist" signifies a desire for theologically ideal living that is untainted by the human fallibility inherent in institutional Mennonitism. Like queer theory, Anabaptism seeks societal transformation, which is why it is beneficial to study the two traditions together.

With the exception of my "Queering Mennonite Literature" chapter in Zacharias's collection that is the basis for this introduction, none of the eight aforementioned classics of Mennonite literary criticism has discussed queer Mennonite literature, in part because it has only recently achieved critical mass. Indeed, writing in 2002, Douglas Reimer laments that queer-themed Mennonite literature "is impossible to imagine."[38] Reimer misses the work of Lynnette D'anna (pen name of Lynnette Dueck), who published five queer novels between 1992 and 2001, but so did other critics in the field. It is only recently that queer Mennonite literature has become more broadly visible.

A few articles mention this growing movement, which first became especially noticeable at the 2015 Mennonite/s Writing conference in Fresno, California. The conference included a panel on "LGBT Fiction" that was attended by nearly one hundred people (almost half of the conference's attendees), and the *Journal of Mennonite Studies* published the papers from the panel in 2016.[39] Two other essays that originated as conference presentations in Fresno about the state of Mennonite literature as a field also mention this panel, acknowledging queer Mennonite literature as a subfield, though not attempting further investigation of it.[40] Gundy's 2016 "Mennonite/s Writing: Explorations and Exposition," an adaptation of his November 2015 Menno Simons Lectures at Bethel College in North Newton, Kansas, is slightly more expansive, including a short "LGBTQ" section at the end that discusses Corey Redekop's *Husk*, Stephen Beachy's *boneyard* [*sic*], and Casey Plett's *A Safe Girl to Love*.[41] Three of the participants from the 2015 panel—Andrew

Harnish, Casey Plett, and myself—also presented queer work at the 2017 conference in Winnipeg.[42] One of *Queering Mennonite Literature*'s goals is to help the momentum from these brief mentions of queer Mennonite literature coalesce in order to make this literature visible and assert its importance within the broader Mennonite literary field.[43]

It is no surprise that Mennonite literature has developed some queer (in the queer theory sense) elements because Mennonitism's values are queer in the traditional sense of being odd or peculiar. In a 1952 article in *Ladies' Home Journal*, Dorothy Thompson, a non-Mennonite writer, remarks on this peculiarity after a visit to the Mennonite-owned Bethel College.[44] A fellow traveler tells Thompson that Mennonites "are queer people" because of their rural sectarianism and how they dress. Thompson argues that Mennonites are not "queer" (which she clearly views as an insult) but that they are simply quiet, upstanding American Christians. However, her conversation partner's naming of Mennonites as queer is appropriate, though for different reasons than he suggests. While many outsiders might think of Mennonites as "queer" because of frequently held misconceptions that all Mennonites still dress plain and "are like the Amish," it is true that traditional Mennonite thinking, which embraces values such as pacifism, simple living, and an emphasis on ethics rather than creeds, is out of step with cultural norms today just as it was seventy years ago. Mennonite theological language views Mennonitism as a "third way" between Protestantism and Catholicism and has a vision of Christian community as an "upside-down kingdom."[45] These Mennonite ideals emphasize a rejection of binaries, the importance of creative approaches to conflict resolution, and the practice of mutual aid, especially in resisting oppression. Queer Mennonite literature helps capture how these Mennonite traits currently express themselves in the twenty-first century. In other words, queer Mennonite writing is in some ways a natural extension of the Mennonite spirit. While many queer Mennonite texts are on the broader literary margins, they are necessary narratives nonetheless. Both the queer and Mennonite traditions privilege this position, as various queer theorists advocate for ways of life that investigate and tell stories of the countercultural or marginal.[46]

In light of these similarities between queer thought and Mennonite thought, being raised to think as a Mennonite means being raised to think queerly in the broader sense (though, as noted below, these Mennonite queer attitudes have not necessarily translated to acceptance of sexual queerness), and thus queer themes are becoming increasingly prevalent in Mennonite literature, which has always transgressively investigated those on the margins.[47]

Braun acknowledges that nonqueer Mennonite literature gave her hope before she came out as a lesbian and then gave her a model to use when she began writing about lesbians because of its portrayals of outsiders.[48] This use of earlier Mennonite literature as a model is evident in the work of writers of queer Mennonite literature such as Braun, Plett, Jessica Penner, and André Swartley, who write explicitly Mennonite literature and perhaps even think of themselves as "Mennonite writers" after having learned to do so from the earlier generation. Penner studied with the Mennonite novelist Omar Eby in college, and Swartley studied with the Mennonite poet Todd Davis and the Mennonite literary critics Ervin Beck and Ann Hostetler (who is also a poet). Likewise, I also studied with Beck, Hostetler, and Davis, and these experiences built a foundation for my current work as a Mennonite literary critic.[49] As I discuss in my examinations of these second-generation writers' works, Braun's *Somewhere Else* and Plett's *A Safe Girl to Love* explicitly mention pieces of Mennonite literature.[50] Similarly, Stephen Beachy's *boneyard* responds to the ur-text of Mennonite literature, the *Martyrs Mirror*. These writers acknowledge that a tradition of Mennonite literature exists and that the academic field that studies it is a legitimate one. Their queer Mennonite literature responds to this tradition, critiquing and enlarging it.

One reason that viewing Mennonite literature through the lens of queer theory can be advantageous is because of the term *queer*'s flexibility. Thomas Piontek contends that "queer" is "a questioning stance."[51] This emphasis on interrogation of the normative is also evident in Mennonite literature. Neither tradition is satisfied with the status quo. The Mennonite tradition claims to embrace those whom society makes Other. However, while Mennonites have historically been culturally Other themselves, this position has largely been lost in North America, and the official Mennonite community now participates in the marginalization of LGBT persons. Engaging with queer theory is one way for Mennonites to return to their radical roots.

Much like queer theory is concerned with outsiders, Douglas Reimer argues that Mennonite literature often shares this concern. He uses Gilles Deleuze and Félix Guattari's concept of "minor literature"—a literature that examines subjects on the margins rather than being ensconced in traditional "conventions"—to argue that Mennonite literature is outside the boundaries of mainstream (i.e., the white, nonethnic canon) Canadian literature. It is fair to say that this argument applies to U.S. Mennonite literature as well. Reimer contends that minor literature is always "political" because it must announce itself in order to be noticed, and this politicization inevitably results in "change."[52] The queer is also always political, thus Reimer's notion of

Mennonite literature as a minor literature is a useful model because one of *Queering Mennonite Literature*'s arguments is that queer Mennonite literature is a minor literature within Mennonite literature itself. Aside from its queer subject matter, this literature's minor characteristics are made evident by the way most literary critics ignore it and by the way it is ghettoized by the literary marketplace, being published by small presses in contrast to the work of mainstream Mennonite writers such as Rudy Wiebe, Miriam Toews, Rhoda Janzen, and David Bergen.[53] It pecks at the boundaries of the field, demanding notice.

Queer theory is also useful for examining the theme of the oppressive use of power and authority within communities. Mennonite theologian Carolyn Schrock-Shenk observes that Mennonites do a poor job discussing how the community uses power in hurtful ways and that this has especially been the case when debating whether or not LGBT persons should be offered church membership.[54] Queer theory presents a solution to this misuse of power by offering a new model for investigating the language of authority (whether religious or otherwise) and thus for both finding ways to subvert it and finding ways to wield it in a healthier manner via its explorations of BDSM (bondage, discipline, Domination/submission,[55] sadism, and masochism), which occurs in fiction by Stephen Beachy, Casey Plett, and Sofia Samatar. Tristan Taormino posits that power relations are everywhere in the real world, but they often go unacknowledged because it is uncomfortable to discuss them, so BDSM is valuable because it makes them explicit.[56] In helping its participants think about power, BDSM can lead to an interrogation of the systemic violence present in society.

BDSM is one element of queer sexuality that does not necessarily fit into the LGBT spectrum because it emphasizes specific acts rather than the gender of one's partner and thereby epitomizes queer theory's distrust of categorizable identities.[57] Patrick Califia argues that BDSM "roles are not related to gender or sexual orientation [. . .] or class" and that these "roles and dialogue become a parody of authority, a challenge to it."[58] BDSM can thus lead participants into a liberating state of mind that illuminates one's conception of the world, not just of sexuality. Anyone can act as a top and anyone can act as a bottom in a BDSM scene regardless of their position within the power structures of society. Likewise, for many BDSM practitioners, the experience of dominating / being dominated and the headspace where one is transported through these acts is central to a scene rather than the characteristics of one's partner. David Halperin highlights another revolutionary aspect of BDSM, contending that it focuses on the entire body instead of just the genitals.[59] This holistic emphasis offers a healthy alternative to the traditional mind/body binary, reminding us that our sexuality should be fully integrated into our lives rather than kept to the side as a shameful act.

Sex educator Madison Young's description of how it feels to play the submissive role has clear relevance for Mennonite literature. She writes that "in order to find [her] true self [as 'queer' and other identities she names], [she] must give in" to her Dominant.[60] This language echoes Mennonite descriptions of surrendering oneself to Jesus, a similarity that is strengthened in Young's observation that when she submits, she obtains a "clarity in which [she] feel[s] that [she is] exactly where [she is] supposed to be, full of purpose and with an internal stillness that exists only in absolute surrender."[61] An important difference between a submissive's surrender and a religious one is that the former is a choice consistently taken with pleasure instead of one that can feel forced in a religious context and is often made with the hammer of guilt and the threat of eternal damnation hanging over one's head. This is not to say that one cannot find the kind of peace that Young describes in religious faith but to suggest that new models and language for discussing this fealty in the Mennonite community are necessary and may be found through BDSM.

In one of the only Mennonite discussions of BDSM, Di Brandt analyzes a bondage pictorial from *Penthouse* to argue that bondage echoes the same patriarchal values found in traditional Mennonite theology, "which depends on the language of submission and obedience to define the nature of faith."[62] I agree that this language is hurtful within the context of religious community, but I also agree with Taormino and Califia that oppressive real-world uses of authority can be subverted via BDSM role-playing. Brandt's concerns notwithstanding, BDSM is actually, as Lewis Call explains, "a set of ethical practices" dedicated to physical and emotional safety.[63] It is a common maxim in the BDSM community that the submissive is actually the one in power because they set guidelines for what the Dominant can do to them. This reversal is only one example of how BDSM interrogates power structures. Take, for example, the case of *boneyard*, where bondage occurs between two males. This context introduces different power dynamics than in Brandt's *Penthouse* example of bound women, and the bondage happens in the flesh rather than with an outside viewer in the Dominant position and an anonymous submissive captive on the page. The intimacy of a real-life bondage scene offers the radical possibilities described by Taormino and Califia, which are less available in pornography.

While the radical openness of queer subjectivity means that it inevitably comes into conflict with communities bounded by strict rules and conventions, queer theory's view of "community" is useful for examining the tension characters in queer Mennonite literature feel between the worldly milieus they participate in and their home religious communities. The traditional definition of community assumes sameness among group members. This is how Mennonites have officially understood it; in the past, some Mennonite groups have utilized the practice of shunning individuals who act transgressively, and in the present, even the two most liberal North American Mennonite denominations, Mennonite Church USA and Mennonite Church Canada, discipline congregations that embrace sexually active LGBT persons.[64]

In contrast to this restrictive form of community, Nikki Sullivan writes that queer theorists redefine community as a space of "fracturing" that allows room for "productive differences" instead of enforcing conformity and "enables [. . .] diversity and the radical unknowability" that this variety brings.[65] For instance, Castiglia and Reed call for "communities [that are] founded in ideals rather than [. . . rigid] identities," a characteristic that the queer and Mennonite communities share.[66] Instead of a grouping based upon a shared identity, queer community is based on a desire to learn from one another through the multiplicity of individual experiences. Indeed, as José Esteban Muñoz asserts, community is an "essential" element of "queerness."[67] One learns how to be queer—culturally, sexually, and politically—from others. This training is akin to the way Mennonites teach ethical and cultural practices. The citational aesthetic I use throughout *Queering Mennonite Literature*, situating the book within both Mennonite and queer scholarly discourses and asking readers to pay attention to the endnotes on the edges of the text, is one way I write like a Mennonite, which also means writing queerly. Melissa Adler argues that this kind of approach to "citationality" is necessary for creating queer intersectionality, which is one of *Queering Mennonite Literature*'s goals.[68] I dialogue with previous writers, acknowledging that without their communal work, my own ideas would not come to fruition.

Unfortunately, the religious body does not always reach its vision of collective harmony. Numerous pieces of Mennonite literature describe the breakdown or oppressiveness of community as a result of an insistence that all members adhere to a single standard.[69] The queer notion of community as a place that is contentious, allowing dialogue despite disagreements, offers a healthy alternative model.[70] The slipperiness of the term *queer* allows the boundaries of its community to be permeable rather than enforcing an inside/outside dichotomy.

While it can learn a lot from queer theory, the Mennonite tradition also offers benefits to the queer tradition through Mennonite literature. *Queering Mennonite Literature* highlights three of these possibilities. First, although queer theory focuses on the necessity of radical societal change, in practice it often has a difficult time moving itself beyond academia and into the broader world. Queer Mennonite literature offers models for how queer theory can return to its socially activist roots by showing how it can cause transformation in an area that it tends to neglect, the realm of religion. Second, Mennonite literature has much to say about two important strategies for achieving social change: pacifism and thinking globally. It shows how pacifism is a queer value and how to bring queer principles into multiple geographical contexts. Third, both traditions have roots in traumatic beginnings. Queer Mennonite literature illustrates how to respond to past trauma in hopeful ways, an approach that is sometimes lacking in queer theory.

Methodology

The book uses close readings of the texts it investigates to examine how Mennonite and queer streams of thought play off of each other. I believe that literature can play a liberating role in our everyday lives, and thus my analysis of the texts looks at how they are all activist texts that should be appreciated by lay readers, not just those of us in academia, and is written with this broader audience in mind. Such approaches are gaining in popularity. Andrew Kopec explains that in literary studies, there has been a visible desire to return to literature rather than just being ensconced in theory, and he also asserts that the use of "close reading" is "a polemical act." My use of close reading is not a rejection of theory but an acknowledgment that theory alone is not enough. These readings also advocate for a broader definition of theory, arguing that the texts at hand make theoretical moves themselves. As Alison Reed argues, one way academic work can lead to social change is if it thinks of "litera-ture *as theory*" because of the way literature reproduces lived experience.[71] While obviously theory can be useful, it sometimes gets so abstract that it loses touch with the gritty reality of everyday life, and reading and learn-ing from literature is one way to bridge this gap. Literature has the power to change us because it allows us to learn about ourselves through the stories of others, opening us up to new experiences; therefore, offering the attention to stories that is inherently a part of close reading helps make oppressed groups visible and helps offer visions of better futures. Thus while it is a queer text, if it is a work of theory, *Queering Mennonite Literature* is a work of Mennonite theory, interested in plain language and the teaching of ethics through story. Part of this plain language involves the occasional use of first person and personal stories mixed in alongside literary criticism, a model I copy from both the Mennonite and queer academic traditions.[72] I use a personal voice, which, as Cvetkovich asserts, is a "queer" act, because this is an intentionally personal project, but it is also an inherently public one because of its status as an activist intervention.[73]

Therefore, a personal digression about the position from which I write is necessary. Gundy notes that Mennonite creative writing and literary criticism often disregard the borders between the academic and the personal, opting instead for a hybrid of genres.[74] I contend that this is in part because Mennonite literature is often transgressive of traditional Mennonite mores, and thus both creative writers and critics in the field (and many people are both) feel the need to justify this transgression to the broader Mennonite community or defend themselves against the collective in print. For me, writing about Mennonite literature always feels like writing about family and is therefore much scarier and more difficult than writing about other literature. The personal thus leaks into *Queering Mennonite Literature* because I am interested in queer Mennonite literature because much of it tells my own story as a Mennonite and as a queer person. I am a middle-class male in my late thirties born to a Swiss Mennonite mother and a Puerto Rican father. I am bisexual and kinky, though I prefer the term *queer* to describe myself because of its openness. I want my two ethnicities and my queerness to be conversant with one another, and the space created by queer theory is one place where this dialogue can happen. Queer theory helps me move toward a healthy understanding of selfhood, and I am open about my queer Mennonite identity in this book because the naming of our queer identities is an essential act of resistance in our homophobic society. Sharing about my life is a way to participate in the archiving of queer memory undertaken by the books I study.

Braun posits in an essay about naming herself as a queer Mennonite that she writes "in an effort to begin the building of queer Mennonite academic history."[75] *Queering Mennonite Literature* takes on this task in order to combat the lack of critical attention queer Mennonite literature has received. I cite very few pieces of literary criticism about the books themselves because there simply is not any to cite in many cases. Plett laments that the lack of queer Mennonite literature is one of the costs queer Mennonites have to pay as a result of Mennonite homophobia, and it is fair to add that the pain of this lack is exacerbated by the paucity of attention paid to the queer texts that do exist.[76] It is true that Mennonite literature has little criticism written on it in general in comparison to other fields in literary studies, but queer Mennonite literature has even less. This book thus serves in part as an archiving endeavor, making queer Mennonite literature visible. Together, the texts it examines form a corpus that is worth studying.

Queer archiving is a necessary act because, as Cvetkovich writes, the materials that would constitute queer archives are often endangered, in part because of institutionalized homophobia in academia and in part because these materials are often objects that might not normally be collected by libraries or other official archiving institutions because they are not seen as valuable or are only available in queer spaces such as sex shops, bars, or bathhouses.[77] While all the texts I discuss here are books (though Miriam Suzanne's novel is unbound), a traditional medium, they share this transient nature because they are marginalized by virtue of being published by small presses and are in some cases already out of print. Therefore, one goal of *Queering Mennonite Literature* is to preserve their existence by drawing readers' attention to them, since objects become archival in an institutional, and therefore more permanent, sense through their documentation. This is an activist move because, as Halberstam asserts, "academics can play a big role in the construction of queer archives and queer memory. Furthermore, queer academics can—and some should—participate in the ongoing project of recoding queer culture as well as interpreting it and circulating a sense of multiplicity and sophistication. The more intellectual records we have of queer culture, the more we contribute to the project of claiming for the subculture the radical cultural work that either gets absorbed into or claimed by mainstream media."[78] It is not enough to collect elements of queer culture; it is also necessary to interpret these elements in order to make them available to a broader audience that includes queers as well as non-queers. Thus along with preserving queer Mennonite literature (as both Mennonite literature and queer literature in general) for future readers, one goal of *Queering Mennonite Literature*'s archiving endeavor is to illuminate queer Mennonite literature's "radical" messages with the hope that readers will apply these ideals to their lives. This illumination is possible through the use of the queer theoretical archive from the past thirty years. Hinojosa laments that a frequent shortcoming of Mennonite scholarship is its failure to examine non-Mennonite archives that might have relevance to

Mennonite subjects.[79] My book is an example of the fruits that can blossom as a result of working with archives relationally.

Like Halberstam, Cvetkovich also argues that critics should experience queer culture rather than just analyzing it. She posits that "the archivist of queer culture must proceed like the fan or collector whose attachment to objects is often fetishistic, idiosyncratic, or obsessional."[80] While queer archiving is an essential public, academic endeavor, it is also a personal one. I am a fan of queer Mennonite literature because it reflects my experiences as a queer Mennonite back at me. As I describe further in chapter 1, my collecting of Mennonite literature is obsessive. I accumulate these volumes rather than just borrowing them from a library because they offer emotional comfort to me as objects when I see them on my bookshelves. One concern of my book is thinking about these books not just as literary texts but also as material objects that make queer Mennonites visible in both the Mennonite community and North American society at large, since queer Mennonite literature helps illuminate a slice of queer experience that has not yet been investigated by the queer theoretical project.

I am specifically interested in the works at hand because I am drawn to their activist nature and because of my strong reactions to them. As I first read many of these texts, I found myself experiencing more and more stress, which manifested itself in heart palpitations and feelings of nausea. For example, *Somewhere Else* moved me to the point where, on several occasions, I had to stop reading because my visceral reaction was so intense that I worried I would have a heart attack if I kept going.

Despite voraciously reading all my life, I have never had these physical reactions to literature before. My feelings were a vivid reminder that personal experience is always connected to broader collective realities and that it is necessary for us as critics to explore how individual experiences with literature relate to the larger issue of working for social justice. The authors of queer Mennonite literature are forced into the role of writers-as-transgressors because of society's continuing homophobia. Braun writes in an email that after *Somewhere Else* was published, she felt "guilt for transgressing (writing about Mennonite queers), guilt for taking up space."[81] This admission that the oppression felt under homophobia does not go away even when one is able to use one's voice to claim discursive "space" is a heart-wrenching reminder of how far North American society still has to go in order to become queer-friendly. As critics, we can help ease this oppression by highlighting queer stories. I write this book to pay homage to queer Mennonite writers for their willingness to speak out against oppression with the hope that my readers will be inspired to read these texts for themselves and take action to ensure that their communities—whether Mennonite or not—become more welcoming to these voices. I am sincere in my advocacy for queer theory as a potential force for positive social change, especially when it is combined with radical Mennonite values. But it is also necessary to respond to real-world oppression, which is not nuanced, on a clear, basic level: homophobia, biphobia, and transphobia are wrong. Therefore, in responding to these oppressions, *Queering Mennonite Literature* is intentionally polemic in its advocacy of social justice. This rhetorical strategy is meant to provoke rather than be rigidly prescriptive, just as queer theory's strength lies in the coexistence of its revolutionary openness and its firm stance against intolerance.

Recent Queer Mennonite Literature

The book examines prose by nine Mennonite authors.[82] The earliest texts, Christina Penner's *Widows of Hamilton House* and Braun's *Somewhere Else*, were published in 2008, and the latest, Sofia Samatar's *Tender*, was published in 2017. While Lynnette D'anna's fiction, beginning in 1992 with *sing me no more* [sic], and Janet Kauffman's 1993 novel *The Body in Four Parts* include queer characters, *Queering Mennonite Literature* focuses on authors of the second generation of Mennonite writers, who were formed in part by previous Mennonite literature and now create work in the field.[83] With the exception of Stephen Beachy, whose explicitly Mennonite work also falls within the second generation time frame, they all began publishing books in 2007 or later and have been formed by the flowering of queer literature over the past thirty years as well as the institutionalization of LGBT/queer studies in the academy.[84] Thus along with placing their work within the context of Mennonite literature, I often note resonances in their work with non-Mennonite queer literature as well. I choose to examine these texts because they epitomize the best of recent queer Mennonite literature. However, a number of other novels could also be included.[85] This plethora of texts shows just how rich the queer Mennonite literary tradition has already become and why the critical attention that *Queering Mennonite Literature* provides is necessary.

Chapter 1, "Building a Queer Mennonite Archive," discusses Christina Penner's novel *Widows of Hamilton House* and the writing of Wes Funk, primarily his autobiography *Wes Side Story*. It illustrates how each writer's narratives document queer Mennonite experience as examples of how queer

Mennonite literature acts as an archive. *Widows of Hamilton House* does this through its investigations of the practice of archiving (its main character is a librarian), and Funk's work does this through the ways it fictionalizes his own experiences. The theorization of queer Mennonite experience in this chapter establishes an important interpretive lens for the rest of the texts examined in the book.

Chapter 2, "Searching for Selfhood in Jan Guenther Braun's *Somewhere Else*," builds on chapter 1's investigations of Mennonite literary archives by examining one of the earliest pieces of queer Mennonite literature. *Somewhere Else* depicts its protagonist Jess's struggles to reconcile her Mennonite faith with her lesbianism in an attempt to claim the identity "queer Mennonite." As in *Widows of Hamilton House*, literature plays a key role in Jess's search for community. Reading feminist writers gives her models for living a queer life. The chapter considers three of Braun's personal essays about her own struggles with this identity to supplement the novel's archiving of lesbian experience. Jess is successful in her quest because she is able to synthesize aspects of the queer community and the Mennonite community, including the importance of literature for each.

Chapter 3, "Queering Tradition in Jessica Penner's *Shaken in the Water*," shares chapter 2's concern with finding and building queer Mennonite history. It investigates a novel depicting a Kansas Mennonite community's rise and decline from 1903 to 2007. The queer relationships in the book occur during the 1910s–1920s, a setting that makes the powerful statement that queer Mennonites have always existed. The novel shows how these relationships, which are censured by the book's homophobic, sexist Mennonite community, offer a vision of liberating community and new understandings of the divine.

Chapter 4, "Stephen Beachy's *boneyard*, the *Martyrs Mirror*, and Anabaptist Activism," also draws on Anabaptist history to help build queer identity. It explores Beachy's 2011 novel, whose protagonist, Jake Yoder, is an Amish adolescent trying to process the 2006 Nickel Mines Amish school shooting by archiving his trauma through his short story writing. The novel's postmodern form, which emphasizes the slipperiness of knowledge, argues for a queer, nonbinary approach to life. The book also argues through Jake's reinterpretation of the *Martyrs Mirror* as a queer text that an active pacifist ethic is a necessary element of queer activism.

Chapter 5, "The Queer Ethical Body in Corey Redekop's *Husk*," continues chapter 4's investigation of twenty-first-century queer Anabaptist male identity. The novel uses the figure of the zombie as a metaphor to illustrate how North American society marginalizes the queer and the disabled. Through its depiction of the gay Mennonite zombie Sheldon Funk as a Christ figure, it argues that using a Mennonite ethic rooted in community is one way to combat this marginalization.

Chapter 6, "Trans Mennonite Literature," discusses two pieces of literature, Casey Plett's short story collection *A Safe Girl to Love* and Miriam Suzanne's novel *Riding SideSaddle** [*sic*]. The two texts, which also belong to the postmodern fiction tradition examined in chapters 3, 4, and 5, draw attention to the need to construct a usable queer past in general and a trans Mennonite history in particular. *A Safe Girl to Love* documents this history in its stories, which include a number of references to Mennonite literature, and *Riding SideSaddle** uses its unique form (it is a set of 250 cards in a box rather than a bound volume) to examine issues relating to the archiving necessary to build such a history.

The epilogue, "The Future of Queer Mennonite Literature," revisits how queer Mennonite literature makes the argument that the ideals of Mennonitism are queer and discusses what Mennonite literature has to offer queer theory. It also discusses how queer Mennonite literature might continue to shape the broader field of Mennonite literature in the future. To do so, it offers a brief reading of Sofia Samatar's essay "The Scope of This Project" and some of her recent fiction to show how it furthers the intersectional work of previous queer Mennonite literature by adding racial identity to the identities queer and Mennonite. Samatar's concept of "postcolonial Mennonite writing" is an essential one for the future of Mennonite literature. Just as *Queering Mennonite Literature* begins with the ideas of a Mennonite of color, Hinojosa, so too does it end with the ideas of a Mennonite of color as one way of acknowledging that "queer Mennonite" is but one Mennonite identity that requires theorization and as a reminder that this text, though it almost exclusively examines white characters, is by a queer Mennonite of color.

One commonality that these books share is that although their many biblical references and frequent theological musings are part of how they show their Mennonite character, they generally have unorthodox theological views of the divine and sexual morality. I do not condemn these views—*Queering Mennonite Literature* is a work of literary criticism, not theology—but instead dialogue with them seriously to see what we might learn from them. The books make ethical arguments of the kind mentioned by Doerksen above: they are Mennonite arguments, though not necessarily Christian. Part of how queer Mennonite literature queers Mennonitism is by broadening the scope of what "Mennonite" and being Mennonite means. The books insist that theological Mennonites are not the only ones who get to define "Mennonite." Such work must be a shared conversation. Sometimes being Mennonite means having an unorthodox faith or no faith at all, but it always means acting ethically in order to build and sustain some form of community. All the books advocate for an ethic that meshes with Jesus's command to care for "the least of these" in Matthew 25:45. Theological Mennonites and other religious readers might be disturbed by some of the characters' actions, but the goal of the stories and my close readings of them is to cause readers to think, not necessarily to agree. Therefore, I generally do not spend time discussing how certain arguments made by the texts differ from Mennonite orthodoxy as defined by Mennonite Church USA and Mennonite Church Canada.

Perhaps, however, it is unqueer to insist on differentiating between literary criticism and theology, to dichotomize them. Perhaps it is better to let them bleed into each other for readers as they may. After all, theologian Mark D. Jordan claims that the best queer theology is influenced by pop culture, including novels and pornography, and he names queer fiction such as Samuel R. Delany's *Trouble on Triton* as theology. Queer theorist Elizabeth Freeman goes even further, wondering whether queer theology must include God at all.[86] These writers remind us that the queer transforms categories, liberating them from rigid boundaries. In a Mennonite context, literary criticism tends to edge into the theological because of religion's role in Mennonitism as a cultural and ethnic manifestation of Anabaptist-Mennonite theology. As a result, Mennonite literature inevitably acknowledges the significance of religious thought and experience even when such literature is avowedly secular. Thus while *Queering Mennonite Literature*'s primary conversation partners come from the literary tradition, one could choose to read it theologically if one so desires. *Queering Mennonite Literature*'s intended audience is anyone—academics and lay readers alike—who is interested in Mennonite studies (especially Mennonite literature), queer theory, or the general study of literature and religion. Theologians and religious studies scholars interested in fields such as queer theology, narrative theology, or theopoetics will also find the book helpful because the queer and Mennonite traditions have many more resonances than people realize.[87] They are not the "oxymoron" that Jess from *Somewhere Else* first finds present in the term *queer Mennonite*.

The protagonists in queer Mennonite literature are queer Mennonites, with their queerness being the most prominent aspect of their hybrid identities, though they also cannot escape their Mennonite roots. The identity chooses them rather than vice versa, and because they attempt to make their peace with it instead of fighting it, they offer hope that their presence will make the larger Mennonite community a less oppressive one. But this is not an act of acquiescence to either Mennonite or societal homophobia. In an essay, Braun claims the hybridity that Jess initially cannot, powerfully asserting, "I am a queer Mennonite."[88] Her statement, echoed in the experiences of characters in the books at hand, shows that the community of queer Mennonites does exist and that it refuses to be ignored. It manifests itself in part through the pieces of queer Mennonite literature that keep appearing, to which *Queering Mennonite Literature* now turns.

Building a Queer Mennonite Archive

Over the past two decades, queer theory has taken what Ann Cvetkovich calls an "archival turn," an examination of the concept of the archive as one way to study queer life across a range of disciplines in the humanities.[1] Queer archiving's goal is to preserve a record of queer experience, whether through formal institutional archives, personal collections of items, interviews, or other means. The concept is intentionally open because it is queer. Part of this preservation takes place in writing, an act that both documents queer existence and creates new queer objects that then become part of the archive themselves. *Queering Mennonite Literature* joins the queer archival endeavor by examining how the texts it investigates document both queer Mennonite life and queer life in general. Two levels of archiving are present in the book: it investigates how the texts it studies archive the everyday ephemerality of queer experience, and it archives the books and their archiving endeavors. In other words, the books are both primary sources themselves and secondary sources documenting queer experience. Kate Eichhorn posits that archiving can function as a type "of applied theorizing."[2] As I explain in the introduction, queer Mennonite literature also functions as theory. Examining its archiving endeavors consequently helps reveal how it achieves its theoretical pursuit.

In order to establish how queer Mennonite literature accomplishes the work of archiving, this chapter discusses books by Christina Penner and Wes Funk that place archives, both physical and conceptual, institutional and informal, at the center of their narratives. Mennonites love archiving, and this affinity makes the previous lack of archiving of queer Mennonite experience especially striking.[3] The archiving in Penner's and Funk's texts is firmly ensconced within both the queer and Mennonite traditions and works to remedy this lack. Penner's 2008 novel *Widows of Hamilton House* does so through its focus on preserving and interacting with the past. Funk's 2014 autobiography *Wes Side Story* does so as an example of how to write about all facets of everyday queer experience, offering readers an archive of queer emotions.

Archiving Queer Space in *Widows of Hamilton House*

Widows of Hamilton House is a modern retelling of Ruth and Naomi's story from the biblical book of Ruth that investigates the relationship between the two women instead of focusing on how they are tied together by their relationships to men (as in the biblical account). *Widows of Hamilton House* recasts Ruth's choice to stay with Naomi as an explicitly sexual love story rather than as a godly act of devotion. It does so within an openly Mennonite context: Ruth's Mennonite family (she's a Reimer) and the story's setting (the Mennonite enclave of Winnipeg). The novel is thus another entry in the long list of activist Mennonite literary texts and an early example of queer Mennonite literature.[4] Eli Clare defines "queer" as someone who does not fit into society and contends that the term is closely related to "exile."[5] These two elements of the queer are especially relevant to *Widows of Hamilton House* in particular and Anabaptist thought and experience in general. *Widows of Hamilton House* is queer not only because Ruth and Naomi are bisexual but also because of how it queers both geographical and conceptual spaces, in part through its explorations of the paranormal. That is, it illuminates the marginalized experiences, both past and present, in these spaces as one way of thinking about the new visions for society that queer theory proposes. Moreover, the novel's emphases on the acts of reading, writing, and book collecting highlight the need to make queer archives and experiences visible, as the novel itself does.[6] Because of its queerness, *Widows of Hamilton House* transgresses traditional Mennonite beliefs, and this transgression is what draws me to write about the book. Its queer elements help me make sense of my own queer Mennonite experiences. I share some of these experiences because, as Cvetkovich contends, "personal testimony" can be an important archival tool.[7] The marginality of queer experience means that sometimes memories rather than physical objects are the only documentation of it left.

While I reread *Widows of Hamilton House* to write this chapter, I felt the same sense of exhaustion I often do when reading queer Mennonite literature. I enjoyed the book because the story was compelling and made me care about the characters, but contrary to how I normally read, it was difficult to read the novel for long stretches of time. I began to procrastinate, finding other tasks to do. I thought to myself that perhaps I should read some more theory that would be helpful for the chapter; perhaps I should read some other non-Mennonite queer novels with similar themes in order to place Penner's within a broader context; or perhaps I should work on lesson plans for the next week. It was difficult to decide which was worse: the discomfort of procrastinating, feeling that I was not being productive in the way I should be, or the discomfort of plunging ahead in the novel. My hesitancy felt like something different from my usual writing anxiety, which I have learned to live with in part because I know it is something many writers share.[8] Even Penner's Ruth feels the need to get away from her own research sometimes.[9] As I read on, I decided that the novel makes me uneasy because it feels too close to my own story, and so to dissect it by writing about it is also to dissect myself in some ways. There is a stress inherent in being a queer Mennonite that I share with Ruth. Casey Plett writes that there is an assumed homophobia in the Mennonite community that is inherently taxing on Mennonite queers.[10] Thus while I find my encounters with queer Mennonite literature to be liberating, these encounters also come with the psychological violence of this homophobia, from the knowledge that the broader community wants to keep these stories marginal.

This sense of unease and exhaustion I experienced while reading *Widows of Hamilton House* was magnified when I first tried to write about it. On the night of 8 October 2016, after fitfully beginning to reread the novel, I dreamt that I was in a farmer's harvested field, and my favorite student (a non-Mennonite) showed me a conservative Mennonite newspaper with an article speaking out against me because of my work on queer Mennonite literature. The rest of the dream consisted of increasingly surreal attempts to escape this landscape. Considering the novel's paranormal elements, which include a ghost moving objects around and the spirits of several former residents of the eponymous Hamilton House appearing during séances and other events, it seems particularly appropriate that I had this dream while working with this text, where Ruth's discomfort about her queer Mennonite identity also manifests itself in a religiously inflected dream in which she gets crushed by a pulpit during the 1997 Red River flood (273). She worries that institutional Mennonite homophobia will snuff out her relationship with Naomi and her sense of self with it.

There are very few bisexual characters in Mennonite literature.[11] Thus I am glad for *Widows of Hamilton House*'s sympathetic portrayals of Ruth and Naomi and for the novel's incisive depiction of society's attempted denial of bisexuality's existence.[12] I myself struggle with whether bisexuality is an adequate term for my sexuality because I dislike that it implies that there are only two genders. Similarly, Ruth feels uncomfortable with using "bisexual" to describe herself (246) and notes that in the eyes of her family, she and Naomi have each "confirmed their heterosexuality" by virtue of having once been married to men (257). Ruth's family views her previous relationship with a woman as a phase she has outgrown when she begins dating a man and then marries him. There is no acknowledgment that even though someone is in a relationship with a partner of one gender, it might still be possible for that person to be attracted to other genders as well.

But Ruth and Naomi form a close bond evocative of the biblical Ruth and Naomi once Naomi's son Lon introduces them. In fact, *Widows of Hamilton House* makes it clear—even to readers who may be unaware of the biblical story—that the novel is a retelling of the biblical narrative by mentioning it openly several times (132–33, 138, 284). When Naomi tells Ruth in Ruth 3:4 to "go in, and uncover [Boaz's] feet, and lay thee down," she is alluding to a sexual act because the word in Hebrew for *feet* is also used as "a euphemism for 'genitals.'"[13] This element of the story gets ignored in traditional interpretations that focus on Ruth's loyal actions and Boaz's generosity, but *Widows of Hamilton House*, by making Ruth and Naomi lovers, makes the story's sexual undercurrents explicit while also arguing that the community of women has revolutionary queer power. The novel echoes the sexual nature of the Hebrew double meaning of feet/genitals in a passage where Naomi touches Ruth on the knee, which is a seemingly innocent gesture in public but for them is a form of "kiss[ing]" (259). The women are wary of showing open affection in their homophobic society but also resist this homophobia by remaining in their relationship despite its taboo nature.

The novel argues that queer relationships can lead to new forms of family. Some may see Ruth and Naomi's relationship as pseudoincestuous because of their initial connection through Naomi's son / Ruth's husband Lon, but the novel rejects such mores, instead focusing on the power of women's relationships with each other, whether sexual or not. Ruth explains that there is not a satisfactory label for her relationship with Naomi but that the important thing is the relationship itself (246), which represents a new form of community that, even if it has a membership of only two, is essentially Anabaptist because it offers a vision of a better world.

Finding Healthy Community

Widows of Hamilton House also investigates issues of Mennonite community boundaries through Ruth's status as an outsider. While the biblical story describes Ruth's entry as a Moabite into the Israelite faith community, the novel describes Ruth's entry as a Mennonite into the worldly community. Of course, in this move, Ruth seemingly leaves something behind, and this is one way the novel queers the biblical story—by questioning what the biblical Ruth lost when she chose to make Naomi's people her own. What kind of pain was involved in that act of loyalty, and was there a part of her that felt disloyal to her original community?

As for Penner's Ruth, she leaves her rural family for the city and embraces the world sexually, through her relationships with women, and spiritually, in her newfound belief in and experiences of the paranormal, which expand her conception of the supernatural. Penner's Ruth is not compelled to abandon all she has ever known. That is, the Mennonite community is not rejected through Ruth's narrative because the novel places her story firmly within the broader Mennonite story. One way it does this is by describing the death of Ruth's grandfather during the Russian revolution (39). Despite the fact that it is frequently retold in Mennonite literature, the story of Russian Mennonite trauma is extremely rare in queer Mennonite literature, which generally focuses on the trauma of being a queer Mennonite instead.[14] But *Widows of Hamilton House*'s inclusion of this common Mennonite literary theme acknowledges that queer Mennonite narratives have a place alongside and within broader Mennonite narratives and that new Mennonite identities, such as queer Mennonite, are legitimately included within the community.

Searching for Queer Space

One way the novel advocates for conceptual spaces for queer Mennonites is by focusing on the relationships between its characters and the physical spaces they inhabit. I find this dynamic in *Widows of Hamilton House* particularly compelling. In recent years, I have begun studying the importance of space—both in literature and in everyday life—as a part of my trying to define the concept of "home," which has been a lifelong struggle for me. I have lived all over the United States: New York City; Lancaster, Pennsylvania; Goshen, Indiana; DeKalb, Illinois; Salt Lake City, Utah; and now Utica, New York. Thus it is difficult sometimes not to feel that there is an impending displacement on the horizon. This sense of geographical rootlessness and, I think, my willingness to be open to the experiences that have led to it are a result of the influences of my Mennonite upbringing. So many of the Mennonite narratives I heard as bedtime stories growing up were about displacement, whether about the early Anabaptists having to hold church in caves, or about my Swiss Mennonite ancestors leaving Europe in search of religious freedom in Pennsylvania, or about Russian Mennonites fleeing to Paraguay after World War II in children's books such as Barbara Smucker's *Henry's Red Sea*.[15] When you are raised in a tradition that teaches you to be "in the world but not of it," it is difficult to ever feel at home. This tension has been heightened for me because of my mixed ethnicity. One or the other of my ethnic identities has been Othered by the culture of many of the places I have lived.[16]

So space is difficult for me, and it is thus not surprising that my afore-mentioned dream involved a vivid spatial element even though I feel safer in my queerness than Ruth does in *Widows of Hamilton House*. My family accepts my sexuality, and I have found a supportive community of scholars in which to pursue my interest in queer literature. But I recognize that I am extraordinarily lucky in these regards, as there are still not enough queer-friendly spaces in either Mennonite life or academia. This is why texts such as *Widows of Hamilton House*, which examine space through a queer lens, are so important. This lens illuminates the way spaces can be transformed as one step toward a liberated, politically queer future. Queer Mennonite lit-erature is an especially fertile landscape for this transformation because, as Maggie Nelson asserts, no matter what kind of space you are in, "nothing you say can fuck up the space for God"; there is always the potential for change.[17] It is always possible for the spaces in which we find ourselves to move us in profound ways, whether through encounters with the divine or the paranormal or something from the secular world. For instance, when Ruth moves into Hamilton House, she has no idea that it will change her life completely, but when it does, she is open to these changes. I try to emulate such openness in my own life.

I have found the concept of psychogeography, which examines how spaces affect individuals psychologically and asserts that the effects of space are political, helpful in my theoretical study of space. Psychogeographer Merlin Coverley observes that "psychogeography concerns itself" with "the act of urban wandering [and . . .] political radicalism, allied to a playful sense of subversion and governed by an inquiry into the methods by which we can transform our relationship to the urban environment." He goes on to explain that "this entire project is then further coloured by an engagement with the occult and is one that is as preoccupied with excavating the past as it is with recording the present."[18] Coverley's explanation suggests that psychogeogra-phy is an appropriate lens through which to examine the depiction of space in *Widows of Hamilton House* because both the novel's urban setting and its investigation of the paranormal play an essential role in its queerness and because "political radicalism, allied to a playful sense of subversion," is an excellent definition of the queer theoretical principles that guide this book. Moreover, Hamilton House's past plays a significant role in the way Ruth and Naomi experience the space.

Ruth moves into Hamilton House, which is an actual house in Winnipeg, after moving to the city from Alberta.[19] The house is owned by a Mennonite-run fair-trade craft store that is clearly based on the Ten Thousand Villages chain, which was started by Mennonite Central Committee. It is significant that the house is immediately established as a Mennonite space, as not only is it owned by Mennonites, but Ruth finds out about the apartment for rent via the "Mennonite Game," since her aunt volunteers at the store. Unlike most pieces of queer Mennonite literature, where the characters struggle to find a Mennonite space where they can be queer safely,[20] *Widows of Hamilton House* allows a queer character to help queer a Mennonite space that by the end of the novel becomes her permanent residence. This permanence is important because while Ruth often feels uneasy about the space throughout the novel, she is able to fight through these feelings (which could be seen as an echo of Mennonites' historically difficult relationships with space as a result of their history of persecution[21]) in order to make the space her home.

The house begins to affect Ruth right away. On her second day living there, she finds a photograph of it that makes her "afraid" and "change[s]" the way her body moves inside the space (13). It takes her a little while to understand why the house moves her in these ways, but Ruth encounters it as a queer space immediately in that it is weird and uncanny. She discovers soon afterward that the original owners, the Hamiltons, held weekly séances there for many years. These séances, which are a queer practice because of their implicit rejection of mainstream views of both the world and the afterlife, fascinate Ruth to the point of obsession.[22] She begins investigating the Hamiltons and ultimately is convinced that the spirit world they believed in exists.

Part of how the house becomes a queer space involves a sexually queer act carried out through this spirit world. Unbeknownst to Ruth, Naomi buys the house and then tries to break up with Ruth and kick her out because she knows that Ruth has felt oppressed by the house. But Ruth, while lying despondently in bed, gets kissed by Lillian Hamilton's ghost, an act that inspires her to go make love to Naomi and stay in the house, which saves their relationship (283). Lillian's ghost insists that the women stay together and thus advocates that the house become a sexually queer space as well as a spiritually queer one. The house's queer paranormal aspects, which liberate the space from conventional mores, allow the women to make it their own.

Explorations of paranormal spaces like the space of *Widows of Hamilton House* occur strikingly often in queer Mennonite literature. For example, Jessica Penner's *Shaken in the Water* includes a yard inhabited by a ghost tiger whose "Voice" is heard by characters across several generations, André Swartley's *The Wretched Afterlife of Odetta Koop* is about attempts to exorcise a homophobic Mennonite ghost from a haunted house, and Funk claims in *Wes Side Story* that he encounters ghosts in his Saskatoon house.[23] I am unsure what to make of this reoccurring motif. While I have never experienced the paranormal myself, I know trustworthy people who swear that they have, and its frequent presence in queer Mennonite literature feels like something more than a coincidence. Perhaps portrayals of the paranormal not only evoke the uncanny qualities of queerness but also offer writers a safe conceptual space in which to discuss queer Mennonites because one must be open-minded to acknowledge the paranormal just as one must be open-minded in order to appreciate queer perspectives. *Widows of Hamilton House*'s paranormal aspects are the earliest and the most positive in queer Mennonite literature, just as the novel is one of the only texts in the field to depict a safe, queer-friendly Mennonite space.

Queer Archiving

Cvetkovich posits that "the history of any archive is a history of space."[24] The relationship between these histories holds true for both finding physical spaces to house archival materials and the act of documenting the emotional archives created through the ways spaces affect their inhabitants. Space and archiving are closely intertwined in *Widows of Hamilton House*, which is part of what draws me to the novel. In fact, a significant aspect of my bibliophilia is my book-buying and collecting (I rarely use libraries) because my books tell the story of my life through the experiences I associate with them; they archive my personhood. My books are the first things I unpack when I move because they help me remember who I am and help me insert myself into a new space in order to make it a home. In my scholarship, I enjoy investigating marginal texts, whether they be books by forgotten authors such as Theodora Keogh or ignored and in some cases out-of-print books by more well-known authors such as Miriam Toews or Samuel R. Delany.[25] I like to think that my collecting of these scarce texts, whether arranging them on the bookshelf or referring to them on the written page, is helping keep them safe from oblivion. My obsession with curating these books makes me wonder sometimes whether, despite my infrequent use of libraries, I missed my calling as a librarian.

Since taking a Mennonite literature course at Goshen College in 2001, building my own archive of Mennonite literature has been a significant part of my book-buying practice. At first I thought I would be able to own a copy of every piece of Mennonite literature, but I soon realized that this would be impossible, because (happily) writers in the field are too active for me to keep up with. But I buy and read as much Mennonite literature as I can because in the broader field of literary studies, it is a marginal literature (especially in my U.S. context) often published by small presses, and I worry about its lasting power. What will happen to excellent texts that deserve study, such as Dallas Wiebe's *Our Asian Journey*, which has been out of print for years, or Miriam Suzanne's *Riding SideSaddle**, which is difficult for bookstores and libraries to shelve or keep intact because it consists of 250 unbound pages in a box?[26] Since 2013 I have been focusing almost exclusively on Mennonite literature in my scholarship in order to help preserve some of these texts. As Cvetkovich explains, "queer cultures" are often "ephemeral."[27] Writing *Queering Mennonite Literature* is one way to combat queer Mennonite literature's archival marginality, helping ensure that its existence remains visible for future use by lay readers and scholars.

Ruth shares my obsession with scrutinizing and archiving marginal texts. She works in a library at the University of Winnipeg, one of the libraries in the book, both public and personal, that serves to symbolize the importance of archiving. In a passage where Ruth is researching in the University of Manitoba archives, she reflects upon who has the power to decide which objects are archived and which are not (100–101). Her skepticism about the official history found in institutionalized archives epitomizes a queer approach to the world, as does her work archiving marginal texts in unorthodox ways.

Two examples of the queer archiving methods Ruth employs are the way she organizes her personal library chronologically by when she reads each book rather than by genre or alphabetically by author and the way she uses random pieces of paper from her everyday life—ticket stubs, receipts, photographs—as bookmarks and then leaves them in the books (54–55). Her library practices make her personal library a repository of her life. The organization of a library, whether personal or institutional, is important because, according to Melissa Adler, it is inevitably a political "statement" rather than a value-neutral act.[28] In Ruth's case, her library makes a statement against Mennonite biphobia. The arrangement of her books is significant because her library records her previous relationship with a woman, Abby, and is thus a physical, concrete, archival manifestation of Ruth's bisexuality. Even though Ruth's family pretends that this relationship did not happen, Abby's inscriptions in the books she gave to Ruth pay testimony to their love.

One of Ruth's queer archiving practices occurs at her job. As part of her work, she goes through boxes of donated books to see whether any of them are worth keeping. As she does so, she imagines the lives of the owners of the donated books (29–30), recognizing that the books carry a history of emotions that makes them more than just physical objects; they also map their former owners' conceptual psychogeographical wanderings. *Widows of Hamilton House*'s portrayal of these marginalized books positions the novel as an archive itself because it pays testimony to all the books that are ultimately forgotten and destroyed. It reminds us that any archive, no matter how extensive, contains gaps and is inevitably incomplete.

Ruth muses about "the current of undesired books that move beneath any city" (17), recognizing in psychogeographical terms that books become associated with the space, the city, they belong to. Just as books themselves create conceptual spaces that affect the headspace of their readers, they also transform physical spaces that, in turn, transform the books themselves because readers will have different encounters with the same text depending on their geographical context. For instance, I am sure that my experience reading *Widows of Hamilton House* as someone who had never been to Winnipeg before reading it was much different from that of a Winnipeg native. These unwanted books, described in the novel as a "current," are a constant flow, lurking like the waters in the rivers of Winnipeg that flood late in the novel. One might get swept away by these books as Ruth ultimately is swept away by one of them.

While the discarded books Ruth encounters contrast with the official, public archive of the library, Ruth—as a result of finding *Intention and Survival*, a real-life volume by the house's original owner, T. G. Hamilton, in a box of donated books that the library rejects—discovers and creates of them an archive about Hamilton House's séances.[29] She documents her obsession with this book and her resulting interest in the house's history in a journal, where she acknowledges that it is difficult to document the "type of [paranormal] history" Hamilton's book tries to preserve, which is part of why she is so enthralled by it (70).

Cvetkovich argues that one task of queer scholarship is to document queer "cultural contexts that might otherwise remain ephemeral because they haven't solidified into a visible public culture."[30] Penner's novel names and makes visible some of these contexts while being one itself. It also com- bats oppressive systemic homophobia by documenting queer Mennonite experience. Ruth writes in her journal that "there are stories that have never been told. Stories so quiet, that when you read them, you will call them unrealistic [. . .] because you've never heard a story about it before." She goes on: "When you choose to listen to a story that hasn't been told, it enters your body like a foreign object." These stories, she contends, include LGBT relationships (243).[31] *Widows of Hamilton House* functions as an archive for these kinds of stories; the novel makes them available so that its readers can no longer say they have not heard them and thus have no frame of reference for them. It makes queer Mennonite stories visible in light of how LGBT persons continue to be discriminated against by the institutional church. Ruth's comparison of marginal stories with an "object" that penetrates and thus changes the body is apt because these stories' rarity gives them an unsettling power that in some cases—including my own experience with the novel—is literally physical.

Ruth's written archive is expanded to become a paranormal archive as well when one of the house's spirits enters her body and causes her to transcribe into her journal a poem by Robert Louis Stevenson—a poem she has never read before and that she assumes is her own creation (293–94). This event marks the archiving in the novel as a queer act because of the way the spirit inhabits Ruth, breaking down the physical barriers of her self and putting her in the role of amanuensis for the good of the community, including the house's spirits and the two women, whom the spirits help remain together.

While Ruth's experience of possession is stressful because of its disconcerting nature, it ultimately benefits her. Likewise, I find that writing through the stress of dissecting my queer Mennonite self while attempting to better understand the novel has been a worthwhile endeavor. Early in the novel, Ruth asks Lon to tell her his "strangest story" (52). This is what Penner does with *Widows of Hamilton House*. She gives us a book that is queer in multiple ways and that readers cannot help but be affected by. I value it because it helps us look for the stories on the margins and sometimes join them. As Ruth writes, "I feel like I tried the normal route [in life]. And it broke my heart" (244). The novel thus argues that we must look to queer ways of living, whether sexually or politically, instead. For those of us from the Anabaptist tradition, this is simply doing what our ancestors have done since the sixteenth century. It offers paths toward a more just society.

The Uncanny Call of Wes Funk

The notion of being "called" to a specific vocation is a significant one in the Mennonite theological tradition. Whether this call comes directly from God in a scene similar to the call of Samuel in 1 Samuel 3 or whether it comes from someone else in the faith community, narratives of call are a common trope.[32] It is thus not surprising to encounter a Mennonite writer using the language of call when discussing how he became a writer. *Wes Side Story* includes two episodes that explain why Funk decided to begin writing. His description of how he fulfilled this call by writing his autobiographically inflected fiction places Funk's work into both the queer and Mennonite literary traditions and creates a conceptual space where the two meet.

When describing how he was called, Funk, while attributing the call to supernatural forces, does not assign this mandate to God. He attributes it to two ghosts. The first of these apparitions is Funk's former lover Keith, who died of AIDS. Funk decides to visit a psychic during a time of questioning in his life, and she raises Keith's ghost, who tells Funk that he is "'supposed to write books.'"[33] While Penner confines the queer practice of séances to the realm of fiction, Funk claims that they have real-life efficacy.

Funk's call to writing is repeated later, when he is browsing in a record store. He is mesmerized by a poster of The Doors' lead singer, Jim Morrison, and "f[eels] a kind of enlightenment. [He] was supposed to write" (104). Funk's choice of words here is significant because he uses religious language, albeit from Buddhism rather than Christianity, to describe his experience. Although he receives his call from a secular source, he is able to respond to it because he has a religious framework through which to interpret his revelation—namely, the idea that some people do receive special calls to complete certain tasks.

Most readers will react incredulously to the sources of these calls. The sources are queer in the sense that they are weird and uncanny, and their unsettling nature will tempt many readers to dismiss the stories' veracity out of hand. After all, who wants to believe that psychics might actually have legitimate powers or that pictures on the wall are going to start giving out messages? The hearing of voices is supposedly something that only the insane experience. Interpreting Funk's claims about his interactions with ghosts thus requires what Abram J. Lewis calls "a hauntological reading," which acknowledges the truthfulness of Funk's experience for him even if readers are agnostic about its possibility.[34] Traditional academic strategies are unable to make sense of his experience. There is no objective evidence to verify that it happened. Theological Mennonites will have theological objections to it because it does not fit within a Christian cosmology, and secular readers will find it scientifically impossible. Therefore, all I can do is acknowledge its existence in the text and let other readers decide for themselves how to relate to it. Funk tells his ghost stories openly and sincerely and leads his life afterward with a sense of purpose that he gleans from them. The apparitional appearances are thus real in their effects whether or not they are real in fact.

Funk's openness to experience a call and respond to it makes the argument that it is necessary to participate in community and that it is possible for the community to give the individual instructions for how to live one's life. While Funk receives his call from the queer (Keith) and secular (Morrison) communities, his openness to the idea that he should take up a new vocation and write explicitly queer fiction in service to others is an act tinged by values from both the Mennonite and queer traditions. Kay Stoner writes about the similarities between these two communities, noting that they are both marked by long histories of oppression and arguing that in working to realize their visions of social justice as "dissenting group[s]," they share community-building activities such as "potluck[s]" and "small group[s]." Even choosing to leave the homophobic church for the queer community echoes the early Anabaptists' choice to leave the state church, as both choices include a belief that a better vision of community is possible.[35] Casey Plett also examines the relationships between queer life and Mennonite life, naming "family, community [. . . ,] the loss of family, the loss of community [. . . , and] [d]isplacement, the destruction of stability" as themes in both Mennonite literature and queer literature.[36] Mennonites and queers share the experience of exile, and these experiences manifest themselves in literature. One way Funk raises this theme in *Wes Side Story* is by depicting how his call gives him a new community, the writing community, to go to once he leaves his homophobic Mennonite community behind. He then uses his position as a writer to acknowledge the influence that both the queer and Mennonite communities have had on him as he archives queer Mennonite experience in his novels.

Aside from its uncanny aspects, Funk's call from Keith is a queer one because of their sexual relationship. Keith's position as a queer martyr as a result of his AIDS-related death adds an element of sacredness to his charge to Funk to tell stories of those on the margins honestly. In effect, he calls Funk to write so that he and others like him will not be forgotten. Funk completes this testimony in part by being open about his relationship with Keith and how it involved barebacking (i.e., anal sex without condoms) rather than the practice of safe sex (82).[37] Funk's willingness to seek pleasure for his body instead of feeling shame about its taboo desires and, just as importantly, his willingness to narrate his pursuit of this pleasure rather than censoring himself help claim legitimacy for these actions and work as weapons against societal homophobia.

Funk's call from Jim Morrison also includes queer elements prefaced earlier in the book by some of Funk's previous experiences with music. He explains that he realized *"it was okay to be gay"* despite his homophobic upbringing when listening to openly queer musicians as a teenager (48, emphasis in the original). Public gay role models helped Funk accept himself, and by relating this story as well as writing his novels, he works to act as such a role model for others, so his work is explicitly activist. He also writes that music "saved [his] life" several times when he was trying to find himself as a young man (43, 68). It is significant that Funk pays tribute to the importance of music and musicians in his life (much more so than he does about specific writers, in fact). Biographical theorist Hermione Lee contends that biography examines "the effects of a life on others."[38] Funk does this regarding his own life later in the book, but he must first explain to readers the influence others had on him so that he could get to a place where he could respond to his call to have that effect. Funk places his narrative firmly within the context of community, which is, once again, a queer and Mennonite move.

Morrison's image serves as a representation of these influences in Funk's life. The erotic way Funk describes him in the poster, as though he is a Calvin Klein model—"shirtless" with "lion-mane hair"—turns Morrison into a queer sex symbol, one so powerful that Funk gets The Doors' logo tattooed on his back soon afterward (104). In light of Funk's transcendent experience, this poster acts as a secular icon, a talisman for Funk as he tries to provide the kind of narrative model to readers that he finds in queer music. As Funk responds to his call from Morrison, he pays homage to the rocker in the title of his first novel, *Dead Rock Stars*, which is about the owner of a record shop similar to the one where Funk encounters the poster. Funk explains in his autobiography that he had always been intrigued by musicians such as Morrison who died young (104). He gives the protagonist of *Dead Rock Stars* this fascination as well.

Wes's Funky Body

Once he received his call, Funk wrote a book of poems and short stories as well as three novels before writing *Wes Side Story*.[39] Examining how he constructs his identity as a writer in the latter illuminates the activist elements in his fiction. *Wes Side Story* begins this construction on its cover. The title, aside from being a campy, and thus queer, musical-related pun, works as a polemical statement because Funk asserts he is telling his "side" of things, that his outsider perspective needs to be heard.[40] The cover image is a stylized frontal portrait of Funk's face by RoseMarie [*sic*] Condon that uses Funk's hair, glasses, goatee, and earrings to define his head rather than depicting his head itself, lending the image a ghostly quality that is appropriate considering his experiences with the paranormal. The portrait has Funk's name where his mouth would go, symbolizing how he speaks himself throughout the book. The portrait's inclusion of Funk's three earrings is important because they are a marker of his outsider status (more on this below) as someone who embraces countercultural movements, queer or otherwise. The cover image repeats on the book's half-title page without Funk's name or the title, so there is just an emphasis on his face, which is significant: he is there, not just as an abstract concept held in language, but as someone who must be seen. In sociologist Arthur Frank's terms, this image helps make Funk "narratable" by inserting a representation of him into the discourse.[41] *Wes Side Story* writes Funk into being so that others will acknowledge his existence despite its marginality. The repetition of the cover image on the half-title page is also important from a Mennonite viewpoint because Funk is not worried about appearing prideful (an especially heinous sin in Mennonite thought) by showing himself twice. He asserts that his presence is important. He is called to share a message and demands our attention as he shares it. The third image at the beginning of *Wes Side Story*, which appears on the title page, is not of Funk but of the title only, in the same font as on the cover but twice as large and with three stars around it. This image names Funk as "fabulous," as a "star," again playing up the campy nature of the book's title.

The cover's emphasis on Funk's corporeal self is continued throughout the book, often in explicit ways. For instance, he mentions masturbating to a photograph of Mick Jagger and shares that his nickname for his penis is "Mr. Wiggly" (29–30, 52). The matter-of-fact tone Funk uses when relating these details indicates that he includes them not to be titillating or salacious but because he believes it is important to be open about the enjoyment of his body as a corrective to North American society's policing of sexuality. Despite its commonality, masturbation is an essentially ephemeral act, so Funk's inscribing of it on the page epitomizes queer archiving. Readers may feel that Funk's inclusion of such details is an example of oversharing at best and scandalously sinful at worst. However, by including them he insists that all of queer life should be visible, even in its most private, everyday moments. As Juana María Rodríguez declares, queer archiving involves "the soiled and untidy."[42] Funk makes it clear that as a queer archive, *Wes Side Story* will document every area of his life.

Queer Failure

One element of Funk's identity as a writer as given in *Wes Side Story* is that he views himself as being on the margins and that he writes to those who are also there. He dedicates the book to "anyone who has ever felt like an outsider" (5). There is an appropriate similarity between this dedication and that of J. Jack Halberstam's book *The Queer Art of Failure*, which is "for all of history's losers."[43] Halberstam argues that "failing is something queers do" but that this act can be powerful because it leads to new unthought-of perspectives and is one of the "weapons of the weak."[44] This view of failure resonates with the Mennonite concept of the "upside-down kingdom" that Jesus references in Matthew 20:16: "The last shall be first, and the first last." Those who are considered outsiders, whether because they are failures or otherwise, have a certain kind of subversive knowledge because they can observe the powerful without themselves being observed, since the powerful treat them as though they are invisible. In acknowledging this group, *Wes Side Story*'s dedication names both Funk himself as marginal and the book as specifically queer because being queer means being on the margins.

Funk establishes his outsider credentials early on in *Wes Side Story*. He begins the book with the story of his father proposing to his mother (9–10). This narrative choice places Funk's story firmly within a community, affirming that the concept of community is an important one for him. But he then shows throughout the book how his experiences have alienated him from this community, both his immediate family and their broader Mennonite milieu. He explains that he was an unplanned child (15), a detail that shows he was never wanted by the community he acknowledges in the book's opening pages. He is constantly at odds with his family, noting simply that he "was different" in his description of a fight with his mother over whether he could take home economics rather than shop class (39). Funk leaves his rural Saskatchewan home after high school, hoping he will find belonging in Saskatoon. This move from country to city, symbolizing a rejection of the faith community in favor of a dalliance with the world, is a common one in both Mennonite lives in general and Mennonite literature specifically and is repeated in Funk's first two novels. Unfortunately for Funk, he does not initially find fulfillment in the city and tries to commit suicide. His family visits him in the hospital but does not offer to take care of him as he recovers, underlining just how much of an Other he is to them (69–71). In light of this near-death experience, it is understandable that when Funk receives his call to write about marginalized lives as a way to help those who reside there, he takes it seriously.

Funk also names himself as an outsider as a writer. He recounts how *Dead Rock Stars* received "17 rejections" before he finally decided to self-publish it (118). This nontraditional publishing choice places Funk's work on the literary margins, in part because literary critics and his fellow writers may look down on it, since it does not have the publishing industry's stamp of approval, and in part because his choice does not give his work access to established distribution channels. Cvetkovich's previously cited observation about the ephemerality of queer cultures certainly applies to Funk's oeuvre.[45] Funk writes about queer culture to preserve it, but his books themselves are ephemeral in that they are very difficult to acquire because of their self-published status, especially now that he is deceased. For instance, as I was writing this portion of the chapter in September 2016, I wanted to purchase a copy of Funk's first book, *Humble Beginnings*, and was unable to find one available online. A search of amazon.ca for Funk's other novels on 8 September 2016 revealed no paper copies of *Baggage* or *Cherry Blossoms*. Just two paper copies of *Dead Rock Stars* and *Wes Side Story* each were available, and Kindle editions were available for only the latter three. All paper copies were being sold by the same small store: Laird Books in Regina, Saskatchewan. On the same date, amazon.com (i.e., Amazon in the United States) had one paper copy of *Dead Rock Stars*, and abebooks.com had one paper copy of *Dead Rock*

Stars available from a New York bookseller and one paper copy of *Cherry Blossoms* from an Ontario bookseller along with copies of those novels and *Wes Side Story* from Laird Books. On abebooks.com, Laird claimed to have twenty copies of each book rather than two (and for some reason, they do not advertise their copies of *Cherry Blossoms* on Amazon), but whether they have two or twenty, these statistics show that Funk's works are rare enough that they risk being lost to literary history, which is one reason I am writing about them. As of 8 September 2016, Funk's website, www.wesfunk.ca, was still up, and there were links to purchase both paper and electronic versions of *Dead Rock Stars*, *Cherry Blossoms*, and *Wes Side Story*, but it was unclear whether a request to purchase one of these texts would be answered, as Funk himself may have been the one to fulfill such orders. A check for his site on 3 July 2018 revealed that it no longer exists.

The fragile availability of Funk's books is an issue shared by queer Mennonite literature as a whole. All the texts discussed in this book are published by small publishers and, as a result of these companies' lack of economic stability, are always in danger of going out of print. Indeed, this happened to Jessica Penner's *Shaken in the Water*, whose first publisher, Foxhead Books, went out of business in 2015, two years after the novel's publication. Happily, André Swartley's company Workplay Publishing, which produces self-published books that have gone through a full editorial vetting process (i.e., it is not a vanity press), published a new printing in 2017.[46] While it is fair to raise questions about self-published books' aesthetic quality, it is also possible to view the move to self-publish as an activist answer to the mainstream publishing industry's perceived reticence to publish queer books.[47] Another piece of queer Mennonite self-publishing, Stephen Beachy's *Zeke Yoder vs. the Singularity*, is one example of such activism. Beachy's 2016 Kickstarter campaign to support his Amish science fiction young-adult novel raised US$1,522, 25 percent more than its goal of $1,200.[48] The campaign's success shows that there is a reading public willing to pay for queer literature. In discussing their Kickstarter campaign for another queer literary project, the founding of *TSQ: Transgender Studies Quarterly*, Susan Stryker and Paisley Currah acknowledge one problem with "crowd-sourced fundraising" is that it is "a technique of neoliberalism, helping shift costs from service providers to consumers in ways that increase profits and decrease benefits."[49] However, this kind of fundraising also helps create a community and allows it to work together to archive its narratives by bringing objects that it deems important into the world. While I wish that I lived in a society that valued literature enough that such fundraising efforts would be unnecessary, I was happy to donate to Beachy's campaign as a form of repayment for the joy and learning his previous books have brought me.

The authors such as those studied here who choose self-publishing are capitalizing on the changing mechanics of the literary marketplace as part of a grassroots, bottom-up movement to make their queer, marginalized stories heard whether academia respects them or not. Funk's sense of calling that he must get his stories out there no matter the cost, even if, as it turned out, it initially meant paying for the printing of his books himself, epitomizes this trend. His choice to self-publish is a queer and Mennonite move because it emphasizes witness-through-story for the sake of the community rather than the sake of fame and profit.

Funk himself occupied the margins of the writing community because he did not have any kind of university degree or formal creative writing training and thus had a difficult time gaining access to the reading and lecture circuit. When viewed through Halberstam's lens of failure as a queer virtue, Funk is perhaps the queerest of all queer Mennonite writers in that he had no academic credentials, rode a bus to work, worked menial jobs, and died after mistakenly taking too much pain medication.[50] His work epitomizes "outsider art" to the point where readers might wonder whether it even deserves the attention of a critical endeavor such as this one.

However, Funk emphasizes in *Wes Side Story* that his work has affected readers just as he is explicit about how visible queer role models influenced him. He shares several stories of meeting strangers on the street who identify him as Wes Funk the writer, and he also notes that *Dead Rock Stars* was included in a university course on gender studies (146, 150). Funk's work achieves a kind of canonization via this inclusion, albeit a tenuous one because it was not taught in an English course. But the fact that it becomes visible enough to enter both popular consciousness and academia is a prime example of "the last shall be first" motif. Despite his failures, Funk shows that his writing accomplishes what he was called to do because people respond to it and it is recognized by those with institutional power. Funk also writes that on multiple occasions, people have told him that reading his books caused them to stop being homophobic because it gave them a better understanding of gay life (128, 204). These accounts show the importance of Funk's stories, including his autobiography, in making queers visible to others. His work has a prophetic effect, causing people to change their lives after hearing his message. As with all prophets, Funk encounters some resistance to his writing, but this resistance helps raise his work's profile. His books become visible enough to be both banned and included in banned books events (191). These incidents illustrate that the queer narratives Funk tells are still revolutionary, necessary ones. His words from the margins carry power.

Funk's Autobiographical Fiction

Funk's transgressive novels include numerous autobiographical elements. The "About the Author" statement from *Baggage* says that he has "dedicated his writing to telling stories that reflect his life," and in *Wes Side Story*, he notes that these autobiographical elements are often queer (128).[51] Valerie Rohy highlights the importance of life writing in "queer literature."[52] It is not surprising that the assertion of self in such writing is often manifested in queer fiction as it is in Funk's work and the texts investigated in chapters 2, 3, 4, and 6 to varying extents. Although Funk takes pains to emphasize *Wes Side Story*'s genre in its subtitle, he approaches writing autobiography and fiction in the same way. All his books use the same plain, chronological prose style to the point where they become generically indistinguishable so that if one did not know any better, it would be possible to read *Wes Side Story* as a piece of metafiction about a character named Wes Funk. Such sameness is not normally the case with novelists' life writing and may simply result from Funk's lack of formal writing instruction.[53] Nevertheless, it works from a queer perspective because of its insistence that the boundaries between genres are made to be disregarded.[54] The queer archiving accomplished in Funk's work is what matters instead. There is always some kind of "truth" in his narratives, factual or otherwise.

Funk's insistence on writing about queer experience makes the connection between real life and the necessity of queer fictional models for the queer community explicit. The protagonists of his first two novels, *Dead Rock Stars* and *Baggage*, are both fictionalized versions of Funk himself. In *Dead Rock Stars*, Jackson Hill looks exactly like Funk, with red hair, earrings, a goatee, and black glasses;[55] in *Wes Side Story*, Funk acknowledges that this character is his "alter ego" (160). Like Funk, Jackson has left his rural hometown for life in Saskatoon but must then figure out how to relate to the community he abandoned. He struggles with constructing an identity that will allow his urban gay self to be in a relationship with a farmer. This plot is an essential one for queer literature because, as Halberstam notes, fiction depicting "queer rural life" is rare.[56] But *Dead Rock Stars* offers an example of how it is possible to find liberating queer rural spaces and thus inhabit a queer rural self. As Lee posits, biography is always concerned with "identity."[57] While, as noted in the introduction, some literary critics wonder whether the field of Mennonite literature should move beyond questions of identity,[58] Funk's writing argues that we cannot be done with the concept quite yet, since those on the margins are forced to contend with their identities because the oppressors use these identities as justifications to oppress them. *Wes Side Story* is, on one level, about Funk's struggle to find an identity for himself, which he ultimately does as a queer writer by writing fictional versions of his experiences.

Baggage is the most autobiographical of Funk's novels, as it explicitly examines queer Mennonite identity. The novel tells the story of Sam Brown. It begins as *Wes Side Story* does with his parents, who discuss the burden of Sam's unplanned conception. Despite the fact that she did not intend the pregnancy, his mother decides that her child will have a "purpose" and that they will name him "Samuel [. . . which] means *to listen.*"[59] In case readers do not immediately make the connection between Sam and the biblical Samuel, his mother's speech makes it clear that he should be read as a prophet. Samuel actually means "name of God" rather than "listen," but Sam's mother's mistranslation reinforces that readers must pay attention to his story. Sam, as *Baggage*'s Funk stand-in, is a prophet, just as Funk depicts himself as a prophet responding to a call in his autobiography.

Sam also references another literary Samuel, Samuel Reimer from Rudy Wiebe's 1970 novel *The Blue Mountains of China*, whose story is contained in the second-to-last chapter of Wiebe's sweeping narrative of Russian Mennonites fleeing the Soviet Union for the more religiously tolerant landscapes of Canada and South America.[60] Entitled "The Vietnam Call of Samuel U. Reimer," the chapter depicts Reimer's call from God to go preach peace in Vietnam and how his Mennonite community refuses to listen to him, which results in his death. While *Baggage* ends on a happier note, its resonance with Reimer's story is significant because of how its themes place it in the broader tradition of Mennonite literature. Funk's writing works to expand the tradition, making space for queer stories and calling for acknowledgment that the kind of lives they portray have been part of the larger Mennonite story all along. *Baggage* shares the oppressive rural community found in "The Vietnam Call of Samuel U. Reimer," but instead of letting this community destroy him, Sam leaves it for the theoretically welcoming arms of the city as Funk himself did.

Aside from its similarities to *The Blue Mountains of China*, Sam's Mennonite background—he notes that his family is "Mennonite" and mentions having cousins in Steinbach, Manitoba, which is also a Mennonite marker for those who know how to interpret it—makes *Baggage* an explicitly

Mennonite text.[61] Sam's character is prophetic because he finds a way to be a queer Mennonite despite his home community's opposition. While Funk's sparse mentions of his Mennonite background in *Wes Side Story* indicate that he experienced a lot of pain from his homophobic upbringing, it is significant that he mentions it at all and that he chose to write an explicitly Mennonite novel. He recognizes the Mennonite community's influence on him. Bernice Friesen also notes that Funk submitted a poem to *Rhubarb*, the journal of the Mennonite Literary Society, before he died.[62] This choice of venue indicates that Funk may have been coming to terms with himself as a specifically Mennonite writer, not only a queer one.

Just as Funk's fiction shares similarities with previous Mennonite texts, it also shares similarities with a set of foundational queer texts, Ann Bannon's five-part Beebo Brinker series of novels.[63] Although *Baggage* is not a sequel to *Dead Rock Stars*, the books share characters and settings in order to portray the possibility of a supportive queer community that is larger than individual relationships. In doing so, they repeat Bannon's creation of standalone texts within the context of a shared world of characters and issues that help make the queer community visible. Bannon's novels remain influential because they are some of the first queer novels to have relatively happy endings in contrast to those in previous queer fiction, since their characters are able to affirm their queer identities rather than being forced to either denounce them or suffer horrible repercussions.[64] Similarly, it is significant that *Dead Rock Stars* and *Baggage* are love stories that end happily because they offer an important hopeful vision for queer Mennonite futures. In these novels, Funk provides the stories he describes struggling to find for himself in *Wes Side Story*.

Reading Funk's fiction through the lens of his autobiography empowers the fiction because the pedestrian, everyday aspects of its narratives are given more urgency through the activist aspects of Funk's call. Despite the various rejections he experiences, Funk shows in *Wes Side Story* that he takes his call seriously and keeps writing, ultimately succeeding in this act. His choice to answer his call helps illuminate some of the intersections between queer literature and Mennonite literature, most notably their emphasis on the search for healthy community, and places his work firmly in both traditions. It remains the task of readers to respond to the fulfillment of Funk's call and explore the queer Mennonite archive that he documents for us, which is useless if left undisturbed. How will we employ his prophetic words?

Searching for Selfhood in Jan Guenther Braun's *Somewhere Else*

Jan Guenther Braun's novel *Somewhere Else*, which is a "fiction[alized]" version of Braun's life, depicts Jess Klassen's struggles to reconcile her Mennonite faith with her lesbianism in an attempt to claim the seemingly contradictory identity "queer Mennonite."[1] Its examination of institutional Mennonite theology is the most explicit of all the books *Queering Mennonite Literature* studies, and thus it pays the most attention to the role Mennonite faith plays in Mennonite selfhood. Happily, by the end of the novel, Jess succeeds in her quest for an integrated identity. But this outcome is in doubt throughout Jess's narrative because of the pervasiveness of Mennonite homophobia combined with the welcoming queer community that Jess finds in exile, which raises the question of why it is even worth hanging onto her Mennonite self. Jess's early act of naming herself as queer in her struggle to find an identity is important. It gives her an initial sense of selfhood that acknowledges her desires while at the same time giving her space to continue to discover and construct herself in a way that works for her because it is not prescriptive. Living as queer and placing the Mennonite element of herself to the side for much of *Somewhere Else* allow Jess to learn how to accept her attraction to women and joyfully embody it. It is only once she takes this step that she is then able to return to a healthier, more compatible version of her Mennonite self.

While *Somewhere Else* is one of the earliest texts studied in *Queering Mennonite Literature*, it remains as relevant as ever because of its realistic portrayal of lesbian life, in terms of both this portrayal's plausibility and the book's mode of writing. Writing in 2017, Sara Ahmed argues that "we need a revival of lesbian feminism" because "living as a lesbian" is a way to "live a feminist life."[2] Ahmed's version of lesbianism insists that being a lesbian is a politically active stance and thus a queer, intersectional one. It insists that two identities that should be natural allies but sometimes are not, queer and feminist, can come together in powerful ways for change. *Somewhere Else* depicts the revolutionary feminism Ahmed calls for through Jess's narrative.

Somewhere Else is also an example of what José Esteban Muñoz calls a "concrete utopia." Unlike an "abstract utopia," a concrete utopia is a queer form that offers visions of the future that stem from real-world political activism. To create these visions, concrete utopias "critiqu[e] the present" by drawing from the queer past in order to offer hope for a liberated future. Queer archives are essential for concrete utopias because of the concept's dependence on the past as a source of strength and hope. This past consists of the everyday elements of queer life: snacking, working, watching movies, going to museums, having sex, and so on.[3] These aspects serve as building blocks for envisioned queer existence. Braun's novel fits Muñoz's framework because it presents an activist queer vision that offers hope that it is possible for the identity of "queer Mennonite" to be a fulfilling one. It does so by archiving both the queer pasts that Jess finds and the story of her early lesbian life itself.

Braun's "Queer Mennonite" Identity

Three personal essays by Braun from 2008, 2013, and 2016 help illuminate why *Somewhere Else* may still be read as a relevant concrete utopia a decade after its publication. The essays archive the fluctuations of Braun's hopes regarding her queer Mennonitism. They move from a position of optimism to one of disappointment and back to a renewed willingness to engage the Mennonite tradition to make it better. The first and third essays were published in the *Journal of Mennonite Studies*, and the second was published in *Rhubarb*. It is significant that Braun chooses to write about her Mennonite self and that the essays appear in Mennonite venues even though it is clear Braun often feels angry and frustrated with the Mennonite community. Her choices show that she is interested in sincere dialogue with the broader community and that she is arguing for space for queer lives within the community. She does not want leaving to be the only option despite that, considering its current doctrine, leaving is the church's de facto solution.

The first essay, "From Policy to the Personal: One Queer Mennonite's Journey," which was published shortly before *Somewhere Else*, is written from a position within both the church community and the queer community. It begins by stating how Braun's Mennonite "people," General Conference

Mennonites, sounded "like freaks" when she first learned about their roots in a Mennonite history course.[4] The essay names the traditional queerness of Mennonites that Dorothy Thompson's *Ladies' Home Journal* article mentioned in the introduction highlights. Mennonites are off the beaten path; we are weird; we do not fit. It is thus especially frustrating when the church does not make space for those among its community who find unorthodox paths of their own. Braun's work portrays the disconnect between the church's ideal of loving those on the margins and its actual oppressive treatment of them. Braun and her fellow queer Mennonite writers use their texts to advocate for this ideal, in part by using the church's teachings to critique it, showing how the community has failed to live up to its vision for itself and must thus find ways to do better.

"From Policy to the Personal" gives a history of denominational discussions about the issue of queer church membership that have resulted in the community's policies of exclusion, including the startling fact that the church tried to suppress queer Mennonite stories it collected while it was studying the issue in the 1980s.[5] Knowledge of such a history illustrates just how important public queer Mennonite voices like Braun's are because of their insistence that they be heard so that queer Mennonite experience is always visible. Despite the church's chicanery, Braun insists on her desire to be included, declaring, "I am a queer Mennonite. My story is indelibly linked to the main narrative of Mennonite history."[6] By tying herself to the community's story, Braun, too, asserts that Mennonitism is queer in some philosophical ways and argues for a place at the table for those of us who are sexually queer. This is space that she claims throughout the essay, even when describing how Mennonite homophobia has negatively affected her life. Braun's essays and novel are statements that she refuses to let the church take her Mennonite identity away from her and that she will not acquiesce to institutional Mennonitism's attempts to silence her life. She ends "From Policy to the Personal" by declaring that although she feels the need to give up her dream to be a Mennonite pastor, "I am a Mennonite, for better or for worse. [. . .] I will not leave."[7] This is an important activist statement because it insists on the queering of Mennonite identity. It asserts, as *Somewhere Else* does, that "queer Mennonite" is a claimable, legible identity worth fighting for.

Discouragingly, by Braun's 2013 essay "Queer Sex at Bible College," the fight to maintain her identity leaves her questioning whether it is even worthwhile to be affiliated with the Mennonite community because of its homophobia. The frequent use of profanity throughout the essay functions as a way for Braun to claim space in the queer community (we queers love swearing!) and to claim space away from her Mennonite community because of her flaunting of the traditional Mennonite emphasis on plain speech and such scriptural prohibitions as not taking God's name in vain in Exodus 20:7. The necessity for this space is foreshadowed at the beginning of the essay when Braun states that her "identity" as a younger person "was very much made up of the fact that I was a Mennonite."[8] While the "was" here indicates the historical past, it also raises the question for readers as we read the rest of the essay of how Braun feels about this identity at the time of writing, casting a shadow over what follows.

"Queer Sex" expands the brief discussion in "From Policy to the Personal" of Braun's time as a student at Canadian Mennonite Bible College (CMBC, now part of Canadian Mennonite University) in Winnipeg.[9] Braun, who by then is aware of her attraction to women, knows that she cannot be both "openly queer" and Mennonite in this setting.[10] Her choice to stay closeted is understandable, a survival strategy that feels necessary at the time. Unfortunately, as the rest of the essay shows, her strategy does not work because she feels further and further alienated by the church's homophobia. Instead, Braun's willingness to name herself as queer in print and let the Mennonite community react however it may is a defiant, activist move that illustrates how the church loses just as much as, if not more than, she does if it rejects her. An unhealthy community is unhealthy for everyone in it, not just those it marginalizes. Braun describes how she was taught the significance of "community" at CMBC, but it was a diseased version that was overrestrictive of individuality.[11] This experience shows that Mennonite claims to care for the oppressed can create a false sense of belonging for those on the margins that is then stripped away when they fail to conform.

However, despite this hypocrisy, Braun is able to separate the liberating ethics of Mennonite teaching from the church's rejection of her. She writes that she "knew that God hadn't left me or judged me, or forsaken me."[12] God is always on the side of the oppressed even if the community is not. Here she claims that one can be not just a queer ethnic Mennonite but a queer theological Mennonite as well, because no institutional church can ever have a full understanding of God, and so queer Mennonites can have just as close of a relationship with the divine as anyone else.

Braun concludes that she must have this relationship elsewhere, though. As a result of the church's oppression, it loses her. The end of the essay is worth quoting at length because of its raw, heart-wrenching power. Braun "came to understand that you can only be told for so long that you don't belong [. . .] before you just leave. So I left. I never meant to, though. I always said I would fight, that no one can take away my baptism, or the fact that I love the church. Now on Sunday mornings I sleep, and sometimes I have sex."[13] The essay condemns the church as a failure because of its disregard for those who "love" it while also being a defiant, proud claiming of Braun's queer identity due to her willingness to publicly acknowledge her sex life. It also includes a kernel of hope that Braun can return to her Mennonite identity because of the use of present tense in the statement "I love the church" and the statement that she did not mean to leave but simply could not take the oppression any longer. So while "Queer Sex" is written with Braun outside the church, it still fiercely claims the identity of "queer Mennonite" not only because of its Mennonite publication context, which indicates a willingness to stay in touch with the institutional and cultural communities, but also because of its status as a lament for how the church fails to live up to its own teachings about caring for outsiders. The fact that Braun takes the time to bother writing such a lament shows that she has hope that the community will change for the better.

Braun's third essay, "A Complicated Becoming," offers possibilities for how this change might occur. It begins by discussing how, through the years, Braun has learned more about identity construction and how one's various identities play off of each other. She posits that building a self means actively choosing to participate in the communities that facilitate the identities that are the most important to a person. Braun argues that this is a Mennonite stance because of "the Anabaptist tradition['s . . .] radical" emphasis on gathering "like-minded weirdos" together.[14] Again, Braun recognizes the philosophically queer aspects of Mennonitism, including its roots in community. Queer Mennonites may be "weirdos," but through efforts such as Braun's to make us visible, we are a presence that the broader Mennonite community can no longer ignore.

Unlike her first two essays, "A Complicated Becoming" hardly discusses Braun's personal faith journey but instead shows how Mennonite literature has helped her reclaim her Mennonite self, giving her hope for change. Braun explains that literature, both Mennonite and non-Mennonite, taught her "a commitment [. . .] to not being acceptable" as a writer. This position means that being "a queer writer [. . .] is not simply a sexual orientation. It is a questioning."[15] Braun's experiences reading Mennonite literature and personally interacting with Mennonite writers teach her the activism that being queer entails and keep her in touch with the version of Mennonitism that the Mennonite literary community represents. The narrative of Braun's encounters with Mennonite literature implicitly makes the argument that the entire field is politically queer, just like Mennonitism as a whole. Braun goes on to say that she continues to draw "strength" from Mennonite literature and also from "the Jesus of Nazareth narrative."[16] Thus she refuses the faith community's rejection of her queerness, arguing that they are not the only ones who have the right to interpret what they presume are only their stories. She finds room for herself in the Jesus story as a queer Mennonite.

Braun declares in "From Policy to the Personal" that she writes it as a starting point for the creation of "queer Mennonite academic history."[17] Ultimately, this seed has resulted in much growth. Braun's choice to put her story into words both in that first essay and in *Somewhere Else* helped inspire me to begin writing about queer Mennonites. Knowing of this work, Julia Spicher Kasdorf then recommended me to Andrew Harnish when he was looking for others interested in queer Mennonite literature, and our meeting led to the "LGBT Fiction" panel at the 2015 Mennonite/s Writing conference.[18] The panel and the subsequent work it inspired, including "A Complicated Becoming" and *Queering Mennonite Literature*, are examples of the queer Mennonite academic work envisioned in "From Policy to the Personal." This progress, despite its slowness—which Braun expresses justified frustration with—shows that the vision originally presented by *Somewhere Else* is still relevant and can function as a queer Mennonite ideal worth striving for.

Claiming Queer Identity in Exile

Somewhere Else begins with Jess encountering a list of Bible verses that Mennonites use to define homosexuality as a sin. When she sees the list, she feels a "silent violence" directed at her that causes her to vomit.[19] By choosing this term instead of a weaker one, such as "discrimination" or "prejudice," the novel immediately illustrates how the church eschews its pacifist ideals through its homophobia, engaging in systemic violence by policing queer bodies. Jess throws up throughout the novel whenever she is stressed because her Mennonite upbringing does not give her the tools to process strong emotions healthily, instead insisting that she deny her emotions so that she can live the meek life the community prescribes. This is a restricting of all bodies, not just queer ones. While I grew up in a Mennonite community that was not as oppressive as Jess's, I was also taught emotional austerity, and I think that training is part of what caused my strong physical reactions to *Somewhere Else* that I discuss in the introduction. I am struck by the similarity between Jess's bodily responses and my own, but they make sense within a Mennonite context: in a tradition that constantly teaches you to deny yourself, how are you supposed to react when you encounter a story that shows you to yourself as queer Mennonite literature shows myself to me? As Mennonites, we are trained to shy away from this visibility.

As a result of the church's violence, Jess realizes she must leave her community. Independently, her parents realize it as well and decide to send her to boarding school in Ontario (30). This act functions as a kind of informal shunning, pushing the issue of Jess's lesbianism to the side and marginalizing her further rather than making space for her in the community she loves. Jess understands what her parents are trying to do and refuses to go. She slips away in the middle of the night instead (34). It is important that Jess leaves on her own terms rather than her parents', who represent the broader church not only in their role as parental authorities but also because Jess's father is the president of a Mennonite college. By depicting him as a church figurehead, *Somewhere Else* presents Jess's struggles as a microcosm of the broader queer Mennonite struggle against institutional Mennonite repression.

Jess knows that leaving via the community's way, still nominally a part of it but really not because of the geographical and emotional distance going to boarding school would create, would simply lead to more emotional violence and the further destruction of her emerging queer self, so she takes agency over her life by striking out on her own. Di Brandt explains that the decision to go into exile from the Mennonite community has been "lifesaving" for members of various groups on the margins of the community, including "independent-minded women [. . . and] gay people."[20] It is evident by the end of *Somewhere Else* that becoming an exile does save Jess's life, and as shown below, Mennonite literature plays an important role in helping her survive the experience. Brandt's poetry actually helps Jess leave home because reading *questions i asked my mother* gives Jess a model for the rebelliousness needed to go against the community's wishes (13). However, as noted in the previous chapter, the choice to leave the community in hope of finding a better one is still a Mennonite move. Jess has learned from her Mennonite upbringing that fleeing when in danger is a logical choice. The stories of persecuted Mennonites that Jess is raised with in Sunday school and at home, which feature Mennonites being ready to leave Russia or Germany at a moment's notice before the government rescinds its decision to let them escape teach her what she needs to do.[21] She packs to leave as though an "army [i]s coming [. . .] in twenty minutes" (18). This mind-set might sound macabre to non-Mennonite readers, but it seems fairly normal to me—I have gone through the same mental exercise a number of times because of being raised with the stories of displacement mentioned in chapter 1. I get nervous every time I go through airport security because I worry that somehow my documents might not be in order. In traditional Mennonite thinking, the world is a terrible, violent place, and one must always be ready to seek refuge elsewhere. Unfortunately for Jess, her Mennonite community itself is violent, so she has to go. She believes that on some level her parents will understand her decision because of the stories they raised her with. Later in the novel, she muses that they did not look for her after she left "because they respected running away as my ancestral right" (61). Jess's sardonic comment shows that even when she is trying to get as far away from Mennonites as possible, she is living a Mennonite life.

When Jess leaves, she buys a one-way train ticket to Winnipeg (36). She, like Wes Funk (and Braun herself), is from rural Saskatchewan, and like Ruth in *Widows of Hamilton House*, she looks to Winnipeg as a place of potential and hope. She thinks she might find welcoming Mennonites there (45). While Jess's logic is flawed because the religious Mennonites she hopes to seek out would belong to the same homophobic denomination as her family, it is an understandable choice for Jess to make because it is fair to say she is drawn to Winnipeg because of its status as a Mennonite mecca: it is a "safe" city for Mennonites to go to if they have to encounter "the world." So her journey into exile away from the church is nevertheless tinged with Mennonite elements.

While Jess struggles to reconcile her queer and Mennonite identities, her act of naming herself as queer in this struggle is important. It gives her an initial sense of selfhood that acknowledges her desires while at the same time giving her space to continue to discover and construct her self in a way that works for her because it is not prescriptive. Living as queer and placing the Mennonite element of herself to the side for much of *Somewhere Else* allow Jess to learn how to accept her attraction to women. It is only once she takes this step that she is then able to return to a healthier, more compatible version of her Mennonite identity. Similarly, Braun felt that if she was "true" to her "queer" self, she "would eventually lose everything" related to her Mennonite involvement.[22] She realized that she had to find a way to reconcile these identities and needed to find a queer-friendly setting in which to do it. Her novel's title emphasizes this setting's necessity for both her and Jess's narratives. They must be "somewhere else" to discover themselves. *Somewhere Else*'s cover, which depicts an airplane boarding pass, emphasizes this journeying.[23]

Jess's move to the city is a common one in queer Mennonite literature and in queer Mennonite experience in general. Like Jess, it was not until I left another Mennonite enclave, Goshen, Indiana, for a city that I was able to begin investigating my queer identity. This identity is a legible, visible one in cities in a way that it is not in rural Mennonite communities. While the books discussed in chapters 3, 4, and 6 illustrate that it is possible to be a rural queer, finding models for how to be so can be difficult.[24] One can find space in the anonymity of a city that is not always available in a small town to think through whether such a taboo identity is applicable to oneself.

55

Although she is unsure what she will find in Winnipeg, Jess is able to explore her queerness right away after leaving Saskatchewan when she gets picked up by another woman on the train, Freya, who takes her home when they get to Winnipeg (43, 47). Freya and her housemates seamlessly integrate Jess into their community, so she finds acceptance right away. It may seem a bit unrealistic that Jess gets so lucky, but her luck functions to assert *Somewhere Else*'s status as a concrete utopia. Her initial success at finding a community gives her the strength to keep exploring her queer self. She and Freya have sex and begin a relationship. In this experience, Jess feels like "a child, being carried in the womb of my new lover" (49). Her sexual initiation is the prelude to her queer rebirth. Her queer self is still gestating but will soon emerge fully. The metaphor she uses echoes Jesus's language of being "born again" in John 3:3, acknowledging the queer ideal of community because of the resonance of being born into a community of believers through baptism.

The sacramental element of baptism is present in Jess's sexual encounters. Juana María Rodríguez asserts that queer sex is a place "where survival becomes imaginable."[25] Sex is an essential part not only of Jess's claiming of a queer identity but of making that identity one that sustains her as a person while in exile. At its best, sex creates a community of two (or more if one enjoys group sex) that offers safety and comfort. It is the kind of act that helps create a utopia. Jess finds this ideal in her erotic encounters with Freya. Throughout much of *Somewhere Else*, there is a shyness present in Jess's narration of her sex life in that she mentions when she has sex but does not describe it. However, there is one scene with Freya where Jess is unabashed about claiming the beauty of women's bodies. She wakes Freya one morning by giving her cunnilingus, and she describes becoming enchanted by the "perfume" of Freya's vagina, admitting that even years later the memory of the smell causes her to "stop breathing" and lose her train of thought (91). The scene is important because it embodies the antithesis of the Mennonite taboo against bodily pleasure that Jess has been taught, both in the gender of her partner and in the specific act, which has no purpose other than sexual gratification. It also writes against the broader societal discomfort with vaginal scent. Jess does not feel squeamish about going down on Freya but does it for her own enjoyment as well as her partner's, finding pleasure in the act's raw physicality.

Aside from her community of two with Freya, Jess enjoys learning from her other housemates. She finds that the house runs in what she recognizes as Mennonite ways. There are emphases on "community, simple living, and civil resistance" (51). Jess sees that the importance of community in Mennonite thought is a good thing even though her actual experience of it was not. Paradoxically, being taught the Mennonite ideal of community while growing up helps Jess realize that her home community is flawed and that she must seek out a better one. She needs a place where openness is practiced, not just preached, and finds it in her house's queer community.

Jess's house community experiences spark my own memories, which are relevant to share here, not to be prideful, but to illustrate the importance of Braun's book for providing a model of how to live a queer Mennonite life.[26] After college, I lived in a Mennonite-owned boarding house, Menno House, in lower Manhattan for two years with ten mostly twentysomething housemates. This experience was essential for my realization that I was queer, because the city atmosphere forced me to be thinking about sex and sexuality all the time. Like me, most of my housemates were in a libidinous stage of life, so intra-house hookups, including a few involving myself, occurred frequently. Similarly, on my walks home every evening, I would be exposed to all my fellow young professionals putting themselves on display as they went for after-work drinks. Being in a new place always requires a mental adjustment, and mine in such a sex-saturated space necessarily meant figuring out my sexual identity, something I had always been discouraged to do in my Mennonite upbringing both at church and in my eight years attending Mennonite schools. Like Jess's housemates, the housemates I came out to were supportive.

Once I acknowledged that I was queer, I wanted to begin exploring my sexual identity just as Jess does, but I had no guides for doing so. I remember reading the listings of gay bars in *Time Out: New York* and wondering what it would be like to go to one but never having the courage to do so. I wish that queer Mennonite books such as *Somewhere Else* had existed at the time as a model for me to figure out both how to explore queer identity and how to retain my Mennonite identity, which I felt quite estranged from even though

I was living with other Mennonites, many of whom were also skeptical about the church. We tried to learn together how to be ex-Mennonites, a status that I was to realize later is an impossibility. At the time, Mennonite literature was the only thread attaching me to Mennonite discourse, something that I had previously been fully ensconced in because, like Braun, I was planning to be a pastor. In an alternate, queer-friendly universe, we might have been seminary classmates.[27] Like Braun and Jess, I learned how to transgress, which is certainly what claiming my queer identity felt like, from Mennonite literature.

The Community of Literature

In both Braun's and Jess's narratives, literature provides the space to begin reconciling the identities "queer" and "Mennonite." After deciding to put off seminary, Braun majored in English at the University of Waterloo, where she discovered "a world" of new ideas.[28] The plethora of perspectives that she found in literature helped Braun claim her queer identity. Similarly, Jess has to go away from the Mennonite community to a secular context in order to find belonging before she can then integrate her queerness with her Mennonitism. Jess finds her first welcoming community in literature by both Mennonite and non-Mennonite authors. As described above, she draws strength from the activist nature of previous Mennonite literature such as Di Brandt's writing before she leaves Saskatchewan. The strong feminist tradition in Mennonite literature has had a major impact on the field, without which queer Mennonite literature would have been much different—if it had come into existence at all.[29] We see this influence especially in Braun's work, including in Jess's reading choices. Through Jess's reading of Mennonite writing, she learns how to look to literature for help in times of need and is able to use this strategy once she moves to Winnipeg. Her citations of feminist Mennonite literature as essential for helping her understand her queer identity show how she embodies Ahmed's lesbian feminist ideal because she is able to make the intersectional move of applying this writing's questioning of gender roles to her investigations of sexual identity.

One of the best things about Jess's house community in Winnipeg is that the residents keep their books in a shared library. Jess spends much of her time reading through it. In an early archiving effort to make queer literature visible, the kind without which Jess's discovery of queer narratives in exile would be much more difficult, Claude J. Summers writes that queer literature is a necessity for queers as a resource because of frequent familial and community rejection once we come out, and he affirms the importance of libraries in providing access to such literature.[30] Jess's access to the house's library, which includes texts that are queer both sexually and politically, plays an important role in her learning how to do queerness in private and in public. Her library investigations are a search for queer narratives that mirror her own experience as she searches for a literary community to replace the real one that has been lost. She draws on lesbian history as archived in various books to find a livable life for herself. Ahmed argues for the importance of books both as learning tools and as physical objects manifesting lesbian existence in her assertion that "you need your favorite feminist books close to hand [. . . .] Kick-ass feminist books have a special agency, all of their own."[31] This argument for personal libraries is not an argument for conspicuous consumption but one that posits that sometimes objects can act as shields against sexism and homophobia, that they can be necessary tools of survival because of how they archive queer experience, reminding their owner that they, the owner, exist within a tradition to draw strength from.

One way Braun's book acts as a concrete utopia is by citing activist literature as the novel itself reveals that it is a queer, activist work. Once she is away from the Mennonite community, Jess reads lesbian stories such as Sarah Waters's *Tipping the Velvet* (73). It is significant that *Somewhere Else* has Jess cite Waters specifically, because Waters's lesbian novels always take place in the past (*Tipping the Velvet* takes place in the late 1800s; *The Night Watch*'s World War II setting is the closest Waters's work gets to the present), thereby showing that women's same-sex erotic relationships have always existed. Braun's novel thus archives an author who is also interested in archiving lesbian experience. In an early critical endeavor to catalog such an experience, Terry Castle contends that society does its best to ignore lesbian narratives, and as a result of this practice, lesbians are "made to seem invisible" in venues such as literature and film.[32] While matters have improved somewhat in North American society in the quarter-century since Castle's statement, it remains relevant, especially within a Mennonite milieu. Ahmed describes how there is still constant societal "disbelief" about lesbians that manifests itself in the questioning of lesbian existence, giving the example of checking into a hotel room with her girlfriend and having the clerk refuse to believe that they want a room with only one bed.[33] In light of such lesbophobia, it makes sense that Jess seeks out books such as Waters's to fight society's erasing of lesbianism and to make her lesbian self visible to herself. Likewise, by telling Jess's story, *Somewhere Else* helps make lesbians visible for the Mennonite community. Ahmed declares that living out an "archive" of antilesbophobia "derive[s] as much from our struggle to write ourselves into existence as from who appears in what we write. This intimacy of standing against and creativity can take the form of a book."[34] Braun participates in this activist narrative formation by putting her personal experiences into fictional form. In this light, *Somewhere Else* is a queer Mennonite manifesto that both reveals the existence of queer Mennonite identities and archives their experiences. Braun's book is an essential building block of the queer past and the possibilities of a queer future for queer Mennonites. Ahmed further claims that when living a lesbian feminist life, "life becomes an archive of rebellion."[35] Jess's story is important because of her willingness to rebel against the unjustness of her homophobic Mennonite upbringing. This choice epitomizes Mennonite radicalism when one considers the Anabaptist tradition's roots in rebellions against various state churches in the sixteenth century.

Along with explicitly queer texts, Jess reads feminist texts such as Margaret Atwood's *The Edible Woman* (87). Like *Tipping the Velvet*, Atwood's book is a feminist coming-of-age narrative that reflects Jess back to herself as she continues to construct her queer feminist identity. She struggles throughout *Somewhere Else* to find other people who care about her in a healthy way—her relationship with Freya sours after a few months—but she is never completely alone because of her reading.

The community of queer literature that Jess encounters in Winnipeg gives her enough of a theoretical underpinning for her queer identity that she feels secure in it when she leaves to go to university. As Jess unpacks her books in Waterloo, she has "a sense of peace" because of how they make the space feel like home (97). They comfort her in an example of Ahmed's concept that feminist objects can be a source of sustenance.

But before she leaves Saskatchewan, Jess steals a book that she finds in her father's library, which plays an essential role in her explorations of literature and identity throughout the novel. This (fictional) text is a poetry chapbook by Martha Wiens, *In the Wilderness*, which contains love poems to a woman (25–26). Thus there is a literary vision for Jess of how to combine "queer" and "Mennonite" from the very beginning of *Somewhere Else*. She takes *In the Wilderness* with her when she leaves Saskatchewan, and it is always there, lurking, even when she largely places her Mennonite self aside while she, too, is in the wilderness.

Jess is at first unsure what to do with *In the Wilderness* because it is too radical for her to process at first. She says that finding a piece of queer Mennonite literature feels illicit, like finding drugs or "pornography" (26, 40). In comparing Wiens's book to pornography, Jess names it as sinful. She is still thinking through the lens of the Mennonite community's view toward queerness, and because she cannot yet quite accept her queer self, she also cannot accept the concept of queer Mennonite literature as a liberating force that could help sustain her life.

However, Jess's comparison of *In the Wilderness* to pornography also includes another element. Despite its socially marginalized nature, pornography often serves as a form of sexual education.[36] Jess's analogy highlights how Wien's book is educational for her. This learning begins right away because when she reads it the night she finds it, she realizes that she cannot "survive" in her "community," that she must leave if she is going to find her queer self. She remarks that even reading such a revolutionary piece of literature, let alone identifying with or agreeing with it, is transgressive because "private reformations are discouraged" by her community (28). The church, as holder of authority, is also supposed to be the holder of truth for each of its members. This belief illustrates why early Mennonite literature such as Brandt's or Rudy Wiebe's or Patrick Friesen's or Julia Spicher Kasdorf's—the list is long—was seen as so rebellious and shocking by the theological community.[37] In the collective's view, the act of claiming a personal voice to talk about the Mennonite community in public flies against standards of humility and epitomizes the sin of being prideful. But Jess realizes that she needs to find a place where she can claim her own queer voice by investigating her hybrid self.

In the Wilderness helps her claim this voice. As *Somewhere Else* continues, there are several scenes where Jess returns to Wiens's collection to read but then ends up writing her own poems instead (76, 127). The book becomes an inspiration for Jess's explorations of herself as she begins writing her own queer Mennonite literature, helping her think about both of these identities. In thinking about Wiens as a possible model for herself, Jess wonders why Wiens chose to stay on the fringes of the community, living at the edge of town in Saskatchewan, instead of leaving (77). Wiens's choice shows Jess that sometimes it is possible to relate to a community even in its imperfections. Jess realizes she might not have to remain in exile for the rest of her life. When Jess comes back to Mennonites, they will not accept her immediately (though, as mentioned below, her family might), but there is hope for things to get better, the kind of possibility that is present as one works toward a concrete utopia.

As a result of what she learns from *In the Wilderness*, Jess decides to write her senior thesis on it (107). At this point, three years after leaving Saskatchewan, Jess is able to embrace queer Mennonite literature just as she embraces her queer self. It is no longer sinfully pornographic. In her choice of thesis topic, Jess tries to build the queer Mennonite academic tradition that Braun speaks of in "From Policy to the Personal." In a concrete utopian move, Braun envisions this tradition by creating *In the Wilderness* for Jess to use as a model despite the lack of such a model for Braun as she was writing *Somewhere Else*. In doing so, she actually wishes the tradition into existence as described above. Braun's success is a perfect example of how concrete utopias can have a real-world impact.

During her research, Jess uncovers some secret family sexual history. When interviewing Wiens, Jess finds out that before Wiens met the woman who inspired her book, she had a child with Jess's father, David (178). The revelation of this relationship helps humanize David because we see that he is not a perfect, faceless church figurehead. Instead, he is a flawed hypocrite who had a sexual relationship before marriage. By including this relationship's story, the novel highlights the need for an openness in the community that will lead to more healthy discourse around all sexuality, not just queer sexuality. Wiens's story also suggests that she is bisexual. Although Jess encounters Wiens's work as a woman-loving-woman narrative, *Somewhere Else*'s depiction of a bisexual and a lesbian building queer Mennonite community together as a part of its queer Mennonite archiving is an important, utopian vision of necessary queer coalition making.

Queer Mennonite Hope

As Jess's queer identity develops, she struggles to figure out whether it can mesh with her Mennonite self. During a difficult time in their relationship, Freya calls Jess "an oppressed Mennonite woman," ignoring the growth that Jess has achieved in claiming her queer self (71). She is still a Mennonite even if she does not want to be. This incident shows how identity is a double-edged sword: identities are powerful when we claim them for ourselves, but they also allow others to put us in a box. The Mennonite box Freya puts Jess in defines "Mennonite" narrowly and does not allow any potential for Jess's queer self to remain in it. In Freya's view, "queer" and "Mennonite" are the opposites that Jess first feels them to be.

But as *Somewhere Else* continues, Jess finds herself being drawn back toward her Mennonite self, partly as a result of wrestling with *In the Wilderness* and partly because she feels that an element of her personhood is missing. One good thing about the Mennonite tradition and how it is taught to those in it is that there is a very definite sense of what happened when and why it still matters today. Jess feels this past tugging at her. She realizes that by denying her Mennonite self, she has "been trying to live without a history" (166). As Jess's drawing on her history to help her leave Saskatchewan shows, such an attempt is virtually impossible in the North American Mennonite context, so she has to find a way to integrate her Mennonite identity into herself because it is impossible to excise it completely.[38]

This integration is initiated by Jess's queer desires. When grudgingly taking a "Bible as literature" course during her final year of university, Jess meets a woman named Shea who gives Jess her number and who, as it turns out, is a Mennonite (110–12). Jess is apprehensive about letting another Mennonite into her life, but her attraction to Shea is strong enough that she invites her over for a midnight date. Jess makes coffee with a French press for Shea, explaining each step of the ritual to her (114–19). Their date activity is significant because it creates community right away. Recalling Kay Stoner's observation about potlucks being both a queer and a Mennonite ritual, the act of sharing coffee, a beverage loved by both communities, creates a queer Mennonite space for the women to inhabit as Jess slowly begins to redeem her Mennonitism.[39] The attention Jess pays to the elaborate process of making the coffee treats it like a sacrament. There is an element of serving Shea that is reminiscent of the way Jesus serves his disciples during the Last Supper in John 13:1–15. It is the women's first communion together. It is also important that this ritual takes place in Jess's house, which, like her house in Winnipeg, is a communal one. Being in a private space allows the women to build community in a way they could not if they were in a restaurant or cinema. They can get to know each other in conversation without the distraction of a movie or someone's crying child two tables over. But the presence of Jess's housemates and their knowledge that Shea is there also give the women a broader community for their relationship to grow in. When Jess is not sure whether she can continue the date because she is nervous about her already strong feelings for Shea, her housemates encourage her and convince her to go back to the coffee. Once Jess returns to the conversation, she uses the language of narrative structure from another of her welcoming communities, literature, to begin to make sense of what her and Shea's relationship might look like, and she tells Shea about Wiens, again reinscribing the space of their date as a queer Mennonite one (119–22). The women figure out how to inhabit their hybrid identity together.

Jess and Shea's relationship is not always easy despite the hopefulness of their first date and their intense sexual encounters because they both still struggle with the psychological weight of Mennonite homophobia. But ultimately the sharing of this oppression convinces Jess that she must confront it directly. Just before deciding to leave Waterloo, she thinks about all the elements of Mennonite ethnicity and faith that she and Shea share (152). The deep realization of their communal bond along with her other positive experiences of community during her exile give Jess the strength to go back to Saskatchewan and face her family with Shea as a queer Mennonite. Jess's return places her within Jeff Gundy's framework of rebellious Mennonites as "lurkers": people who journey away from the community and come back to participate in it irrevocably changed, with feet in two worlds.[40] The end of Jess's exile benefits both her and the community because she will be able to teach it what she has learned and change it, even if slowly, for the better.

Muñoz argues that "utopianism represents a failure to be normal."[41] Being utopian means looking past the life possibilities society presents to oneself in favor of looking toward seemingly unimaginable alternatives. Braun does this by writing *Somewhere Else* and by acknowledging its real-world genesis through her dedication of it to previous queer Mennonites, placing the book firmly within the context of community (199). Likewise, Jess envisions utopia by reconciling her queer and Mennonite identities. She does not live up to her Mennonite community's standards for her but instead lives up to her own in order to create a fulfilling life for herself. When she returns to her family, she insists that they make space for her queer self. By doing so, she acts as a hopeful prophet for Mennonites, sharing what she has found on her journey away and giving the community inspiration for change.

3

Queering Tradition in Jessica Penner's *Shaken in the Water*

Kansas native Jessica Penner's 2013 novel *Shaken in the Water* depicts three generations of a Kansas Mennonite community as they struggle with the theological boundaries the tradition places on them. The book shares its family saga through date-stamped, nonchronological chapters that jump back and forth between characters from all three generations. It is a difficult book because of this mazelike structure, but this difficulty is ultimately rewarding because its postmodern form emphasizes the need to make things new in liberating ways. The novel's women are especially afflicted by theological restrictions as they struggle with how their community works to police their bodies. But they resist this oppression by reclaiming their bodies for physical pleasure, sometimes with each other, and are helped in this fight by a mysterious, ghostlike tiger and its "Voice" that comes to them in times of need. This feminist reclamation of bodies is epitomized by *Shaken in the Water*'s two central characters, Agnes and Nora. The novel uses their stories to simultaneously act as a critique of Mennonitism and an affirmation of it through the ways it writes back to the Mennonite literary tradition, claiming space in it for queer female bodies.

Agnes Funk is the first of *Shaken in the Water*'s characters, and her story, which shares the book's title, stretches from 1903 to 1997. All the novel's important characters are tied to Agnes in some way. Her centrality to the book's fragmented narrative, which is emphasized by the fact that it begins and ends with chapters from her perspective, indicates her importance for the novel's ethical message. Much of this message comes from the way the book examines Agnes's body.

Shaken in the Water highlights Agnes's body immediately with a description of her "Tiger Scar," a mark on her back that is painful whenever it is touched.[1] From birth, Agnes's body is marked as Other both from herself, in that she is never able to be completely comfortable in her body because of the pain always lurking in any potential movement, and from the community, in that her mark sets her apart physically like a veiled mark of Cain. But this constant reminder of her corporeality also contains some positives for Agnes. Instead of being able to embrace the traditional mind/body split that was a favorite of Mennonite namesake Menno Simons and has been a part of Mennonite thinking ever since, Agnes is grounded in the world because she has to pay attention to her body. This experience gives her a different, less restricted view of the world than the one most of her fellow Mennonites share.

65

One element of Agnes's bodily awareness is her experiences of its possible pleasures. As a child, she often runs around naked because clothing hurts the scar (34). These are moments of youthful joy for Agnes that allow her to stave off the community's repression of the body longer than most of its members are able to. As becomes clear later on in the novel once the mysterious tiger comes on the scene, Agnes's Tiger Scar is a mark from the divine. Viewed in this light as a gift rather than as a blemish, she is meant to experience her body in nontraditional ways, and it is the community that is in the wrong for forcing her to wear clothes and marking her nudity as being somehow shameful. The community never attempts to create flexibility in its standards of propriety to accommodate Agnes's unique body. Thus while Agnes does eventually join the church, she is never quite in step with it, recognizing that its standards are not always healthy.

But before she joins the church, Agnes finds a secret spot, a gully with an abandoned barn, where she goes to run naked when she feels the need to let her scar breathe (35–36). Katherine Schweighofer notes that farmland's vastness can offer privacy for sexual exploration that is otherwise difficult to find in rural communities, offering space for liberating sexual encounters.[2] This is what Agnes finds in the gully. It is a space for her to have agency over her own body whether her nudity is sexual or not, an agency that the community would deny her both as an adolescent (she is her parents' property rather than her own) and as a woman. This is not to say that the novel argues for a complete rejection of community, because Agnes shows her desire to be part of the community by sometimes singing hymns when she is alone in the woods (37), creating her own version of church. But it does argue for more flexibility for members of the community to search for the divine in their own way.

Agnes and Nora: A Love Story

The gully is also where Agnes meets Nora Harder, the love of her life and *Shaken in the Water*'s most important character. Nora stumbles upon Agnes singing naked and, instead of being horrified, quickly takes off her clothes as well (38). This overture toward friendship immediately helps create a community of two between the girls, which is important because they find a safe space with each other that they do not experience in the broader community. Like Agnes's, Nora's body is marked as Other because she is deaf, and the two are able to support each other in bearing this oppression. Agnes can share her need to be naked with Nora, and Nora can share her desire to communicate with Agnes, as right away they begin figuring out their own shared language of signs (40, 95). This breaking out of the community's official, patriarchal language into a new women-defined one is a concretely utopian queer act in that it completely rejects the terms of discourse posited by the community for something heretofore unimagined. The bonds of this new discourse community are so strong that, as explained below, they last for the entirety of Agnes's earthly existence.

The affinity between Agnes's and Nora's bodies is sealed the first time they meet each other, when Nora touches Agnes's scar. Nora's touch gives Agnes a vision of a woman who kisses her and gives her a gown to wear that does not hurt her scar (40–41). This supernatural vision offers up the possibility that Agnes will be able to find peace—which is different from healing—with her scar and her body as a whole. It is significant that Agnes's vision includes the queer act of the kiss as well. The angelic woman names female-female sexual acts as good through her kiss, signifying that *Shaken in the Water* affirms queer sex as liberating rather than sinful. The fact that this vision comes from Nora also identifies her as having a special relationship with the supernatural, which is explored further later on in the novel. The gully is thus affirmed as a sacred space where Agnes and Nora may experience the divine in an unfettered way.

The gully's status as a queer space is affirmed on another day when Agnes and Nora meet there. They work on creating signs for different parts of their bodies, and in the process, they end up naked again, and Nora gives Agnes an orgasm when she touches her scar (96). The scar is transformed from a deformity into a locus of sexual pleasure. This is a powerful re-visioning of Othered bodies because it affords them an erotic agency that society often tries to deny. It is also significant that only Nora has the key to unlocking the scar's power, because we see that Agnes's body is women-oriented. Years later, on Agnes's wedding night with Nora's brother Peter Harder, he thinks that Agnes is shy in bed when she does not want to have sex, but it is actually because she does not love him, and thus the scar hurts when he tries to caress her (16). He is never able to give her an orgasm despite having a name that male porn stars would kill for (152).[3] The scar is a barrier in their sexual relationship because Peter does not have the power to touch it in a way that gives pleasure. It acts as a reminder of the healthy relationship Agnes and Nora had while also highlighting how unhealthy Agnes's marriage is. She marries a man because it provides economic security and the Mennonite community does not give her another option for her life.

The flowering of Agnes and Nora's friendship into a sexual relationship, which is the healthiest one in the novel, is one of the most important occurrences in all of Mennonite literature because it makes the claim that there have always been queer Mennonites even though the community has repressed their stories. Agnes and Nora's relationship acts as what Ann Cvetkovich calls an "imaginative archive," an archive of the real but unknown.[4] It documents the queer Mennonite relationships that must have existed in the past but left no historical trace. While *Shaken in the Water* is not the first piece of queer Mennonite literature, its chronological setting is the earliest for a queer relationship.[5] Therefore, not only does the novel write back to the Mennonite literary tradition (as shown below) by having Agnes and Nora's relationship function as a stand-in for all the queer Mennonite relationships that have been lost to history, but it also writes back to and revises the entire tradition of Mennonite homophobia, claiming a queer Mennonite voice.

Although the book portrays Agnes and Nora's sexual relationship as positive, Agnes herself feels it must be kept secret even after Nora's death because of the community's homophobia. After Peter's death in the early 1970s, Agnes burns her only photograph of Nora along with all her journals about their relationship because she does not want her children to discover them after she dies (67–69). She does not know what to do with the story of her and Nora because she has no models in her Mennonite context with which to analyze it or affirm its goodness, so she destroys its archival record.

Nevertheless, the fact that their story is told by the novel shows that these stories must be told, that they require an audience.

Agnes and Nora and Peter: A Love Story?

While Agnes has the Tiger Scar from birth, it predicts her relationship with Nora because of Nora's transformation into the tiger when her human body dies (341; more on this death below). Thus Nora is present in bed with Agnes and Peter, not just because she is the only one who could touch the scar pleasurably, but because the scar is her mark on Agnes; it is Nora's physical manifestation. Read in this light, the Agnes-Nora-Peter threesome is noted right at the beginning of the novel when the scar is first described.

The concept of a love triangle is helpful when examining the relationships among the three. In an early work, queer theorist Eve Kosofsky Sedgwick, referencing René Girard's work on love triangles, notes, "The bond that links the two rivals is as intense and potent as the bond that links either of the rivals to the beloved."[6] This is certainly true in Agnes and Peter's case, as they are married to each other for five decades because they each remind the other of Nora and their relationships with her (134). She is constantly present, even in death.

But unlike the common love triangle of two men fighting over a woman, *Shaken in the Water* presents a woman and a man fighting over a woman. Agnes and Peter realize they are rivals for Nora when the three are still teenagers. When the two women begin seeing each other, Peter realizes that something is up and spies on them. He becomes "jealous" of their shared language because he "love[s]" Nora and decides to teach her to speak in order to steal her away from Agnes (124–28). While Peter realizes this is wrong, and while he is perhaps the least sympathetic character in the novel because he tries to destroy the women's relationship, it is significant that he sees Agnes as a legitimate rival rather than dismissing the relationship as an immature phase with no real emotional weight attached to it. Unlike the rest of the Mennonite community, Peter is able to understand that taboo relationships can be just as meaningful as officially sanctioned heterosexual ones because, as discussed below, he also has taboo desires. Meanwhile, Agnes tries to convince Nora not to go through with the lessons because she wants Nora for herself and wants to protect Nora from the teasing of others because of her disability (98–101). Agnes is afraid of what will happen to their community of two if Peter is let in. She recognizes that Peter, as a carrier of patriarchal authority, is her oppressor, and thus she must fight against him at all costs.

Nora's response to this competition for her attention is striking. She chooses neither Peter nor Agnes but instead gleans pleasure from both relationships. Nora's bisexuality offers an openness that echoes the novel's openness to the goodness of a variety of sexual expressions. While her relationship with Agnes is healthier than hers with Peter, which is signified by the fact that the book gives Agnes the honor of being present at the miracle when Nora's human body is destroyed and she is transformed into the tiger-Voice (341), Nora's insistence on loving both of them rather than acquiescing to their competition over her by choosing a "winner" argues for new, peaceful relationship models. The love triangle is a queer one not only because of its woman-woman relationship but also because of Nora's refusal to play by the usual rules of such frameworks. This re-visioning of the triangle model that uses a female-female relationship as its axis is, as Terry Castle argues in a response to Sedgwick's work, a tool for dismantling sexism and homophobia.[7] While it ends tragically early as a result of Nora's death, Agnes and Nora's relationship proves that it is possible for women to be happy without men (something that Mennonite theology still does not acknowledge) and provides a model of healthy queer relationships for readers that the women themselves do not have and must make up as they go.

I speak of a love triangle between Agnes and Peter and Nora not only because of the scar that marks Nora's constant presence in the marriage but also because Nora and Peter have sex numerous times before her death (130–31). It is safe to assume that nearly all readers will initially react with horror to this coupling because it breaks the incest taboo. However, *Shaken in the Water* unsettles this reaction by portraying the relationship as consensual and pleasurable for both siblings. When Peter tries to end the relationship early on by naming it as "sin," Nora asks, "How is this a sin? It feels right" (121–22). Peter is unable to provide a convincing rebuttal because Nora is correct in naming bodily pleasure as beautiful, as a gift from the divine. She has already experienced this pleasure with Agnes and does not understand why the community would make laws restricting the pursuit of this pleasure with others.

While most readers will agree with Peter that his relationship with Nora is wrong, and while I am not going to argue that *Shaken in the Water* claims that consensual incest is acceptable, it is significant that the novel questions this taboo and investigates whether there might ever be a form of allowable incest. Schweighofer observes that traditional farm life includes "almost zero privacy" with a lack of individual bedrooms and a lack of time to oneself because of the ubiquity of chores. One consequence of this constant

69

proximity to family members is that older siblings often become teachers of sexual education to younger siblings.[8] These conditions of farm life make space for the incestuous in ways not experienced in urban settings, thus raising the question of whether incest's violence is the same regardless of geographical context or whether it can mean something different in a rural context. We see this in the case of Peter and Nora, where Peter teaches Nora many things that the community refuses to teach her because of her deafness. Like Schweighofer, Cvetkovich also investigates whether it is possible to view incest in new ways. She contends that incest is a queer topic and that a "queer healing practice would turn negative affect or trauma on its head, but by embracing rather than refusing it."[9] Thus while Cvetkovich agrees with the conventional view that incest is inherently violent, she also shows in a discussion of Dorothy Allison's *Bastard Out of Carolina* how the incest in that novel, which is utterly horrific and on the surface makes no claims that there is anything positive about it, nevertheless results in some good because it leads to the protagonist Bone's claiming of her own sexuality through her fantasizing about BDSM as a way to cope with her trauma.[10] Similarly, R. Victoria Arana documents a long history of literary sibling incest stories stretching from ancient Egypt through the twentieth century, contending that these portrayals are usually positive.[11] The incest between Nora and Peter is also depicted as much less violent than one might expect—there is the systemic violence that Peter wields in his maleness, but the actual sex act is enjoyed by both parties and at times is initiated by Nora—and my argument here is inspired by both Cvetkovich's and Arana's in that I also see that some good comes from this taboo sexual expression in Penner's novel.

Shaken in the Water rewrites incest as a negative event into a positive one for Nora because it helps Nora further embrace her marginalized deaf body. Queer disability theorist Eli Clare observes that North American society discriminates against people with disabilities by assuming that they are "asexual" beings.[12] Thus *Shaken in the Water*'s portrayal of Nora's sexuality is liberatingly transgressive not only for its women-loving elements but also for its depiction of the possibility of a person with disabilities being able to have an active sex life. Clare also asserts that it is essential for marginalized bodies to be represented in literature.[13] *Shaken in the Water* is one of the few Mennonite texts that does this.

The depiction of Nora's relationship with Peter also offers a new sexual ethic that counters the traditional Mennonite repression of bodies: If it feels good, how can it be a sin? Some readers might find this approach to ethics a bit too laissez-faire, but Nora celebrates the pleasure her body feels in an unrestricted way because Nora's family has not taught her the concept of sin (121–22). Because of her disability, they do not treat her as fully human, as a being with a soul that can be judged. The novel thereby uses Nora's moral innocence as a device for exploring the dynamics of incest in a way that does not condemn her for enjoying sex with Peter and also argues for new examinations of the relationship between bodily pleasure and moral codes. If anyone sins in the incest, it is Peter, not Nora, but her ethic of taking pleasure in the body as a form of worship wants to include him in the act's sinlessness too. Claiming her body's pleasure and taking agency by naming this pleasure as good is a revolutionary feminist queer act. It is a liberating way for her to experience her body, and the novel argues in favor of this act while not necessarily arguing in favor of consensual incest as an acceptable practice. Arana asserts that sibling incest narratives are always about "the relationship between authority and creativity."[14] Nora and Peter's relationship is a creative act in that it allows Nora to enjoy her body even though her broader community, beginning with the rest of her family, shuns her body because of her disability. It makes space for Nora to learn how to support others later on as the tiger when they transgress in ways that cause the Mennonite community to unreasonably persecute them. The novel therefore makes a statement about how the Mennonite community affects those it treats as Other.

When considering whether to condemn Nora and Peter's relationship, it is also necessary to consider the importance of the community's role in Nora's behavior. The community marginalizes her because of her deafness and does not give her membership through the teaching of theology or ethics. The church allows Nora's family to refrain from taking her to church because the family is embarrassed by her (121). Alison Kafer writes that disability is seen as a kind of "failure" in North American society.[15] Nora's family and the church take this attitude toward her in general. They do not bother to teach her the community's beliefs because they view her deafness as a characteristic that makes her less than human and thus do not see the point of helping her develop. As a result of this neglect, Nora finds her own practices that work for her, which is a liberating move, and the community also loses its right to judge her, since they have already rejected her through no fault of her own. If theological Mennonite readers are disturbed by Nora's view of her and Peter's relationship, by association they only have themselves to blame. Plus, of course, the novel wants to make readers uncomfortable with the incest it portrays because this uneasiness opens up room for change.

If readers are made uncomfortable by Nora's sexuality, perhaps they will do more to help cultivate healthy attitudes toward sexuality in their own communities.

Shaken in the Water reemphasizes its desire for readers to rethink incest and thus, by extension, all policed sexual expressions by including a second incestuous relationship between Agnes's son Johan and his niece Imma (who is close to him in age; there is not the extreme power imbalance that this relationship normally implies). Again, this relationship is consensual, and again the community is more at fault than the relationship's participants because one reason Imma is drawn to Johan is that he tries to help her escape her abusive father while the community turns a blind eye to the violence. Imma and Johan's relationship is another example of how the novel argues that the content of a relationship is what is important, not necessarily the identity of its participants.[16] The relationship between Agnes and Nora is the healthiest one in the book. The incestuous relationships between Nora and Peter and Johan and Imma are the second healthiest, and the other heterosexual relationships are all unhealthy. So *Shaken in the Water* argues that it is ridiculous to discriminate against nonheterosexual relationships when heterosexuality is no guarantee of happiness. There must be room for love, which should be the basis around which community is built anyway, to find its way where it will.

Nora's Transformation

There is a negative aspect of Nora and Peter's relationship that must be considered, however: Nora becomes pregnant (131). One result of her family treating her as subhuman is that she does not receive any kind of sexual education, even of the rudimentary kind that Mennonite mothers would have sometimes passed down to daughters at the time. Aside from the moral censure that giving birth out of wedlock will bring upon Nora and her family, even if she wants the baby, she will have no means of supporting it.

But instead of allowing Nora's pregnancy to come to term and allowing it to act as a kind of scarlet-letter rebuke of her transgressive sexual actions, *Shaken in the Water* ends Nora's earthly life. While she is taking shelter in a barn during a storm, she begins going into labor, a position that is an obvious allusion to the Virgin Mary giving birth in a stable in Luke 2:7 and that further serves to name Nora as a sympathetic character. Lightning strikes the barn, burning it to the ground. As the barn collapses, Nora is transformed into the tiger and speaks briefly to Agnes for the first time as the Voice before running away (341). Nora's death or, more accurately, her transformation does not feel like a punishment. Instead, *Shaken in the Water* gives a twist to the traditional literary punishment of transgressive women mentioned in chapter 1 by depicting Nora's transformation as a form of liberation because she becomes the Voice. She literally gets a voice, something that her family and the broader community continually denied her, and this voice is more helpful in the community than God's-as-interpreted-by-the- Mennonite-community is. As the Voice says to Agnes's son Tobias when he asks why it manifests itself to some members of her family, "Some people need a little more attention—attention God can't spare" (65). By giving this attention, Nora as the tiger-Voice is actually concerned about the poor and the oppressed. For instance, she keeps Agnes's daughter Huldah company when the church shuns Huldah for refusing to wear her covering and protects Johan's wife Ellen as a girl when she confronts her heroin-addicted father (86, 93). In contrast, the book's Mennonite community is interested in marginalizing people who do not follow its restrictive guidelines rather than healing the margins. Nora as the tiger-Voice is able to have much more influence over the community than if she had lived, even if she had lived a supposedly sin-free, godly life.

When readers find out that Nora is the tiger (a fact that is revealed long after the tiger makes its first appearance), it not only changes how we see Nora, but it also changes how we see Agnes because it gives a new interpretation to her scar. The scar becomes a symbol of how she and Nora were destined to be together. Nora's mark is on Agnes from the moment she is born, and they are fated to find each other in the gully, and Agnes is fated to be haunted by Nora throughout her earthly life until returning to the gully for that life's end. Nora and Agnes's intertwined fate is akin to what God says to Jeremiah in Jeremiah 1:5: "Before I formed thee in the belly I knew thee; and before thou camest forth out of the womb I sanctified thee, and I ordained thee a prophet unto the nations." They are tied together as prophets for their Mennonite community, arguing for a healthier view toward bodies (especially women's bodies) and acceptance of queer sexualities.

Their uncommon passings accentuate their status as prophets. The supernatural elements of Nora's transformation are echoed in Agnes's end. Huldah, who sometimes has the gift of prophecy, tells Agnes that she is about to die (252). The preordained element of her death by the divine is a showing of favor because of its uniqueness and thus an affirmation of Agnes's life. Agnes goes to get naked in the gully, where she meets with Nora one last time, and as she thinks of Nora, she has an orgasm and hears the Voice, which takes her (370–72). The end of her earthly life resembles that of Enoch in Genesis 5:24 or Elijah in 2 Kings 2:11, which indicates that readers should view Agnes's life with favor. The fact that Agnes has one last orgasm from Nora as an element of her passing shows that not only are the women not condemned for their sexual activities, but they are affirmed by them. Their relationship is the healthiest in the book because it is based on unconditional, nonjudgmental love.

Shaken in the Water and Kansas Mennonite Literature

The novel is a hopeful one because of the liberating elements of Agnes's and Nora's stories, but it feels anti-Mennonite. When I taught it to non-Mennonite students in a course about postmodern American fiction in 2016, several students remarked on how critical the book is of Mennonites, and they worried about whether Penner is still able to attend a Mennonite church as a result of writing it. Happily, the community has not shunned Penner because of her novel, though I did share with my students the story of Rudy Wiebe, who had to leave the Canadian Mennonite community for a time after he published his first novel.[17] My students' observation is not without merit, however. None of the nontransgressive significant characters in *Shaken in the Water* is sympathetic, with the exception of Agnes's grandson Jeffrey, who dies at the end of the only chapter in which he appears (212–13). Yet the book is still hopeful about the Mennonite community because of the way the novel places itself firmly within the Mennonite literary tradition and thus affirms that there is hope for the Mennonite community's future.

It inserts itself into this tradition by writing back to a small but significant strain of U.S. Mennonite literature, Kansas Mennonite literature. This strain begins with Gordon Friesen's 1936 novel *Flamethrowers*—which, as noted in the introduction, is one of the foundational texts of North American Mennonite literature in general—and stretches all the way through to work by contemporary Mennonite writers such as Penner and André Swartley. Friesen's book includes the first instances in English of what have become common Mennonite literary themes, such as fleeing from Russia, comparing Mennonites to Jews, and feeling the physical results of the violence of strict religiosity.[18] It also includes a Mennonite young person who leaves the community in an attempt to find a better life, as Tobias does in *Shaken in the Water*. This attempt is a failure, as Peter in *Flamethrowers* discovers that his Mennonite upbringing has stunted him irrevocably, and he is thus unfit for a fulfilling existence in the non-Mennonite world. Neither community offers him happiness, and like *Shaken in the Water*'s Peter, he is the opposite of the strong foundation that his biblical name would imply. The novel's other transgressive character, Isaac, who is a poet, unlike *Somewhere Else*'s Martha Wiens is ineffective in making change in the community and ends up broken down and bitter. Unlike Agnes and Nora, who are able to find space to wrestle productively with the community despite its attempts to grind them down, Peter and Isaac fail completely to find livable spaces despite the advantage of their male privilege.

The Kansas Mennonite literary tradition continues in Dallas Wiebe's works, especially his narratives involving the character Skyblue (who is, as Hildi Froese Tiessen writes, Wiebe's fictional "alter-ego"), which include the 1969 novel *Skyblue the Badass* and a number of stories about Skyblue spread throughout Wiebe's four short story collections.[19] *Skyblue the Badass* is a significant text because it was the first piece of U.S. Mennonite literature to make an impression in the mainstream literary community.[20] It was published by a major press, Doubleday, and an excerpt was first published in the prestigious *Paris Review*, where Wiebe continued to publish throughout the years.[21] Like Wiebe's subsequent stories, the novel is written in the high postmodernist style—self-referential, more interested in language games than in traditional plot—epitomized by the work of writers such as John Barth and Donald Barthelme that was ascendant at the time.[22]

The Skyblue narratives use a postmodern form to break away from the Mennonite tradition of plain discourse guided by Jesus's teaching to "let your communication be, Yea, yea; Nay, nay" in Matthew 5:37. But this form is not used to any productive effect that challenges the status quo; it is all shine and no substance. The Skyblue narratives are ultimately about a privileged heterosexual white man whose life is pretty good overall. In contrast, Penner's book uses its postmodern form to critique the tradition while still remaining in contact with it. Penner tells Julia Spicher Kasdorf in an interview that *Shaken in the Water*'s fragmented form is an attempt to "try to build something beautiful and proud" out of "tragedy," which I read as being the novel's Mennonite community's oppressive standards.[23] Via the slow building of Agnes's and Nora's queer selves throughout the book as a result of its nonchronological form, *Shaken in the Water* makes it clear that their new vision for ways of relating to bodies is its primary message. If the book were constructed chronologically, the women's stories would be sequestered toward its beginning and would thus lose much of their ethical force. *Shaken in the Water*'s other postmodern characteristic, what Ann Hostetler calls its "magical realis[t]" elements, Nora's transformation into the tiger-Voice, is also important because it helps many of its characters (and, by extension, readers) discover nontraditional ways of encountering the divine.[24] This openness to the miraculous is certainly not present in Wiebe's Kansas work, which, as the *Skyblue the Badass* dust jacket asserts, is about "the inevitable defeat that is life."

Friesen's and Wiebe's texts, as attempts to move away from the Mennonite tradition, focus on the male experience with nary a strong female character in sight and are devoid of hope as far as the Mennonite community is concerned.[25] While they both include brief mentions of same-sex attractions, these passages portray queer love as nonsensical at best and as utterly sinful at worst, with none of the liberating, revolutionary aspects present in *Shaken in the Water*.[26]

In contrast to Friesen's and Wiebe's, Penner's critique of the Mennonite community is a constructive one. However, Penner initially expected to move away from the tradition as well. She explains that when she began writing fiction, she decided she was not going to write about Mennonites, but the Mennonite stories came out nevertheless.[27] This ambivalence about the tradition and seeming inevitability of joining it anyway is significant because it shows a desire to change the tradition. While Penner is now firmly, voluntarily ensconced in the Mennonite literary community—she presented at the 2012, 2015, and 2017 Mennonite/s Writing conferences, for instance—*Shaken in the Water* argues for new directions within the tradition through its positive depictions of queer sexuality. This is a move that neither *Flamethrowers* nor the Skyblue narratives make. *Shaken in the Water*'s depiction of queer Mennonite women would be moving if read in a vacuum, but read within the broader context of Mennonite literature, it becomes even more powerful because of how it is a feminist narrative and how it offers visions for ways queer Mennonites can make space for themselves within the community.

4

Stephen Beachy's *boneyard*, the *Martyrs Mirror*, and Anabaptist Activism

In 2010, the North American Mennonite denominational publisher Herald Press published an anthology edited by Kirsten Eve Beachy, *Tongue Screws and Testimonies*, that contains fiction, poetry, and essays that respond to the ur-text of Mennonite literature, Thieleman J. van Braght's *The Bloody Theater or Martyrs Mirror of the Defenseless Christians Who Baptized Only upon Confession of Faith, and Who Suffered and Died for the Testimony of Jesus, Their Saviour, from the Time of Christ to the Year A.D. 1660*, or *Martyrs Mirror*. Beachy's book epitomizes the upswing of interest in the *Martyrs Mirror* and the subject of martyrdom in general in recent years from both creative writers and literary critics as modern-day Anabaptists investigate the role of literature in their lives. One of the stories in *Tongue Screws*, Chad Gusler's "OMG!! Geleijn Cornelus Is Hott!!," features a young Mennonite woman who is surprised to find one of the *Martyrs Mirror*'s illustrations erotic.

As part of this recent upswing, in 2011 another Beachy, Stephen Beachy, published a novel called *boneyard* that takes this erotic revisioning of van Braght's text to the extreme. *boneyard* uses an example of modern-day Anabaptist martyring along with some new ways of reading the *Martyrs Mirror* to reflect on how we should interact with both martyr stories and the ever-growing presence of violence in American society. It argues that while it is important to acknowledge martyrs' memories, it is also necessary to focus on how to prevent violence, whether physical violence or systemic violence such as homophobia, rather than only on how to respond to it. As John D. Roth notes, the *Martyrs Mirror* has often been reprinted in times of political strife for use as a "polemical" text; similarly, *boneyard* takes a queer activist stand against violence in American society.[1]

boneyard is ostensibly a partially burnt manuscript written by Amish teenager Jake Yoder and transcribed by Beachy.[2] As the manuscript's supposed editor, Beachy makes a number of interjections into the text via footnotes. From now on, I will differentiate between this Stephen Beachy, the mostly realistic character in *boneyard*, and Stephen Beachy, the real author of *boneyard*, by referring to the former as "Beachy" and the latter as Beachy.

Nickel Mines and Martyrdom

The memory of five Amish schoolchildren killed in a school shooting in Nickel Mines, Pennsylvania, in 2006, haunts the novel. *boneyard* attempts to respond to the shooting through Jake's tortured stories, which are presented as individual short stories but combine to form an at least semicoherent longer narrative. The novel's fragmented, postmodern form is significant, as it questions whether the book even has a right to exist or whether the tragedy it depicts is so horrible as to be unspeakable.[3] How does one write about a violent massacre without somehow valorizing that violence, and how can one write against that violence when one is writing within the same culture that produced the violence? *boneyard*'s form also functions to ask, If it is appropriate to speak about the tragedy, how should we do so? Although the novel fits into the postmodern fiction tradition, which may be accused of being overly theoretical to the point of mere gimmickry and political apathy, *boneyard*'s treatment of a real event illustrates its status as an activist text. "Beachy's" act of saving Jake's writing about the shooting is an assertion that the massacre must be discussed for healing to occur, and in this way *boneyard* acts as a memorial for the shooting victims, in part by archiving Jake's queer responses to their deaths.

The novel draws on the *Martyrs Mirror* to accomplish these objectives, deriving inspiration from the big book's status as a teaching text. Aside from the written martyrs' stories, the current English edition of the *Martyrs Mirror* includes fifty-five illustrations of its subjects by the engraver Jan Luyken, and most of these pictures depict gruesome deaths via methods such as drowning, being buried alive, and being burned at the stake.[4] *boneyard*'s two halves are named for van Braght's text, with book 1 called "Martyrs Mirror" and book 2 called "Bloody Theater." Book 2 includes twelve reproductions of illustrations from the *Martyrs Mirror*, a fifth of the larger book's total. "Beachy" writes that the placement of these images throughout *boneyard* is exactly as Jake had them in his manuscript.[5] Therefore, the images are one of the most reliable elements of Jake's narrative.[6] The *Martyrs Mirror*'s text helps illuminate the shooting victims' presence in *boneyard*, while its illustrations play a major role in Jake's stories.

boneyard only mentions the five shooting victims about half a dozen times throughout its three hundred pages. Two of these instances are in the "Note from the 'Author'" (quotation marks in the original), which is written by "Beachy," though all the information he gives about the shooting is factually accurate. Three other instances occur in footnotes (61n10, 193n49, 269n81). The victims are hard to find in the book; they are not mentioned in the main body of the novel's text itself. The first mention of the victims is in *boneyard*'s short description of the shooting. A single paragraph describes the location of the shooting, the timing of events in the schoolhouse leading up to the shooting, the number of students (all girls) who were shot, and possible motivations for the shooter's actions (9–10). In other words, the information included in this paragraph is unremarkable. It simply condenses all the facts about the shooting that could be found in any news article on the event.[7]

However, this description's inclusion in the novel's second paragraph signals the event's importance for the text. It colors everything that comes after it. The violent sexual fantasies in Jake's stories rub up against the real-world violence in the schoolhouse, interrogating the glorification of violence in American society. In doing so, *boneyard* shifts the interpretive narrative created around the shooting in its aftermath. Julia Spicher Kasdorf writes that the media chose to emphasize the Amish community's decision to forgive the shooter rather than viewing the shooting as an example of an ongoing epidemic of violence against females in our society.[8] However, the novel asks readers to focus on the violence itself rather than the response to it. It raises questions such as, Why is it permissible for someone to easily, legally gain access to the weapons necessary for such a massacre? Why do we live in a society that has done nothing to stop the epidemic of school shootings that was already in full swing at the time of the Nickel Mines shooting and has worsened since then? By fetishizing the Amish's response to the tragedy, the discourse around the shooting has chosen to ignore its broader context within a violent America, but *boneyard* asks us to think about this context by placing Jake firmly into the world through his queer sexual fantasies and membership in a rock band. He reminds readers that the shooting's meaning is much messier than most interpretations would have it be.

The novel also interrogates the values taught by the *Martyrs Mirror*.[9] It is easy to make the connection between the self-sacrificial ethic of the figures in van Braght's text and the victims of the shooting. For instance, one of the survivors tells the story of how her older sister asked to be shot first, apparently with the hope that this might somehow help save the others.[10] While many would read this as a heroic tale of the kind that Jess is raised with in *Somewhere Else* (and the stories in *Martyrs Mirror* are often likewise read as such), *boneyard* questions whether the valorization of such stories and their black-and-white approach to violence fails to acknowledge how complicated violence is and how we are all implicated in it to varying degrees. "Beachy" questions the usage of the term "hero" with regards to the shooting in a footnote (193n49). But at the same time, this questioning is itself questioned by the fact that it occurs in a footnote about the shooting that is completely unrelated to its referent in the main body of the text. The story of the shooting is obviously important, but here it is treated as being so unspeakable that it can only appropriately be mentioned in a seemingly irrelevant note. The text does not make it easy for us as readers to figure out what we should do. It is up to us to struggle toward an interpretation of the novel, and this struggle implies that this is how we should approach or, in the case of the *Martyrs Mirror*, reapproach all texts in order to make them relevant to our twenty-first-century lives. This kind of approach is queer because of its rejection of a belief in absolutes that lead to clear-cut answers.

"Beachy" writes that when he first met Jake while visiting Nickel Mines after the shooting, Jake, an alumnus of the school, claimed that one of the victims was his sister. "Beachy" quickly discovers that this assertion is a lie, and thus he wonders if he can "believe anything" Jake tells him (10). In immediately questioning Jake's trustworthiness, *boneyard* questions its own legitimacy because it is, after all, allegedly Jake's manuscript. Aside from being a familiar poststructuralist move highlighting the fallibility of language, this querying illustrates the problematic nature of assuming that narratives such as that of the shooting are straightforward. While the basic facts about the event can be known, the interpretation of those facts is still in question. Similarly, as will be seen, Jake discards the usual interpretation of the *Martyrs Mirror*, showing us that even the most traditional texts are candidates for re-visioning. The fragmented, circular nature of *boneyard* constantly reminds readers that there is no such thing as a simple story. "Beachy" himself even gets confused about the story he offers to the public, as, although Jake has not lived in Pennsylvania for years and writes his stories while in the sixth grade in Iowa (10), "Beachy" refers to the shooting victims as Jake's "class-mates" (62n11).

Reinterpreting the *Martyrs Mirror*

boneyard's repetitious form draws inspiration from two very different sources. The first is, again, the *Martyrs Mirror*, which retells the same basic story over and over, describing the unjust nature of each martyr's persecution and extolling their steadfastness in the face of death. Each chapter in book 1 of *boneyard* also retells the same basic story, with similar characters, shared names and locations, and similar sexually infused plotlines. Aside from mimicking van Braght's book, this element of the novel is a nod to queer novelist Kathy Acker's work, of which "Beachy" is a fan (114n26). Acker often repeats passages verbatim in her fiction. An example of this repetition occurs in her novel *I Dreamt I Was a Nymphomaniac Imagining*, where the nearly two-page-long paragraph beginning "Last night I dreamt I was standing" is repeated four times in a row. Likewise, in Acker's *Don Quixote*, there is a section where nearly every paragraph is repeated between two and four times.[11] Jake's stories do a similar thing, most notably in the description of male authority figures as "a stern man, not without a certain appeal" (e.g., 27, 44, 127). This connection of *boneyard* to both a traditional Anabaptist text and the work of one of the most important writers of postmodern fiction shows the necessity of having multiple teaching texts in one's life, as drawing on only one set of stories is inadequate. Jake needs stories from both traditions to help him navigate his life. As will be seen, once he encounters the kind of queer, sex-infused discourse found in Acker's work, he is able to discover new relevance for the *Martyrs Mirror* in his life.

boneyard's use of repetition, which includes its reproduction of images from the *Martyrs Mirror*, is also a way of questioning narrative itself and how one tells stories about atrocities. The reader keeps battering at the novel's narrative, trying to extract truth from it, but at the same time, the truth of the narrative cannot be pinned down. The story in book 1 of the novel just keeps getting rewashed in each chapter. As Jake says at the end of book 1, "Wherever you go it is the same cities and the same desert and the same river" (170). This sameness, which he echoes in his stories, may be read as indicating that some kind of truth is contained in them, but this truth is difficult to pinpoint. The searching for truth is the important thing, not the conclusion one makes about it.

This emphasis on the story itself rather than what the story can teach us is evident in *boneyard*'s portrayal of the Nickel Mines victims. The novel seemingly portrays the dead schoolchildren as martyrs in the traditional *Martyrs Mirror* sense: they are innocent, they choose to go willingly to their deaths instead of attempting escape, and they die because of their religious beliefs. I do not mean to sound like I am blaming the victims here. Rather, I mean to say that like the martyrs from van Braght's text, the victims exercised agency by making the choice not to resist, because to do so would have been an act of violence. The victims' actions (i.e., the decision to choose not to act) embody the spirit of Jesus's command to "do good to them that hate you, and pray for them which despitefully use you, and persecute you" in Matthew 5:44, a passage that Anabaptists have traditionally used to justify their belief in nonresistance. Although, as Kasdorf notes, the police believed that the shooting was not a hate crime against the Amish, the shooter would have known that the schoolhouse was an easy target because the Amish belief in nonresistance precluded the presence of any kind of security.[12]

However, unlike the stories told in the *Martyrs Mirror*, which often include details such as letters written by the martyrs, accounts of their trials, and descriptions of the weather at the time of the martyrs' death, the children's story receives very little explicit attention in *boneyard*, and thus it is difficult to draw an easy moral from it.[13] Despite "Beachy's" brief description of the shooting, readers must bring information about the shooting from news accounts to bear in order for Jake's despair about the shooting and subsequent loathing of his writing to make sense. The victims' fleeting presence in *boneyard* pays homage to their memory, but perhaps more significantly, they serve to open up space for Jake's much more complicated interactions with the *Martyrs Mirror* in book 2, which in turn lead to the sexual themes in his manuscript, which lead to his attempted destruction of it after the shooting.

Like many of the *Martyrs Mirror*'s readers, Jake is more interested in the book's illustrations than its text.[14] However, he is not interested in them for the artistry of Luyken's etchings or because they provoke theological reflection. He is interested in them because they involve bondage, a major theme in his fantasy life. This interest gets established in Jake's first story from book 1, which depicts the Jake character (who is at least similar to the Jake in book 2, though they may not be the same; in other words, Jake fictionalizes himself just as Beachy fictionalizes himself) taking a vocabulary test involving BDSM terms such as "manacles," "spread-eagle," and "spanking" and ending up bound for several days in his Language Arts teacher's barn while he is used as a sex slave (32–35). In this story, Jake's mother reads him the *Martyrs Mirror* every night before bed (26). Jake is thus aware of the traditional usage of van Braght's book as a tool for theological instruction, but once he is able to interact with the book himself in book 2, which is written as a memoir-esque account of his teenage years, he finds another kind of value in it. He uses the *Martyrs Mirror* to glean erotic inspiration for his stories. Jake writes that during puberty he would masturbate to the illustrations several times per day because they "were the only pictures of half-naked men I had access to" (191–92). Jake is gay and living in a homophobic community—he himself is a martyr in this sense—thus he must take whatever opportunity he can find to explore his sexuality.[15]

His desperation to do so leads him to discover the erotic undertone of some of Luyken's etchings, an interpretation of them that may not be as far-fetched as it first seems. During the question-and-answer time at the end of the "LGBT Fiction" panel held at the 2015 Mennonite/s Writing conference at Fresno Pacific University, Lauren Friesen claimed that there is an oral tradition among Dutch Mennonites that Luyken was sexually attracted to men. It is impossible to know whether this story is true or not, though its persistence through the centuries may indicate that it is. If it is true, then the illustrations are a queer text regardless of Jake's use of them in the same way that texts by writers from Mennonite backgrounds are considered "Mennonite literature" even if they do not include explicit Mennonite content.[16] It would make sense if Luyken's attraction to the male form would work its way into his art, because even though it might seem inappropriate to eroticize martyrdom, a body being martyred is still, after all, a body and thus something that retains erotic possibilities. Jake seizes these possibilities inscribed into Luyken's illustrations for his fantasies. The depiction of Jake's fantasizing plays an important role in his queer identity because of fantasizing's significance in queer life. In a homophobic society, the realm of fantasy within one's own head is one of the few safe spaces to envision queerness and the desires it entails and to embody them, albeit alone, through masturbation.

Readers of the *Martyrs Mirror* may find Jake's reinterpretation of it shocking, but the big book's spirit of radical transgression, which is also a queer value, actually fits perfectly with Jake's attempts to explore his sexuality, which his community views as wrong. Luyken's illustrations are so viscerally powerful (whether in an erotic way or not) that Kirsten Eve Beachy does not include any of them in *Tongue Screws and Testimonies* because she worries that they will overshadow the anthology's writing![17] The etchings demand a response, but like any piece of art, they do not dictate how one should respond to them, which leaves room for Jake's perhaps surprising interactions with them. While Jake's use of the images as pornography is liberating for him, Stephanie Krehbiel explains that she finds them oppressive because twenty-first-century society already offers numerous images of "splayed, exploited bodies," and she does not need even more of them from her religious texts.[18] These two perspectives are not necessarily contradictory, however, because gay pornography works differently than heterosexual pornography.[19]

Jake's stories, and his use of the *Martyrs Mirror* as inspiration for those stories, are exercises in seeking truth in places where religious authorities claim it cannot be found. Paul Martens and David Cramer contend that there is an inherent tension in the Anabaptist tradition between its advocacy of radical challenges to institutional religious authority and the potential misuse of this radical rhetoric: How does the community discern which radical critiques of it are worth listening to and which ones are correct to dismiss?[20] Some readers of the *Martyrs Mirror* will feel that *boneyard*'s reinterpretations of it fall into the latter category, but I disagree. Viewed through Anabaptism's radical lens, Jake's stories epitomize the spirit of queer Anabaptism. Jeff Gundy calls the *Martyrs Mirror* "an act of resistance," a phrase that also aptly describes *boneyard*.[21] This "resistance" in van Braght's book makes it a queer text in the political sense. It is a text that questions society's power structures and looks for inspiration in society's margins. Thus it makes sense that *boneyard*, which is queer both in its political stance and in its portrayals of sexuality, would use the *Martyrs Mirror* as a spark for Jake's physical and written explorations. The novel functions as a kind of literary criticism on the *Martyrs Mirror*, teasing out themes that most readers would miss and making them available for archiving through Jake's writing.

Jake's usage of van Braght's text might seem scandalous, but his appropriation of it as pornography is an incisive commentary on the gratuitous nature of many of the *Martyrs Mirror*'s illustrations and the way readers have traditionally responded to them. The illustrations are titillating for those who read the *Martyrs Mirror* as a religious text (i.e., pacifist Amish and Mennonites) because they depict the taboo subject of violence. Jake reveals the close relationship between sex and violence in his sexualized use of van Braght's book. He queers the book by focusing on the "buffed" physique of the men in the images instead of the faith-based actions that lead to their deaths (177). Similarly, "Beachy" quotes Antonin Artaud's assertion that there is "nothing more erotically pornographic than Christ" (221) and in a footnote discusses the thin line between pain and pleasure, noting that the loss of blood can lead to feelings of euphoria (218n58). The *Martyrs Mirror* illustration that inspires this observation (reproduced in *boneyard* on page 219) shows an early Christian martyr, Pelagius of Cordova, having his arms chopped off. However, the most striking element of this picture is not the blood flowing down from Pelagius's wounds or his severed arms on the ground. It is how androgynously pretty he looks.[22] His closing eyes are framed by extravagantly long eyelashes. He is topless, and the lines of his pectoral muscles are overly rounded, sporting prominent nipples, making them look like women's breasts. How can a teenager such as Jake think pious thoughts when confronted with such an alluring, available body? Of course, Jake brings a twenty-first-century gaze to seventeenth-century art, but nevertheless, whether intentional or not, erotic subtexts clearly exist in some of the *Martyrs Mirror*'s illustrations.[23] Jake merely makes them plain by documenting his sexual activities and, in doing so, shows that these subtexts may be read as queer as well.

The discourse surrounding Pelagius's image in the novel offers yet another example of *boneyard*'s slipperiness and unreliability. Jake explicitly references Pelagius's story (218), but Luyken's etching of Pelagius is not one of the illustrations included in Herald Press's edition of van Braght's book, which, as I show in note six of this chapter, is almost certainly the one Jake has access to. (There is no copyright notice in *boneyard* acknowledging where the images come from.) Is Jake using the *Martyrs Mirror* as written erotica as well?[24] Is he reading—or perhaps simply viewing—the 1685 Dutch edition? Or is this just a gaffe on Beachy's part? The barely noticeable ways such as this in which *boneyard* deconstructs itself while also teasing apart van Braght's text are what make it such an intriguing novel.

As Robert Zacharias asserts, "Any engagement with a foundational communal narrative—even the writing against it—ultimately serves to affirm its importance."[25] *boneyard* acknowledges the importance of the *Martyrs Mirror* as a foundational text for Anabaptist storytelling even as it appropriates van Braght's text for its own purposes. In doing so, *boneyard* places itself within the Mennonite literary tradition while also being firmly ensconced in the queer literary tradition.

There is also a model for Jake's queering of the *Martyrs Mirror* in the "slash fiction" movement, which is a genre of fan fiction that, according to Jane Ward, takes texts that are not explicitly queer and "rewrite[s] or reanimate[s them] with queer themes and images."[26] This rewriting helps make visible the presence of queer persons in settings where they have traditionally been silenced. Viewed through a slash lens, *boneyard* may be read as *Martyrs Mirror* fan fiction that makes plain the presence of queers in the Anabaptist community.

One of Jake's stories describes the *Martyrs Mirror* as being "full of pictures of men and women in pain" (63). While it is true that most of the book's pictures depict either torture or executions, it is incorrect to say that it is "full" of these pictures.[27] On average, there is approximately one illustration for every twenty-two pages. But this misstatement shows how for Jake the *Martyrs Mirror* is only about the illustrations as a form of pornography. He is not interested in its religious instruction even though he ultimately chooses to join the Amish church. Instead, he wants to know how he can get the most out of his body while it is on earth. Kasdorf calls the *Martyrs Mirror* a "book that shows us what bodies are for," and Jake agrees because it helps him learn about his desires.[28] But he rejects the book's hatred of bodies, the idea that bodies are only good for sacrificing, which Kasdorf names and also questions, instead boldly asserting that bodies are for pleasure. In his fantasies about and brief actual explorations of BDSM, Jake explores how pain can be pleasurable. Although he is unable to explicitly name what he learns, he comes to the realization that is common knowledge in the BDSM community that, aside from the physiological similarity of the body's responses to pain and pleasure, being bound and voluntarily subjecting oneself to pain can be pleasurable because it is a form of "play."[29] It is a voluntary letting go of whatever power one has in everyday life in order to experience complete submission. In the bottom role that Jake fantasizes about, he fulfills Jesus's command in Matthew 5:44 to be humble and submissive in the face of persecution, but this is a way of celebrating his God-given body instead of renouncing it. Like Nora in *Shaken in the Water*, he insists that sexual pleasure is good rather than sinful. While in a sense the martyrs in the *Martyrs Mirror* choose their pain in that they accept torture and death rather than recanting their subversive faith, Jake's mimicking of their sacrifice, which ends in a happier way than their stories, is an act that affirms the beauty of life in the world and calls us to appreciate it as a gift. Jake's questioning of the *Martyrs Mirror*'s ethic of self-sacrifice is not new.[30] But his reclamation of it for pleasure is just as radical and liberating of an act as the martyrs' profound theological transgressions.

At another point in book 2, Jake asks, "How do you convey grief without theatrics?" when confronted with another's death (196). This question is an essential one when considering the *Martyrs Mirror* because its illustrations dramatize the deaths of their subjects, (inadvertently) taking away the focus from the martyrs' faith and instead focusing on their bodily sacrifice.

Van Braght's book is thus pornographic in that it is gratuitous and decadent, whether in its visual elements or its physical size.[31] The martyrs become fetishized.[32] It is this spirit that is part of what makes it easy for Jake to use the book in a sexually pornographic way. Jake's question is also relevant to *boneyard*'s attempt to respectfully respond to the shooting. The victims deserve to be memorialized, but does celebrating them as martyrs unfairly reduce their memories to one specific event? Jake's text questions how martyrdom is portrayed and how we talk about tragedy.

boneyard's Witness

However, Jake's feelings about his questioning stories change after the shooting. "Beachy" explains in both "A Note from the 'Author'" and a later footnote that Jake believes the depictions of bondage in his stories in book 1 (which were apparently written before the shooting) "caused" the shooting (12, 68–69n18). Book 2 includes two stories about school shootings that are very similar to the Nickel Mines shooting, including one in which Jake escapes from the schoolhouse just before the massacre begins, which echoes the real escape of one of the schoolchildren before the shooting (231, 269). While the actual shooting is clearly on Jake's mind, he is unable to write about it himself, instead merely mimicking it in his fragmented fiction. His stories archive his trauma from the event by illustrating his inability to write directly about it. Even this writing-as-therapy is not enough to assuage Jake's guilt. He cannot shake the belief that the massacre is a divine punishment for his fetish in both its written and physical forms. Therefore, he attempts to destroy his stories by throwing them into a bonfire, from which "Beachy" rescues them before they are fully consumed (12).

"Beachy" acknowledges that the manuscript was so damaged in the fire that much of it was "completely illegible," thus necessitating his own additions to the text to make it readable (12–13). This leads to the question of whether "Beachy's" assertion that the manuscript is primarily Jake's is true or not. It may be that Jake does not actually exist and that "Beachy" has made the whole thing up. This possibility is raised by *boneyard*'s editor, Judith Owsley Brown, in an "Editor's Note" that immediately follows "Beachy's" author's note (15–17). Brown then engages in an exchange of footnotes with "Beachy" in an attempt to prove that Jake does not exist and that "Beachy" is mentally unstable.[33] Through this war of words, *boneyard* questions whether it has a right to exist in light of the tragedy that it references and in light of the similarities between Jake's BDSM fantasizing and the real-life use of bondage as a prelude to the shooting. Can one continue to write after the trauma of what some have called "the Amish 9/11," or is silence the only appropriate response?[34]

In answer to this question, *boneyard* again takes its cue from the *Martyrs Mirror*. The early Anabaptist community could have fallen silent in the face of unjust, gruesomely violent persecution but instead chose to preserve the stories of its fallen in order to learn from them. As a result, when van Braght compiled his book during a time when persecution of Anabaptists had lessened, he found no shortage of stories to include.

Similarly, the real Stephen Beachy preserves the memory of the shooting's victims by writing about them while also acknowledging that writing about an event is not the same thing as comprehending an event, as the postmodern form of his novel shows. Ultimately, nothing is certain about *boneyard* other than its references to the very real events in Nickel Mines. Nevertheless, "Beachy's" act of saving Jake's writing about the shooting is an assertion that the massacre must be discussed for healing to occur. As Roth argues with regard to the role of martyr stories in the twenty-first-century Anabaptist community, there should be space for a "right remembering" of past victims.[35] But *boneyard* also asserts that the shooting is a symptom of America's deeper illness: its obsession with violence and its fetishizing of guns. Jake's queering of the *Martyrs Mirror* in book 2, his insistence on reading it in a secular rather than a religious manner, is an argument that action should be taken to ensure that the modern-day martyring of innocent victims such as those from Nickel Mines will end. *boneyard* posits that this kind of queer political advocacy is the best memorial we can give to those who lost their lives. Instead of focusing on martyrdom, we should focus on how to prevent the violence that brings it about.

The Queer Ethical Body in
Corey Redekop's *Husk*

Corey Redekop's 2012 novel *Husk*, about the gay Mennonite zombie Sheldon Funk, uses the figure of the zombie to investigate the plight of both the queer and people with disabilities in North American society in order to argue for an ethic of openness and acceptance toward the Other. *Husk* is a weird book. Sheldon is a kind of Christ figure in that he rises from the dead and saves humanity from those who attempt to attain immortality by nefarious means, but he is also an avenging angel who constantly craves a cannibalistic Eucharist. He has eternal life, but this eternal life is not a good thing, because it comes not through salvation but via some unexplained supernatural occurrence that leaves him in an earthly limbo. Throughout *Husk*, Sheldon struggles against the violent impulses of his zombiehood in an attempt to reclaim some of his humanity. The ethics taught to him by his Mennonite upbringing help him place his empathy for others and concern for the human community above his own destructive desires. Along the way, *Husk* highlights those on the margins to advocate for social justice. It does this via all the metaphoric and symbolic weight that Sheldon's body carries throughout the novel because the book calls for an intersectional approach to ending oppression.

Making the Marginalized Narratable

The three major elements of Sheldon's identity in *Husk*—gay, zombie, Mennonite—all play a role in the novel's argument. I examine each of these aspects in turn, but it is first important to acknowledge how powerful the act of sharing Sheldon's story is as a form of witness to the Othering he experiences. Sociologist Arthur W. Frank posits that without narratives about themselves, people (in Frank's example, the disabled, which is relevant in Sheldon's case, but the principle can also be extended to other oppressed groups) become marginalized, and thus to combat this Othering, they need to be made "narratable."[1] *Husk* makes Sheldon narratable because he tells the story of zombiehood from his marginalized zombie position. While zombie narratives are legion, zombie narratives told from the perspective of the zombie are not. It may be odd to think of zombies as oppressed—they want to eat our brains, after all—but this is why it is so important to have a story told from their perspective. Unlike the way they are usually portrayed in zombie narratives as enemies who must be destroyed, the zombies in *Husk* are clearly oppressed. For instance, Sheldon receives "death threats," and the captive zombies he discovers at the end of the novel are kept in a pen, starving, instead of being put out of their misery.[2] Unlike most zombies, including the rest of the zombies in *Husk*, Sheldon has retained his human thinking capabilities, and he uses them to make the plight of zombies visible to readers.

The way Sheldon tells his story is also important. He uses a matter-of-fact tone, describing his zombiehood in a calm, collected manner. Usual zombie characteristics such as walking haltingly or eating human flesh are present, but they are not there for shock value; they are simply there as a part of Sheldon's everyday life. There is no cure for Sheldon's zombiehood; he cannot go back to being fully human, so instead he tries to do the best he can with his new situation.[3] While others label Sheldon as a "freak" (158, 186), he does not accept this demonization. He is different, yes, but he does not let this difference overwhelm his sense of self. Instead, he builds his new body into his narrativizing project and gets on with his life as a struggling actor. This outlook is therapeutic for readers in that we get a new perspective on zombiehood and for Sheldon because, as Frank writes, telling our stories of medical adversity helps us cope with that adversity.[4] Sheldon's refusal to follow conventional zombie narrative tropes makes his story a queer one, not only because he is gay, but in the sense that it is peculiar, that it messes with boundaries. His story's uniqueness, its newness, offers conceptual space for new liberating visions of how to relate to the Other.[5]

Part of the power of Sheldon's narrative comes from his open discussion of his sexuality. Sheldon admits that even though he had an active sex life before becoming a zombie, he still feels hindered by his Mennonite background when it comes to sex (67). The struggle to embrace his queerness is akin to Jess's in *Somewhere Else* because the Mennonite community is unsupportive. Sheldon's mother enforces this divide. Although she names him as a "sissy" (90), she tries to ignore his homosexuality. She asks him if there are any "girls" he wants to tell her about (88). This question silences his personhood and makes him an exile because he will never be able to fully fit within his family or the broader church community without fulfilling the heterosexist norm of marriage.[6]

But Sheldon fights against the homophobia he encounters in both the Mennonite community and society at large by sharing about this persecution rather than being silenced by it. One example is his audition for the "homosexual" roommate part in a reality TV show just before he becomes a zombie. The show's casting director dismisses Sheldon as "not gay enough!" and wants him to be stereotypically lispy and feminine (38–40). Sheldon is so marginalized in this instance that others will not even recognize his marginalized identity, let alone do anything to end his oppression. His gayness is erased because it does not fit the oppressor's stereotype of it. Queerness here is seen only as a commodity, not as a legitimate human identity. This marginalization continues for Sheldon even after he becomes a celebrity due to his zombie status. He gets turned down for the lead role in a romantic comedy because he is gay, and the director worries that this might hurt the film at the box office (198). In this instance, instead of being rejected because he is too marginalized to matter, Sheldon is rejected for the opposite reason: because his homosexuality is too visible. He is damned if he does and damned if he doesn't, with homophobia on all sides. Again, though, it is significant that instead of remaining silent, Sheldon shares how his sexuality is capriciously policed by society.

Sheldon also tells readers that at times he did sex work to support himself when acting jobs were scarce (48). This is a significant detail because he does not feel ashamed of his actions but wants to give readers the entire picture of himself. In a Mennonite context (and often in broader society as well), homophobia stems in part from a general unwillingness to talk about sexuality at all, which leads to unhealthy attitudes about the body that are especially hurtful for women and sexual minorities.[7] Sheldon fights against this silencing and does not repent of his sex work, refusing to shame those who engage in it.

Happily, Sheldon does receive some affirmation of his sexuality. Although he cannot have sex as a zombie, he begins a "live-in" relationship with a fellow actor, Duane, whom he helps publicly come out (197). Through Duane and Sheldon's coupling, which is a mix of love, mentorship, Duane being Sheldon's personal assistant, and Sheldon finding Duane appetizing (he wants to eat him, literally, though of course there is the resonance of "eating" someone in the sexual sense), *Husk* argues for an openness to new relationship models. In the words of Lauren Berlant and Michael Warner, Sheldon and Duane engage in a "world-making project" through their unconventional relationship, creating new modes of interaction, an act that helps sustain "queer culture."[8] Sheldon's sharing of his and Duane's story is essential because it helps give a voice to the possibility of this new world; it refuses acceptance of the status quo and is thus a politically queer act. Although his mother and many others would deny that it is possible for Sheldon to find domestic happiness because he is gay, he and Duane are able to think creatively and find an arrangement that works for them.

There are also several fetish websites run by "corpsers" devoted to Sheldon (146), and he is offered work in pornographic films once his zombiehood becomes public (177). Some kinky segments of society support him, so he is not alone, and he functions as a rallying point for sexual outlaws. Although one might argue that Sheldon's sexual objectification is oppressive, Eli Clare writes that there is a fine line between sexual objectification and becoming an active "sexual subject," especially for sexual minorities.[9] Those who are sexually interested in Sheldon—who, like he does, fall under the umbrella of "queer"—find him praiseworthy and offer him a healthier kind of celebrity than those who mock him on daytime talk shows. It is significant that the corpsers see Sheldon—that they acknowledge his existence and accept him for who he is—unlike his mother or the casting director who rejects him because he does not fit a stereotype. All this discussion of Sheldon's sexuality and his sexual appeal is an important part of making him narratable.

It is clear from the way that Sheldon's open discussions of his sexuality are politicized that *Husk* is firmly ensconced in the queer literary tradition, and there are a number of ways the book explicitly converses with the zombie narrative tradition as well, besides being about a zombie. Redekop places *Husk* into this longer tradition in the acknowledgments, where he thanks "every author, actor, and director who brought zombies to life" (viii). Although *Husk* is a novel rather than a screenplay, the choice to give Sheldon the profession of actor acknowledges the influence of zombie films and television shows on the narrative models Sheldon has to work with in trying to understand his experience when he wakes up undead.

Another explicit reference *Husk* makes to the zombie narrative tradition is to the ur-text of zombie narratives, Mary Shelley's *Frankenstein*. Aside from Sheldon's first name's similarity to "Shelley," which gestures to the relationship between the two books, there are more similarities between Sheldon and Doctor Frankenstein's creature than between Sheldon and other zombies because Sheldon still has his reasoning faculties. When Sheldon tells us about getting back home from the morgue and trying to reassemble his dissected insides, he pays special attention to describing how he staples his heart into his chest, and when he does so, he says he feels "Frankensteinian" (51–52). Of course what Sheldon actually means here is that he feels "Frankenstein's creatureian." Sheldon's repetition of the common mistake of thinking that the creature is named Frankenstein rather than that being the name of his creator shows how attuned Sheldon is to television and movie portrayals of zombies, but *Husk* wants us to think of literary zombies as well.

The similarity to Doctor Frankenstein's creature goes deeper than just the way he and Sheldon are roughly reconstructed. It is essential for Sheldon to have his heart back in place. Sheldon's human life ended because of a heart attack (45), so his decision to put his heart back in even though he no longer needs it to function is one way he helps reconcile himself with the memory of his death and indicates his decision to try to live as human of a life as possible as a zombie. The act of stapling his heart in also serves as a symbol to show why he worries about ethics throughout the book. Unlike most zombies, unwittingly participating in the apocalypse, Sheldon has a heart in the metaphorical sense of being a good person. He is on the side of the humans, not the undead, and thus he tries to hold himself to human ethical standards, attempting to be nonviolent and feeling remorse when he fails. This sense of morality is what ties Sheldon to Shelley's creature more than to other zombies in literature or film. Doctor Frankenstein's creature is undead like other later zombies, but unlike the zombies in most zombie narratives, he is literate, he desires a place in human society, and he is unjustly persecuted by humans. Like Sheldon, it is only when these oppressive acts are committed against him that he resorts to violence. As Daniel Harris writes, zombies in their usual role as villains are "dehumanize[d]," providing cannon fodder for the good guys in movies or teenagers playing video games.[10] *Husk*, in contrast, is a revolutionary zombie narrative. All of its zombies, including those who, unlike Sheldon, are of the mindless variety, are viewed through Sheldon's first-person narrative as beings who deserve love and care. The scene toward the end of the book where the villain Lambertus Dixon shows Sheldon his holding pen of starving zombies who have no hope of release or permanent death is heartbreaking and makes it possible for readers not to mind when Sheldon eats Dixon's brain later on (242, 277–78). Although it shares similarities with traditionally derided zombie narratives from pop culture and often engages in a kind of lowbrow gross-out humor,[11] *Husk* also asserts through its references to *Frankenstein* that it has serious things to say.

One new thing *Husk* adds to the zombie narrative tradition is how in focusing on Sheldon's experience rather than that of the humans who are terrified of him, it uses zombiehood as a metaphor for how North American society treats people with disabilities.[12] Queer disability theorist Alison Kafer defines the "disabled" as people who "have faced discrimination" for bodily reasons, whether they have "mobility impairments," "mental illness[es]," or "chronic illness[es]" such as "HIV/AIDS."[13] Sheldon fits within this definition because people react with revulsion to his body throughout the novel. His agent, Rowan, the only person who claims to care for him besides Duane, only does so because she wants to profit off of him. She threatens to turn him in to the Centers for Disease Control if he does not play up his terrifying features for the media (187). She treats him as a one-man freak show rather than as a being deserving of humane treatment.[14]

Sheldon also has physical conditions that, while they may be normal for zombies, feel like disabilities to him because of his retained human consciousness. He has trouble breathing, speaking, and walking; he has a restricted diet; his body is aging and decaying much more quickly than it did as a human; and he cannot have sex because he is unable to get erections anymore because he no longer has any blood and because his sense of smell is altered, so he can no longer smell pheromones, only the smell of flesh as meat.[15] Sheldon's in-between state of having a human brain within a zombie's body also presents psychological difficulties as he attempts to redefine who he is. The world sees him only as a zombie, as Other, so he occupies a disconcerting middle ground. Although he thinks of himself as human, he is a kind of superzombie because he has the power to telepathically control other zombies, whom he calls his "children" (258). While he wants to be seen as a human, he also uses his powers for the good of the zombie community, and these actions are a recognition that he belongs in that community as well.

Sheldon also experiences body-based discrimination because, as a zombie, many people see him as monstrous, not only in his visage, but also in his potential deeds. Clare explains that society has often seen people with disabilities in this way.[16] The problem for Sheldon is that while he may look to other zombie narratives to help understand who he is, everyone else does the same thing, and they equate him with the zombies in horror films rather than with Doctor Frankenstein's creature.[17] Many others do not find Sheldon monstrous, but this is because they think he is merely "a fraud" (150). Just as when he fails to get the television part because he is "not gay enough," his self gets erased by those who believe he is a fake because they refuse to see his perspective. As often happens, the oppressors in this scenario attempt to define the oppressed, refusing them a voice. However, Sheldon refuses these hurtful outside definitions of himself by sharing his narrative with readers and thereby broadening our understanding of what a zombie can be.

Husk uses the metaphor of zombiehood to discuss another type of disability as well, that of aging. Kafer notes the disability studies maxim that "whether by illness, age, or accident, all of us will live with disability at some point in our lives."[18] With this in mind, all readers should appreciate *Husk*'s activist treatment of disability and should also recognize how ableism and ageism intersect, as the elderly in North American society are certainly discriminated against because of their bodily appearance. Sheldon uses the language of zombies when he discusses his mother and her fellow residents in the dementia ward of her nursing home. He calls the dementia floor "the floor of the walking dead" (90), which references George A. Romero's classic 1968 zombie film *Night of the Living Dead*.[19] The residents are out of sight, utterly marginalized because they are being kept in a de facto prison as those outside wait for them to die. Despite being the undead, Sheldon is much more alive than those in the nursing home because at least he has some agency left. His view of those with dementia stems from a place of compassion rather than callousness. He wonders why humans are willing to put their pets out of their misery but not their family members (86–87). As an authority on death because he has experienced it and as a zombie whose only path to a second death is through violence (since *Husk* employs the traditional zombie trope that the only way to kill zombies is by destroying their brains), Sheldon realizes that sometimes death is preferable to life. Thus *Husk* makes a statement about the powerlessness of the aged in North American society, questioning the insistence that life must be preserved at all costs even when one's quality of life is gone. This is one way the novel expresses its uneasiness with the concept of eternal life as a reward.

The third major element of Sheldon's identity, his Mennonite self, is more subtly dealt with than the first two. Sheri Klassen claims that "*Husk* is not a particularly 'Mennonite' Mennonite novel" because its subject matter is not very Mennonite.[20] However, just as it takes pains to explicitly place itself within the tradition of zombie narratives, the novel places itself into the Mennonite literary tradition in some significant ways. Although Sheldon identifies as a "Menno-not" (87) and *Husk* thereby explicitly references the Mennonite literary tradition by alluding to *Mennonot*, the Mennonite aspects of his identity influence his life as the undead.[21] Elsewhere, Redekop, who names himself as a "Mennonite writer," wonders whether his Mennonite last name is enough to make him a Mennonite, but in *Husk*, Sheldon's last name is an important symbol of two of his identities: Mennonite and zombie.[22] "Funk" is both a common Mennonite name and a nod to the fact that as a zombie, his body is "funky" because it smells and is decomposing.[23] While, as I argue below, Sheldon is unable to conceptually get away from his Mennonite upbringing despite no longer being a theological Mennonite, he is also linguistically unable to get away from being a Mennonite because of his name. He uses the pseudonym "Gary Jackson" as an actor, but once he is revealed as a zombie, this identity is stripped away and he becomes famous as "Sheldon Funk" (e.g., 153).

Aside from this explicit Mennonite marker, Sheldon is also the kind of rebellious character found throughout Mennonite fiction.[24] Jeff Gundy writes that Sheldon is "the most transgressive possible 'lost Mennonite'— not only worldly, an actor and gay, but a zombie and a cannibal to boot."[25] While I question the appropriateness of using the term *cannibal* in Sheldon's case below, Gundy is correct that even in attempting to run away from the Mennonite community, Sheldon makes a stereotypically Mennonite move. His Mennonitism is an essential part of his identity even though he tries to deny it. At one point Sheldon remarks on his "standard submissiveness" in his interactions with others (127). This personality trait also marks him as a Mennonite because of Mennonites' traditional advocacy of *gelassenheit*, or yieldedness, as an approach to life and their practice of being "the quiet in the land." Even when he becomes a celebrity, Sheldon just wants to have a quiet life with Duane rather than asserting his fame for profit. For someone engaged in one of the most stereotypically worldly professions, he is not especially enthusiastic about actually being in the world.

One element of *Husk*'s Mennonite nature is that it is rife with biblical allusions and metaphors, which are evident immediately. As Klassen notes, Sheldon is "born again" at the beginning of the novel.[26] There is an immediate twist to the Christian concept of resurrection, though, because Sheldon does not have a new heavenly body but instead a decaying, partially dissected one. His awakening is supplemented a chapter later by the story of his death, and thus right away *Husk* highlights that it engages theological issues and raises a theological quandary: What happens after death? For Sheldon, the answer is an earthly purgatory that he must negotiate, a second chance that could go well (as it generally does for the first two thirds of the book) or end horribly (as it does for the last third). Sheldon looks for "theolog[ical]" explanations of what he is (139), and while he finds none that are satisfactory, it is significant that he turns to theology as a possible answer after his resurrection. By doing so, he reclaims some of the Mennonite self that he has tried to shed because his Mennonite upbringing is what has given him the tools to search out and read theology.

The travails Sheldon faces as a zombie once again make him an in-
between character because while he faces the challenges a human would face in their everyday life, by virtue of his resurrection, he is also a Christ figure. *Husk* places him in this latter position in several ways. Sheldon remembers the time between his human death and his zombie resurrection, and he describes it by saying, "I was everything [. . . .] There was no I. There was only all" (3). His otherworldly experience echoes both John 1:1 ("In the beginning was the Word, and the Word was with God, and the Word was God") and Revelation 1:8a ("I am Alpha and Omega, the beginning and the ending"). Somehow during the time before he is resurrected, Sheldon glimpses eternity and his oneness with all of creation. He is able to transcend death in a twisted way by becoming the undead. But instead of reveling in this power, Sheldon instead questions why he has received it. He muses, "There had to be a purpose behind all this. Classically, people do not arise from the grave without there being an overarching theme behind it" (27). Sheldon recognizes immediately that there are parallels between himself and Jesus, and indeed, he does find himself in a position to save the world later on, but when he first thinks about his resurrection, all he wants to do is go back to his regular life. He is not interested in exploring his new supernatural powers, such as being mostly immortal and being able to incapacitate people just by speaking to them. He just wants to blend in and be a human again. In his refusal throughout much of the book to use his powers as a zombie, Sheldon is also similar to the prophet Jonah, who just wants to be left alone instead of heeding God's call. Sheldon struggles with the old superhero adage "with great power comes great responsibility" because he does not understand the reason for being given his powers (which *Husk* never explains), and thus the unasked-for responsibilities that come with them weigh heavily on him.

Sheldon tries to live a "normal" life even after he is revealed to the world as a zombie. However, when one of his fellow guests on a talk show expresses doubt about his condition, he opens up his chest cavity and shows her his zombified innards, allowing her to prod his intestines (159–61). This passage again places Sheldon in the position of Jesus because it references John 20:25–28, in which Thomas needs to touch Jesus's wounds after the resurrection in order to believe that it is really Jesus. Sheldon offers the world proof of his zombiehood not to gain followers but with the hope that people will simply acknowledge his existence and let him lead his life. He fights his role of savior as long as he can.

There is one last biblical allusion tying Sheldon to Jesus after Sheldon finally uses his powers for good to save the world from Lambertus Dixon. Dixon forces Sheldon to bite him so he will gain eternal life as a zombie, but in the ensuing fight, Sheldon gains the upper hand and begins to eat Dixon's brain when Dixon tempts Sheldon with the idea of shared world domination in a scene akin to Jesus's temptation by the devil in Matthew 4:1–11 (276–77). When Dixon makes this offer, Sheldon has a similar vision of the entirety of the world and time as he did just before he woke up as a zombie. He tells us that he sees all the divine power in the universe and that he "could have become a god" (278–79). Sheldon could be truly immortal, not just undead—a kind of messiah—but he knows that this is too much power for one earthly being to yield and so, like Jesus, he rejects the offer. By doing so, he saves the world twice: first by destroying Dixon and second by yielding up his power by seeking his second death. Harris shows that most zombie narratives are postapocalyptic, but *Husk* reverses this trope because Sheldon actually prevents the apocalypse at his own cost.[27]

But before that conclusion, Sheldon also wonders whether he is the bringer of the apocalypse, a kind of antichrist. Early in the novel, he thinks he might be "the beginning of the end of life itself" (75). It is interesting here that Sheldon speaks of ending life because he is still alive in a sense, but he acknowledges that his weird in-between state is difficult because he does not understand it yet. We as readers are as much in the dark about what and why Sheldon is as he is, but this unknowability is what allows him to be used symbolically in so many ways in service to the book's various forms of activism.

Dixon takes a dimmer theological view of Sheldon's being as well. He notes that Sheldon's voice is actually made up of seven different voices and that it could be the voice of God or the devil (222–23). This ambiguity is like that of the seven voices in Revelation 10:3–4. Just as the seven voices' message is kept secret, so too is the reason for and power behind Sheldon's resurrection. Whether Sheldon's voice is heavenly or hellish, it is from an otherworldly plane, and unlike Sheldon, Dixon recognizes the power that entails. Dixon wants Sheldon to serve him as an antimessiah to help Dixon conquer mortality and the world. He tells Sheldon, "You are death made flesh" (232), reversing the naming of Jesus as "the Word [. . .] made flesh" in John 1:14. This is literally true of Sheldon, as the people he has killed and eaten have become his flesh, but as I discuss below, he at least has a moral compass, unlike Dixon.

Dixon also mocks Sheldon for refusing to take advantage of his powers, asserting that Sheldon could have convinced people he was the messiah if he was not gay, but no one "could imagine pledging fealty to a son of God who enjoyed getting fisted" (224–25). It is striking that in this homophobic statement Dixon specifically names such a taboo sexual activity. The novel thus sets up Dixon as an explicitly antiqueer character because he is completely closed off to the kind of liberating, transgressive queer relationships discussed earlier. In case readers somehow had not yet divined *Husk*'s politically queer message, it becomes blatant here because Dixon is portrayed as utterly evil. The book uses Dixon, who believes in the Bible (223), to symbolize the homophobia still found in many Christian groups, including Mennonite denominations. In his power-hungry lust for immortality, Dixon also represents the institutionalization of Christianity within political structures of power. Sheldon's fight against Dixon is therefore a Mennonite one because it echoes the belief in the separation of church and state held by many early Anabaptists.[28]

Husk's Ethics

Most of *Husk*'s biblical allusions are easy to notice for those who have read the Bible, and they are clearly intentional. However, the novel never explicitly mentions the Bible aside from Dixon's previously cited statement. This lack of discussion indicates the purpose of all the allusions. Their implicitness places them in a secular context, and the book's refusal to insist on religiosity while still taking an explicitly ethical stance makes the argument that ethics is important for everyone, wherever one might get one's ethical principles from. Sheldon asserts early in the book that whether we believe in religion or nothing at all, "all we really want" is for someone to tell us that everything is all right (17). The basic question Sheldon tries to answer throughout his story is how to be. What models should he use for constructing a "good life" when he is already dead? Everyone asks these questions, whether in a religious framework or a secular one. Sheldon tries to create some new queer models for living with Duane, and he also draws from the ones he has from his Mennonite background. Whatever choices one makes in seeking a good life, *Husk* insists that they be made from an ethical standpoint.

The obvious question regarding Sheldon and ethics, though, is this: How can Sheldon be considered an ethical being? By the end of the novel, he eats at least a dozen people! This is true, but by contextualizing this violence within other elements of Sheldon's zombiehood, it is possible to see how he tries to act ethically and how the novel calls for us to also live ethically as a result. While *Husk* is in many ways written as a realistic, mimetic text and while much of its activism is made possible by this realism, it is also essential to examine the effects of its fantastical zombie elements on its ethical argument for readers. The novel gives us a main character who is in an untenable ethical position. Sheldon must eat humans or decompose (19), which would be, in effect, a second death for him, though it is worse than death because he would still be conscious but no longer have a functioning body with which to enjoy that consciousness. The book puts Sheldon in this position to cause readers to think about what ethical responses to evil might look like in the twenty-first century. What would one do if put in Sheldon's place? It is fair to assume that the majority of readers would like to claim that if they were conscious zombies, they would not eat human flesh because it would feel too much like cannibalism, which almost everyone considers unethical. Readers who have been taught the central Mennonite belief of pacifism would also object to eating humans because of the act's violence. And from a traditional Mennonite perspective, Sheldon and Mennonite readers have the answer to his ethical conundrum. If he has read the *Martyrs Mirror* or other Mennonite martyr narratives, he knows that when following one's moral beliefs will lead to one's death, the only possible choice for a faithful person is to accept that death.[29] As Luke 9:24 says, "For whosoever will save his life shall lose it: but whosoever will lose his life for [Jesus's] sake, the same shall save it." But Sheldon rejects this Mennonite teaching, admitting that he ate "ten or so people" before finding a doctor who was able to grow synthetic human muscle that he could feed on instead (202). Sheldon does receive punishment at the end of the novel, whether for his refusal to lay down his life or for other reasons, and it is possible to read this retribution as an affirmation that Sheldon is an unethical character.

However, although Gundy argues that "no one would take [*Husk*] for a serious exploration of nonresistance," I do want to argue that it advocates an ethic informed by pacifist principles.[30] The first person Sheldon commits violence against is the morgue attendant who is in the middle of dissecting him when he wakes up from the dead. Sheldon breaks the attendant's arms in order to get away but tells us, "There was no malice in this," just pure zombie instinct, and he "feel[s] bad" afterward (9–10). Thus right away Sheldon reveals himself as someone who believes in nonviolence. He does not try to justify his actions to readers but simply describes them because he wants to be honest about his story. Later on, when Sheldon considers eating his mother because he is angry with her for her homophobia and he also wants to end her dementia-ridden misery, he realizes that although eating humans is "now an essential part of" him, it is wrong of him to decide who deserves to die and who does not (93–94). He still tries to apply an ethical sense to his actions and refuses to put himself in the place of God despite his extraordinary powers.

The descriptions Sheldon gives of eating people read like cannibalism, and Sheldon feels afterward that they are indeed cannibalism, but at the same time, despite his human consciousness, he is no longer human, so *cannibalism* is not quite an accurate term. Human flesh is the food that Sheldon's zombie body craves. If he is going to eat, he does not have a choice about what he eats, so there may be room for understanding his actions. Paradoxically, the more humans he eats, the more human Sheldon is because it is this flesh that keeps him from decomposing and allows him to pass as human. Aside from feeling remorse, Sheldon tries to be ethical even in his eating of others, making sure he can eat the entirety of his victims by keeping them frozen in order to make several meals out of them (105). As a zombie, his Mennonite thriftiness is still intact.[31]

Sheldon's nonviolent principles are also displayed when he is offered the opportunity to work as a zombie-cyborg for the military. Doing so would halt the decaying of his body and bring him even more celebrity status, but Sheldon refuses to be a weapon for the government (203–4). He believes in the ideal of a peaceful world, placing the common good above his own by refusing to participate in the destruction wreaked by war. This choice acknowledges the role the military plays in supporting hegemonic systems of power that result in systemic violences such as homophobia.

Although Sheldon eats people out of necessity, he has imbibed the pacifist ethics taught to him to the point where they are still at the core of his being. In depicting Sheldon's struggle to be ethical, *Husk* illustrates that believing in pacifism is one thing, but being completely nonviolent in one's actions all the time is another. Like the rest of us, Sheldon fails to live up to his own ethical standards sometimes. He kills way fewer people than his powers would allow him to, though; for a zombie, he is incredibly nonviolent.

Husk also complicates the easy equation of nonresistance as good and violence as bad by manipulating our ethical responses as readers. It is difficult not to get excited when at the end of the novel Sheldon allows another zombie to eat the treacherous Rowan and when he eats Lambertus Dixon's brain to prevent him from taking over the world (278–80). Unlike the previous deaths he has caused, Sheldon is unrepentant about the villains' demise, but these deaths feel like justice, and we are happy that Sheldon is able to get revenge on the people who have destroyed his life while also preventing a zombie apocalypse. Although Sheldon says earlier that it is wrong for him to decide who should and should not die, it is easy for us as readers to decide that Dixon and Rowan are deserving of death as punishment for their actions. If we condemn Sheldon for being violent, we must condemn ourselves for supporting his violence as well. Readers, and especially Mennonite readers, might feel bad for reacting this way, but it is important that *Husk* raises the issue. The book is an ethical, Mennonite one because it raises this violence-related thought experiment, not because of Sheldon's personal decisions regarding the issue, though the fact that he describes how he feels about the ethics of his actions is significant.[32] The novel urges us to think about how to respond to violence in the twenty-first century in new ways, implying that ideas about peace and martyrdom from the sixteenth and seventeenth centuries might need updating, if only because these ideas assume the issue is always black and white.

The novel's ending offers one last commentary on Sheldon's choices. After the fight with Dixon and his henchmen, Sheldon decides his life as a zombie has gone on long enough. He has one of the other zombies rip out his brain from his broken body and throw it into the desert (286). However, this does not kill Sheldon's consciousness because his brain is not destroyed. Sheldon tells us that he decided to preserve his brain because he "just didn't want to be eaten" (298). He refuses to be a zombie Eucharist, and in doing so, he dooms his consciousness to eternal life. He cannot move; he cannot see anything; he can only think. Sheldon thus ends the book in a kind of hell, but it is a hell of his own making; he does penance for the deaths he has caused. In a twist on the traditional Mennonite martyr narrative, Sheldon is able to escape his martyrdom by others, but he then chooses to martyr himself. Unfortunately, heaven is never really an option for him because the only way out of the hell he ends up in is his second death. So there is no real hope for Sheldon, and *Husk* thereby turns the traditional Christian goal of achieving eternal life on its head. This reversal implies that it is necessary to focus on living ethically while on earth rather than worrying about whether those actions will lead to a happy afterlife. Despite Sheldon's damnation, he remains a sympathetic character because, rather than trying to justify his actions, he acknowledges that on some level it was wrong to kill all those people even though it felt like he did not have a choice. It is this likeability that allows the novel's messages about social justice to impact readers.

Husk ultimately argues through the story of Sheldon's body that those who are marginalized are like zombies: not really there and ignored as individuals, just as Sheldon's brain ends up ignored in the desert. The novel's implied message is that readers must work to end this marginalization by tending to those on the margins, whether queer, disabled, or otherwise. While Sheldon's attempts to live ethically may stem from his pacifist Mennonite upbringing, *Husk*'s call to care for the oppressed is one that we can all heed no matter what identities we inhabit.

Trans Mennonite Literature

Trans Mennonite literature is one of the newest trends in the recent flower-ing of Mennonite literature. This chapter examines two examples: a short story collection that is openly trans and a novel that is probably trans and has a trans sensibility. The two texts draw attention to the need to construct a usable queer history in general and a trans Mennonite history in particular. Casey Plett's 2014 short story collection *A Safe Girl to Love* documents this history in its stories, and Miriam Suzanne's 2015 text *Riding SideSaddle*: A Novel* uses its unique form to examine issues relating to the archiving neces-sary to build such history.

Trans Mennonite Life in *A Safe Girl to Love*

A Safe Girl to Love depicts transnational (Canada/U.S.), transcultural (Mennonite/non-Mennonite and urban/rural), trans women as they attempt to integrate their various identities into livable selves. The book's stories investigate the search for healthy community and the violence felt when communal acceptance is absent. *A Safe Girl to Love*'s characters seek solace in the trans community because they only encounter persecution in the Mennonite community and mainstream society, even among so-called friends. While these two communities may seem antithetical to one another considering the frequency of Christian transphobia, one of the ways the book is revolutionary is in how it shows that they share numerous common values. It explicitly references Mennonite literature and queer literature, arguing that a new tradition combining both of these is possible. J. Jack Halberstam writes that "the dilemma for the transgender character [. . .] is to create an alternate future while rewriting history."[1] Similarly, Zeke in the story "Not Bleak" argues for the necessity of this creative act when she asserts that

Mennonites "don't even know it's possible" to transition between genders.[2] Therefore, Plett has to write trans Mennonite stories in order to make trans Mennonites and trans people in general visible. Plett's characters struggle to create the new, welcoming future envisioned by Halberstam while also claiming a space for themselves, and not all of them succeed. The book begins writing a necessary trans history by archiving trans experience even though this experience is often difficult at best because of widespread transphobia.

Most of *A Safe Girl to Love*'s eleven stories depict the search for community through a conventional realist style that offers open-minded treatments of transgressive subjects such as BDSM and sex work, but the collection also includes three stories written as darkly humorous manifestos for how to live a trans life. This postmodern mix of approaches makes a politically queer argument about both the necessity for a transformed society and the importance of trans literature as a tool for building that society.

Two of *A Safe Girl to Love*'s stories—the first, "Other Women," and the longest, "Not Bleak"—include explicitly Mennonite characters. It is significant that the collection begins with a Mennonite story and that the two stories take up nearly 40 percent of the book. The first story gives a Mennonite tinge to the rest of the collection, coloring the other stories' depictions of community and transphobia and inserting the book as a whole into a Mennonite context. The Mennonite protagonist of "Other Women," Sophie, and the Mennonite antagonist of "Not Bleak," Zeke, are two of the most developed characters in the book. Thus while all of *A Safe Girl to Love*'s portrayals of trans experience are important, the book privileges its explorations of trans Mennonite lives.

The collection's Mennonite presence is emphasized in the book's references to Mennonite literature. One of the nonexplicitly Mennonite stories, "Portland, Oregon," begins with an epigraph from Miriam Toews's *A Complicated Kindness* (93). "Not Bleak" also references Toews's *Summer of My Amazing Luck* in its use of the uncommon name Lish, the name of a primary character in Toews's book, for one of its characters. Also in "Not Bleak," a non-Mennonite character, Liam, reads some of Sandra Birdsell's work, which Zeke "had really loved—rabidly, in a sort of creepy-obsessive way" (174). Her level of devotion is described as being akin to the "obsession" discussed in the introduction that Ann Cvetkovich deems necessary for those who would archive queer experience.[3] In this case, Zeke archives Mennonite experience, trying to figure out how her queer self can fit into it. Of course, readers must already know that Toews and Birdsell are Mennonite authors in order to recognize these references as Mennonite ones. They function as a special insider message for those already familiar with Mennonite literature, acting as both an homage to the Mennonite literary tradition and a claiming of space within that tradition, an insistence that queer Mennonite voices must be heard.

Like most of *A Safe Girl to Love*'s stories ("Portland, Oregon" and "Real Equality: A Manifesto" are exceptions), the dialogue in "Other Women" and "Not Bleak" has no quotation marks around it. This stylistic choice symbolizes an openness to new ways of thinking that the book advocates throughout. It queers genre conventions, arguing that the transformation of society envisioned by queer theory will necessitate new forms of art. As shown below, *Riding SideSaddle** shares this argument.

"Other Women" is an appropriate beginning for *A Safe Girl to Love* because it sets up some common themes for the rest of the collection's realist stories, as shown in the following relatively lengthy close reading. It is the second-longest story in the collection in part because it takes time to lay out the variety of prejudices trans people face and to correct commonly held faulty assumptions about trans people. One of these is that trans people's sexual orientation is somehow also inherently tied to their gender. The story shows that this is not the case through Sophie's erotic encounters. Sophie is open to sexual experiences with different genders even though she claims to prefer women (9). In fact, she refuses to answer when her cousin asks whether she dates women or men, and the story culminates in a night when she is intimate with both a woman and a man (17, 25–32). Sophie is more interested in whether her partner listens to her desires and respects her transitioning body than in their gender; the act and how it is performed is more important than who it is performed with. She rejects Megan in favor of Mark because he does a better job of letting Sophie explore her desires. It is significant that Mark's sexual orientation also remains unnamed (9, 15). He is attracted to Sophie as a person, not specifically as a man or woman. Sophie's lack of knowledge about his sexual preferences allows her to relax around him and ultimately accept his advances. The openness present in these interactions is invigorating rather than threatening. While the amorphousness of openness may be scary, which is why boundaries can be comforting and are often defended vigorously, the lack of limits can also allow for the possibility of revolutionary change. Seeing one's romantic partner as a person rather than as a man or woman begins to erode the gender binary that is central to homophobia and patriarchy.

"Other Women" also examines the search for community. Sophie returns to her home in Winnipeg from Portland in an attempt to figure out where she fits because she has found that transphobia is the same on both sides of the border. Her search for a welcoming community, however, is thwarted throughout most of the story. For instance, although Sophie's mother tries to be understanding of her transition, asking whether Sophie is safe from transphobic violence in the United States, she also worries that the trans community is a "cult" (10, 18). This comment is offensive in part because it implies that being trans is a choice, even though Sophie explains throughout the story that she has always felt like a woman. Her family members are unable to see that while Sophie can choose just how she would like to perform her femininity, she has always known that her self is better expressed through this gender. Similar to her mother's reluctance to accept Sophie's identity, members of Sophie's family refuse to come to Christmas dinner simply because she is there (14). They prefer to sacrifice their experience of community rather than opening the community to those who are at all different from them. As such, their transphobia is detrimental to themselves as well as Sophie. We see the negative aspect of the traditional Mennonite concept of community here, as Sophie's family participates in an informal shunning of her. In fact, this shunning is even worse than the formal kind because it is chosen voluntarily by Sophie's family instead of being forced upon them by church leadership. Just like Jess's family in *Somewhere Else*, Sophie's relatives try to deny that the identity "queer Mennonite" is a possibility.

The place where Sophie should find an unconditionally loving and accepting community, church, is likewise an unwelcoming space. While Mennonites have a long history of being persecuted exiles themselves and thus should be especially cognizant of Jesus's mandate to embrace those on the margins of society, the congregation in "Other Women" refuses to do so. Even worse, it conveys its lack of welcome to Sophie via her family. Sophie's mother implies that Sophie will not be welcome at church because her transition might be too controversial for the congregation to handle and might put the family in a bad light, so Sophie asks whether she should sit apart from the family during the Christmas service, and her mother agrees. Sophie complies by using her hair to hide her face so that the older congregants will not recognize her and waiting out in the car after the service for the rest of the family to finish greeting their friends (13–15). Sophie is constantly asked to accommodate others even though she interacts with those who should welcome her. The scene's critique of Mennonite transphobia is symbolized by Sophie's physical location: she is on the outside in the cold because there is no space for her within the community's warmth. Due to its fear of difference, the congregation neglects Jesus's command to welcome the stranger. It betrays its central teaching in order to protect its boundaries.

In contrast, Mark's acceptance of Sophie throughout the story even though they have just met shows that there is hope for her to find a safe, nurturing community. He tells her that he does not care about her being trans but is simply attracted to her (30). The inconclusiveness of the story's end as they are in the middle of sex offers the possibility that Sophie has finally found an accepting community, even if it is only with one other person. "Other Women" affirms the importance of community while arguing that one should not remain in a community that denies one's full selfhood. The story acknowledges that it is sometimes better to choose exile over self-negation, a process that offers those on the margins the difficult but necessary opportunity to emerge as fully realized individuals who can then return to the community and share what they have learned, transforming it for the good.

The oppressive use of power within the Mennonite community is immediately thrown to the forefront in "Other Women" as Sophie describes her decision to adopt her new name even though her mother, her extended family, and some of her friends would prefer to silence her trans identity by using her dead name (1, 13, 17, 21). Sophie refuses to give up her voice, but it is a constant fight. The process of always needing to be on guard against those who wish to use her former name, and the act of correcting people when they do, takes a toll. She must undertake this task alone because no one is willing to do it for her. She just wants acceptance, to be able to blend in instead of constantly being treated as Other. Instead, Sophie's mother is only able to use euphemistic phrases such as "your new lifestyle" to describe her child's gender (10), and this partial acknowledgment is just as frustrating as no acknowledgment at all because it still treats Sophie as though she is somehow abnormal. Sophie's grandmother also attempts to silence her new identity, refusing to talk with Sophie about her transition and attempting to hide behind religious authority by slipping a Bible verse into Sophie's boots (18). "Other Women" shows, via this episode, that the Mennonite community and society as a whole need new language for explaining individuals' relationships to collective norms. The story implies that the healthy aspects of Mennonite community have fallen away in favor of a view of community as an entity that exists primarily to enforce an us/them divide. Building community becomes an exercise in power rather than in welcoming mutual aid.

Geographical space plays an important role in *A Safe Girl to Love*'s depiction of searching for community. Although the collection explores rural and urban spaces in Canada and the United States, none of these spaces are welcoming for trans people. The transnational element of the book is highlighted in "Other Women" by other characters' references to Sophie as an "American" because she used to live in the United States, even though she is a native Manitoban (10, 13, 21, 24). The other characters use "American" as a code word for Othering Sophie as a way to hide their general uneasiness with her female self. They are not actually worried that she might become an "American," but they are worried about her being a woman. In two instances, Sophie tries to combat this marginalization by turning it into a joke, threatening to cause a U.S. invasion of Canada if others do not curb their taunting (21, 24). She uses the mantle of fake military power to protect herself from having to openly confront her so-called friends' new dislike of her. Her attempts to create community through humor ultimately fall flat because her conversation partners still end up being transphobic to her face.

"Other Women" also introduces the theme of frank sexuality via its ending, with the last fifth of the story dedicated to two sex scenes. In the first, Sophie and her longtime best friend, Megan, are turned on by each other and engage in satisfying foreplay that involves Megan giving Sophie nipple torture (25). However, Megan gets frustrated when Sophie cannot get an erection because she is on estrogen. Megan then fellates Sophie, who resists and ultimately refuses to have sex with Megan because it reminds her too much of her old masculine self (26–28). Instead of listening to how Sophie feels and working together to find a nontraditional way for the two of them to pleasure one another, which would symbolize a better version of the drug-addled sex they had before Sophie's transition (4), Megan quits. The passage shows how deeply ingrained her transphobia is even though she has tried to eradicate it. She can only focus on Sophie's penis instead of her entire person. The end of the story, however, provides an affirming experience when Sophie has sex with Mark. He repeatedly tells her how beautiful she is and listens to what she says feels pleasurable (30–32). As noted above, this scene offers hope for the acceptance of trans persons. Sex can create a space where the construction of gender is stripped away, leaving two bodies focusing on their acts instead of their societal labels, whether secular or religious.

"Not Bleak" continues the critique by "Other Women" of Mennonites by portraying its primary Mennonite character, Zeke, as unsympathetic because she is a thief. However, she herself is oppressed by the Mennonite community's transphobia. When Zeke visits her grandfather, she feels the need to present as male because she worries about how he will react to her as a woman (140–41). The story shows that being part of an oppressed group does not inherently make one a good person while at the same time arguing that the Mennonite community bears some responsibility for Zeke's thieving because she steals to fund her transition process. If her Manitoba Mennonite community would support her—and it is clear that they could financially (151)—she could stay in Canada and benefit from its cheaper health care, but because she is forced into exile in the United States, she must fend for herself.

Zeke's uneasiness with other Mennonites is further seen when she asks the story's non-Mennonite narrator, Carla, to go with her to see her grandfather and Carla asks why she does not ask Sophie, who is back from Canada, to go with her instead because Sophie is also a trans Mennonite. Zeke responds that Carla is the only one in town that she "trust[s]" (141). Her rejection of Sophie as a possible ally shows just how much Zeke has been scarred by Mennonite transphobia: she is unable to trust even other queer Mennonites. While Sophie's presence in "Not Bleak," which takes place after "Other Women," shows that she has left her Mennonite community again because of its rejection of her, it is striking that she is able to find community elsewhere and Zeke is not. Sophie feels safer in the non-Mennonite trans community in North Dakota, but Zeke's bad experiences with community in Manitoba cause her to reject the trans community as well. Instead of building a true friendship with Carla that might lead to her eventually feeling comfortable with Sophie and others in their town, Zeke destroys her ties to Carla by stealing from her. Considering Zeke's choice not to come out to her grandfather as trans, perhaps it is not surprising that she is unable to find a home in the trans community. While it is necessary to respect Zeke's choice because she is in a traumatic emotional situation and it is unfair to insist that she accept the martyrdom that would probably come with outing herself, it is also important to acknowledge that Sophie is able to gain access to a healthy trans community because she fully claims her trans identity.[4] This unabashed claiming gives her a conceptual home to go to when Mennonites reject her.

In contrast to the Mennonite community's rejection of Zeke and her rejection of the trans community, Carla feels that she has a healthy trans community in her small North Dakota town. She enjoys her job at a bookstore; has a good relationship with her trans boyfriend, Liam; and has a network of other trans friends. Carla tries to build this community by mentoring Zeke, who is younger and less experienced in a variety of ways. Carla says that it is "really beautiful" to watch Zeke grow as a person (134). There is more hope at this point in the story than anywhere else in *A Safe Girl to Love* because Carla is at peace with herself and is able to use this position of emotional strength to guide Zeke in her journey toward a path whereby Zeke can get to a good place too. Even when they are in a potentially dangerous situation after encountering some transphobes on the street, Carla is able to protect Zeke, and they get revenge on the men by zapping them with silly string (163–65). Although Zeke ultimately rejects Carla's community-building efforts, the vision of a positive trans community that "Not Bleak" offers is an example of Muñoz's concrete utopia discussed in chapter 2 because it posits that this kind of community is possible despite widespread transphobia.

This emphasis on the importance of queer community is echoed in Zeke's reading choices, which is part of what makes her ultimate rejection of community so perplexing. Aside from reading Mennonite authors, she also reads Miranda July. Like Jess in *Somewhere Else*, Zeke realizes she must go outside of the Mennonite tradition to find queer literary models. Carla tells us that she dislikes July (132), which could be read as an argument for readers to reject July's work as well because Carla is the more likable of the two characters. However, the act of referencing and commenting on another queer writer shows the story's awareness of working in the queer literary tradition. It is important to note that July's queerest book, *The First Bad Man*, which involves a kinky relationship between the two main female characters and in which the work of queer icon David Bowie plays a significant role, was published after "Not Bleak" takes place, so it is possible that Carla would have a more positive view of July's work now.

One reason queer literature is important is its role in documenting queer history. Halberstam remarks on "how difficult transgender history has been to write in general."[5] *A Safe Girl to Love* works to offer fictionalized versions of pieces of this history. In "Not Bleak," we briefly get some of this history through Lish's story of having known Adrienne from "Portland, Oregon" in the 1990s (174). This intra-collection reference works differently from Sophie's appearance in "Not Bleak" because of the time difference. "Not Bleak" takes place not long after "Other Women," whereas it takes place about twenty years after "Portland, Oregon." Lish's storytelling thus simultaneously acts as a form of trans community building, making broader connections between different trans enclaves (in Mennonite terms, she plays a trans version of the "Mennonite Game"), and a form of archiving trans experience, reminding Carla that her trans journey takes place within a context that has history even though it is one that transphobic society would like to deny.

BDSM is another common subject in the Mennonite stories and some of the non-Mennonite realist stories in the book. In "Other Women," Sophie asks both Megan and Mark to be rough with her during their sexual encounters, begging Megan to torture her nipples and hold her down and wanting Mark to pull her hair and "split [her] open" with his large penis (25, 31–32). Sophie's lack of commentary about her masochism—she simply tells readers what acts she desires from her partners without framing her desire at some point by saying "I like pain" or "I'm a masochist" or "I'm a bottom"—is an assertion that it is not remarkable, that even though society sees it as taboo, she does not have to respond to such marginalization. Some readers may find the sex Sophie has shocking, but that is their problem, not hers, because her desires are met.

In "Not Bleak," Carla is less coy about her bottoming as she leisurely describes all the aches and bruises she has obtained after a night "with a [. . .] mega-top woman from the [nearby] Christian college" (138–39). Here the story offers a window into BDSM culture by accurately describing how bottoms often wear the physical markings they receive from their tops as badges of honor, as objects to be savored as they relive the experience of receiving them.[6] The way Carla happily lingers over her residual pain makes sure that readers cannot miss her kinky proclivities, something that it might be possible to do with Sophie's descriptions of sex in "Other Women." This passage comes right after Carla mentions people buying E. L. James's kinky bestseller *Fifty Shades of Grey* at the bookstore (138), a signal for readers that in case they are unsure of how to read the depiction of the sexual encounter that Carla describes, it is one where pain brings her pleasure.[7] It is also significant that Carla's partner is "Christian." "Not Bleak" asserts that Christians (including, by extension, Mennonites) can be kinky, that kinkiness is not just a worldly practice.[8] Carla's interfaith coupling is an example of the queer community building that occurs throughout queer Mennonite literature. The two identities benefit from encounters with each other.

While the Mennonite stories' depictions of BDSM are relatively brief, the entire plot of "How Old Are You Anyway?" centers around it. While the protagonist Lisa works as an online dominatrix via camera, she likes to be dominated in real life (38–39). The story tells of Lisa's flirtation with a new neighbor, Tam, which culminates in Tam coming over after they run into each other at another neighbor's party. Tam intuits that Lisa is a bottom, and they proceed to have an encounter that includes Tam torturing Lisa's nipples, choking her, tying her to the bed, and sitting on her face (48–51).

The description of these acts focuses on Lisa's physical responses, which are intense and at times consciousness-altering. The depiction of her unabashed pleasure is a corrective to traditionally negative Mennonite views of the body. It also acts as a remedy to the way the men Lisa performs for objectify her body, giving her full ownership over herself. While they fetishize her because she is a woman with a penis, she gains agency as a subject by letting Tam top her because in BDSM, it is always the bottom who is actually in control.

Lisa decides to have sex with Tam because Tam looks "so incredibly incredibly kind" (47). Lisa finds in Tam the human connection that she has spent the first half of the story claiming she can do without. Tam is one of the "safe girls to love" referenced in the book's title. Lisa senses correctly that it is safe to make herself physically vulnerable with Tam even though a cardinal rule of BDSM is not to let your partner restrain you at your place the first time you play with them.[9] While it is a mistake to consider "How Old Are You Anyway?" erotica (a term I do not use disparagingly) because it is too plot oriented, its overt sexual focus makes a powerful statement about documenting uncommon sexual practices as one element of constructing queer history. Fictional portrayals of BDSM are necessary because of their refusal to accept mainstream society's attempts to silence alternative sexual expressions. The story also illustrates how BDSM is an ideal community-building activity—even if, as in this case, it only builds a community of two—because of the level of trust necessary between partners to avoid injury. The top must trust the bottom to be honest about how much pain is too much, and the bottom must trust the top to have the bottom's safety as their utmost concern. The story's apparent focus is sex, but it is actually just as much about this building of community—something that is lacking in Lisa's life because she is trans and her former friends have rejected her (39).[10] In contrast, Tam sees Lisa as a whole person because she does not care about Lisa's trans status. This lack of Othering on Tam's part makes a relationship between the two women possible.

The treatment of BDSM in "Lizzy & Annie" is unique in the collection because it is the one story that portrays an extended kinky relationship within the story itself rather than single meetings.[11] The women's relationship begins after they meet up at a reading and Annie brings Lizzy home and lets Lizzy top her, an encounter that once again includes nipple torture (64, 68). This recurring act in A Safe Girl to Love's kinky scenes functions to tie them together to help readers notice BDSM as a significant subject throughout the collection.[12] Similarly, the reference to literature on the night Lizzy and Annie meet emphasizes the other literary references throughout the book. Although "Lizzy & Annie" does not mention any specific books or authors like some of the other stories in the collection, the literary setting for the beginning of the women's relationship is important because it is another example of acknowledging that the book is influenced by and makes itself a part of several literary traditions. Lizzy and Annie are not just part of the trans community; they are part of a literary community as well.

As in "How Old Are You Anyway?" the community created by the women's relationship is just as important as the sex they have. They begin seeing each other weekly for sex (73). Although Lizzy wishes they could see each other more often, she realizes how lucky she is that she has someone who "trust[s]" her with their body and that she can trust with hers (85). It is difficult for her and Annie to find intimacy in a transphobic world, but they are able to create a refuge for one another.

The BDSM elements in "Lizzy & Annie" are also unique because Lizzy is a top, whereas the rest of *A Safe Girl to Love*'s kinky characters examined here are bottoms (Lisa's virtual topping of men in "How Old Are You Anyway?" is an economic practice rather than her kinky preference). The characters' preference for the bottom role has Mennonite undertones. Nguyen Tan Hoang's concept of "bottomhood," which is not only a sexual position but also "an ethical mode of relationality," posits that the vulnerability that is an essential part of this position makes space for liberating work to occur.[13] Bottomhood is similar to the Mennonite ideal of *gelassenheit*, or yieldedness. Unlike *gelassenheit*, however, which is taught as a form of self-effacement, bottomhood claims a transgressive power for its subjects because it asserts that the giving up of power is itself a powerful act; the bottom exchanges one form of power for another. An "upside-down kingdom" ethic akin to that in Mennonite thinking is present here. After all, it is no accident that one of the most common pieces of BDSM furniture is the Saint Andrew's cross, which allows kinksters to reenact the yielding of self practiced in the crucifixions of Jesus and various early Christian martyrs. Hoang argues that this transaction is a "joyful" one.[14] While the Mennonite characters in *A Safe Girl to Love* experience their Mennonite communities' insistence on submission to transphobic practices as oppressive, they and the other bottoms feel this joy in their sexual experiences, which are one bright spot in their difficult lives.

Trans theorist Julia Serano observes that construction of gender is "non-consensual,"[15] and her idea is relevant for discussing the BDSM in *A Safe Girl to Love*. BDSM play is centered around consensuality in order to keep its participants safe by giving them a sense of control and ensuring that it is pleasurable for all involved. One role of BDSM in Plett's stories is as a way of working through the nonconsensuality of assigned gender for the trans characters because while the construction of everyone's gender is nonconsensual, the pain of this forcing is not felt by cis people, since we are able to just go along with it. BDSM play can be a moving experience because it allows participants to claim power in the moment, something they may not have access to in broader society. For *A Safe Girl to Love*'s trans characters, BDSM's consensuality gives them an agency over themselves that the transphobia they often encounter does not. When they are in the bedroom, they do not have to define their gender for anyone but can instead focus on pleasuring their bodies.

A Safe Girl to Love's realist stories also share other themes, including heavy alcohol and drug use, the importance of place, and most prominently, difficulty finding fulfilling work because of the stress of facing employers' and customers' transphobia. These employment struggles often lead to characters performing sex work.[16] This trend, as Serano documents, is based in fact.[17] As mentioned above, Lisa in "How Old Are You Anyway?" cams online. In "Not Bleak," Carla reveals that she has acted in pornography, and it is implied that Sophie sometimes does outcalls (175, 162).[18] Adrienne from "Portland, Oregon" drives for "an escort agency" (103). These jobs are described without moral condemnation, though none of the characters speak about their work positively, since it is dangerous because most forms of sex work are illegal in North America and thus come with the risks inherent in black-market activity. The book's depictions of sex work also are much less detailed overall than its depictions of other sex-related activities, though their frequency signifies the importance of the subject. They remind us that, as Juana María Rodríguez emphasizes, "sex is a labor issue."[19] Sex is not private even in one's own bedroom, but it is always regulated by the violence of capitalism and the laws that enforce it.

Despite sex work's sinful reputation, the collection's inclusion of it is rooted in a Mennonite ethic. Mennonites claim to be on the side of the poor and the oppressed, and if this ideal is lived out, it means being on the side of sex workers by recognizing their humanity and caring about their safety because of their marginalized position both legally and in mainstream discourse in North American society. Like *Husk*, *A Safe Girl to Love* enacts this advocacy through its portrayal of sex work simply by acknowledging that sex workers exist and by telling their stories. Plett herself has "been a sex worker."[20] As with Wes Funk's willingness to discuss his sexual behaviors referenced in chapter 1, it is important that Plett is willing to be open about her own experiences without shame and that she writes about sex work in *A Safe Girl to Love* in a manner that is not sensationalistic or tawdry but acknowledges sex workers as whole persons in a way that society generally does not. The brevity of the book's mentions of the subject in comparison to its more detailed examinations of other elements of the characters' lives shows that the characters are not defined by their work, which is once again a reminder that none of us is reducible to a single identity.

The Manifesto Stories

A Safe Girl to Love offers three how-to stories that serve as manifestos for finding a livable trans life: "Twenty Hot Tips to Shopping Success," "How to Stay Friends," and "Real Equality (A Manifesto)." While only one of the three is written explicitly as a manifesto, all three perform the function of "supporting a cause, propounding a theory or argument" that the *Oxford English Dictionary* attributes to the word *manifesto* because they define trans experiences in the first two, which make arguments about how to approach stressful aspects of trans life, and define what it supposedly means to be "queer" in the third.[21]

"Twenty Hot Tips to Shopping Success" uses ironic humor as a strategy for shielding the hypothetical transitioning trans woman to whom it is addressed from the emotional trauma of beginning to present as a woman. After starting with suggestions about which stores to shop at, the story's third step for buying a first female outfit is to "go home" and drink to comfort "yourself" about the enormity of the task (33–34). The trauma of this experience is common enough in trans life that *Riding SideSaddle** also brings it up, as the narrator wishes for a store with "attractive clothes for heavyset queers."[22] The guidance in "Twenty Hot Tips to Shopping Success" to leave without buying anything is, of course, a piece of advice that would never be included in the kind of magazine article that the story mimics. These articles simplify life, telling readers that if they merely follow the often consumeristic steps the articles advocate, their lives will be perfect. The story's ironic tone is thus established immediately through its step-by-step form. It also illustrates right away that transitioning is difficult because of societal pressures against it.

The following steps encourage "you" to return to the store the next day in a Xanax-induced haze to begin browsing for clothes in earnest. You are instructed to think up all sorts of excuses for looking at skirts in case someone asks about it (34–35). Saying you are trans is not an option. The story acknowledges here that, aside from the fact that it can be dangerous to reveal one's trans identity to others, one struggle trans people face is that, because they have grown up in a transphobic society, they have their own transphobia to conquer in order to accept their trans selves. The story's tone is ironic because, while some of its tips may really be helpful, what is needed is a how-to for getting through the emotional strain of fighting transphobia, which is so severe that the story suggests a sexist, homophobic response to dealing with it. If your roommate interrogates you about where you were, you should "tell him you were nailing chicks. Such banter is unusual for you. If your roommate comments on this, inform him that he is a fag" (36). Of course the story does not actually advocate for homophobia or sexism, but this advice shows how scary it can be to transgress gender norms. You are instructed to hide the taboo act of buying a skirt by pretending to be macho and hiding your pain from society's forcing of masculinity on you by questioning someone else's masculinity instead.

Despite this low point, "Twenty Hot Tips to Shopping Success" ends on a hopeful note. You feel satisfied with how the skirt looks on you and are willing to let your roommate see you in it when he asks if you want to get burritos (37). Here the story actually functions as a helpful how-to because it asserts that no matter how difficult transitioning can be, one can do it successfully, and it is worth it. Therefore, although it is the second-shortest story in the collection, it is also one of the most important because it is the most positive overall.

It is clear in "Twenty Hot Tips to Shopping Success" that the act of finding clothes that fits one's female identity is traumatic. Kathryn Bond Stockton documents how queer persons are often "martyred for clothes" because our preferred fashion choices do not match with societal expectations for femininity or masculinity. Stockton explains that this martyrdom leads to "psychic" distress that manifests itself in "cloth wound[s]," a feeling of pain as a result of the clothes one is forced to wear instead of one's ideal outfit, and that being able to recognize these wounds in others is itself a queer act.[23] Her martyr language resonates strongly with Mennonite experience. As chapter 4 shows, being a martyr is one of the most central Mennonite narratives. The issue of clothing has certainly been a traumatic one for North American Mennonites that has included aspects of martyrdom. Up until the last few decades of the twentieth century, most Swiss Mennonites dressed "plain" (lapel-less "plain coats" for men and prayer coverings and figure-concealing "cape dresses" for women), and in more conservative congregations, some still do.[24] I grew up hearing stories from my mother about how good it felt to stop wearing the covering once she graduated from high school and moved from Harrisonburg, Virginia, to New York City, where the Mennonites had less stringent regulations about plain dress. In speaking with my mother's three sisters and a sister-in-law about when they stopped wearing the covering, they all discussed it as a freeing, positive moment in their lives, and my youngest aunt recalled being ecstatic when my grandfather, who worked for Eastern Mennonite College (now Eastern Mennonite University) for more than thirty years, was able to stop wearing the plain coat and could wear a regular suit and tie to work instead.[25] I have heard similar stories throughout my life from older Mennonites about how oppressive dressing plain was for them.

While it is primarily Swiss Mennonites who have dressed plain and Plett is writing from a Russian Mennonite perspective, in the broader public imagination, all Mennonites dress plain.[26] "Twenty Hot Tips to Shopping Success" draws on this stereotype to access the history of clothing trauma that the story's character experiences in their trans Mennonite context. Dressing plain felt oppressive to many Mennonites because it marked them too extremely as Other in the world as an enforced form of showy self-righteousness: I dress plain, so clearly I must be godlier than you. In contrast, the story's character tries to blend into the world as much as possible by buying clothes at the mall. The title epitomizes this grasping for worldliness. Mennonite authorities would not traditionally approve of any "hot tips" for "shopping" because the "success" that the speaker yearns for could be read as a form of the sin of pride, and "hot" signifies a potentially sinful eroticism. But the speaker's directions for achieving this success serve a communal purpose just as plain dress did. The cloth wounds present in the story signify it as a queer story in the way it tries to build a community by offering aid to those who do not know how to begin visually claiming their female identities.

"How to Stay Friends" describes "your" attempt to reconcile with your ex-girlfriend after she broke up with you once you began transitioning (54). Like "Twenty Hot Tips to Shopping Success," it seems to simply offer a set of steps to follow for navigating a common trans experience—meet at a favorite restaurant, make cheery small talk, get a drink together after the meal—but actually makes an argument about a broader principle for how to try to live one's trans life successfully. Unlike the previous story, "How to Stay Friends" uses no humor and is depressing because your ex is a jerk who continues to use the wrong pronouns for you and constantly makes light of the difficulty of trans existence (55–57). The story highlights the importance of building and maintaining community through your attempt to talk with someone who has wronged you. However, like "Other Women," it also argues that you should not continue these attempts that are ultimately harmful to yourself if the person who has wronged you does not admit their wrongdoing and remains transphobic. The story teaches that in this case, you should not worry about "how to stay friends" but instead let the friendship die unless your ex apologizes and acknowledges her role in harming the relationship. In Mennonite terms, the story posits that sometimes a form of shunning is necessary in order to preserve one's emotional health.

"Real Equality (A Manifesto)" is written as a speech by "a white queer cis woman," "Jilo Bombastier," from Brooklyn (88). Her last name's play on "bombast" signals to readers right away that they should be skeptical of her ideas because they will be puffed up without substance. Her identification as a white Brooklynite indicates that she is a member of the gentrifying hipster hordes that have plagued the borough in recent decades, obliviously pushing up rents and making it even more difficult for the economically marginalized to survive. Bombastier's choice to highlight her cis privilege when describing herself is also worrisome in *A Safe Girl to Love*'s trans context, as unfortunately LGB persons are sometimes transphobic. While she claims to be "a gigantically huge trans ally" (90), the fact that she needs to make such a claim indicates that she actually is not an ally, because she is about to make a transphobic statement. Indeed, as the "Manifesto" goes on, it becomes clear that despite claiming the label of queer for herself, Bombastier is queerphobic in general. She rails against queers "sequestering ourselves into gayborhoods" and being "ghettoized" in LGBT studies sections of bookstores (88–89). Instead, she wants queers to assert their right to the "equality" of the manifesto's title by assimilating, refusing to insist on "the nuance of our histories or desires" because "we are all the same" (91). This is a grossly incorrect definition of the social equality that marginalized groups strive for. Equality does not mean sameness in terms of one's identity; it means having the same access to legal rights and recognition of one's full humanity rather than being discriminated against as Other.

All Bombastier's suggestions are ways to make queers less visible, which is incredibly dangerous in a homophobic and transphobic society that already wants to erase us. LGBT studies sections of bookstores and efforts to archive queer history are necessary so that the queer community is visible to those who might need its refuge. Queer texts offer models for and language about being queer that can show LGBT persons coming from homophobic contexts that they are not alone. For instance, when I first experienced an attraction to another man in high school, I did not have the language I needed to process those feelings. I did not know what the term *bisexual* meant, and no one in my Lancaster, Pennsylvania, Mennonite milieu was going to teach me. As I say in chapter 2, it was not until I moved to New York City after college that I was able to realize that I was queer. My interactions with texts that I encountered in queer spaces such as the Bluestockings feminist bookstore and the Museum of Sex were essential in helping me come to this realization.[27] Similarly, having queer-friendly public spaces, whether they be feminist bookstores, cafés with queer open mic nights, or "gayborhoods," is also important for sustaining the queer community. Characters from several stories in *A Safe Girl to Love* experience threats to their physical safety because they can be read as trans (e.g., 81, 163). These instances illustrate that safe spaces are precious commodities that require nurturing rather than the dissolution Bombastier advocates.

The title "Real Equality (A Manifesto)" references Serano's "Trans Woman Manifesto" and especially "Barrette Manifesto," which has the same satirical tone as Plett's story and calls for "true equality," a phrase that Plett's title riffs on.[28] The story makes these citations plain when Bombastier mentions her trans ex-girlfriend, whom she will "call [. . .] Julia Serano" (90). Bombastier dislikes this Serano because Serano acknowledges her "rage" caused by the oppression she encounters as a result of homophobia and transphobia, and Bombastier thinks that expressing it gets in the way of the assimilation she advocates (90–91). But Bombastier is mistaken because it is natural for oppressed persons to feel rage about their oppression. Rage is not the problem. What can sometimes be problematic is the way that this rage is expressed. For instance, from a Mennonite perspective, acting out in violence would not be an appropriate response to one's rage. But using rage as a catalyst for social activism, as the real Julia Serano does throughout her germinal book of trans theory *Whipping Girl*, is an example of how to turn anger into something productive.[29]

Likewise, *A Safe Girl to Love* takes difficult elements of trans life and makes something powerful and ultimately beautiful out of them. Its characters keep fighting to claim their humanity despite transphobia. At the end of "Not Bleak," Carla says she likes her life (177). While many of the book's characters are not quite at that point yet, the collection shows that a happy trans life is possible, even for trans Mennonites.

Miriam Suzanne's *Riding SideSaddle** is a perplexing object. It looks more like a card game than a book. While its subtitle calls it a "novel," and thus I will use this term to refer to it, it is tempting to call it either a novella or a short story because it is only about five hundred lines long. It is unclear whether *Riding SideSaddle** should even be called a book because it is a set of unbound cards collected in a 3⅛ inch by 3⅛ inch by 5⅛ inch cardboard box. There are 6 cards of front matter and 246 of story.[30] The cards are unnumbered, though some of them have hashtags at their bottom right-hand corners to indicate which characters they are about or, in some cases, to indicate that they are excerpts from a book, *Margaret Clap's Book of Last Words*, written by one of the characters, and when I reference these cards, I will give the hashtags found on them in parentheses. However, around half of the cards have no hashtags and thus have no content for a parenthetical citation. Therefore, when citing these cards, I will either give a detailed description of their content or quote them directly.

Riding SideSaddle*'s unruly form gives readers an extraordinary amount of agency in creating the story. Readers may read the cards in whatever order they wish. This is a radical characteristic even when compared to other novels with unusual formats. For instance, B. S. Johnson's *The Unfortunates*, a well-known example of the "book in a box" genre, is unbound as a whole, but each chapter is bound together, and the first and last chapters are marked as such, imposing a slight sense of order on the reader. In contrast, Suzanne's novel's completely open form invites the reader into a dialogue as cocreator of the story, creating a community with them.

The blurb on the front flap of *Riding SideSaddle**'s box, which is also the text of one of the cards without a hashtag, explains another reason for this form: "It's hard to say exactly what happened first." If one reads the novel as memories of the unnamed narrator, who identifies with the hashtag #me, then its form is much more realistic than that of conventional realist fiction because reminiscing does not happen chronologically; it happens piecemeal, here and there, wherever one's mind happens to go. The novel is messy, just like life.

Despite this über-realism, because of its uniqueness, *Riding SideSaddle**'s form becomes just as important to the reading experience as its content. When I first read it, I had a hard time concentrating on the text because I was worried about not dropping cards on the floor, I was distracted by the film of paper dust left by the cards on my fingers, and I admit, even though I read the novel in the random order it came in, I was constantly trying to reorder the cards chronologically in my head. I could not just relax like I do with other books and let the novel's story wash over me, transporting me into its world. Instead, I had to keep thinking about its form because the act of picking up a card from the stack, reading it, and flipping it over onto the stack of cards that I had already read—which happened at a quick pace because most cards only have one or two sentences on them—was much more disruptive to my mental processes than the occasional turning of a page. I was excited to read the novel because of its queer subject matter and because it is always exciting to read a book by someone I know (Suzanne and I were students together at Goshen College in the early 2000s), but it is difficult to read. It feels like work.

Riding SideSaddle* contains barely enough detail to make a story. One can only sketch an outline. The fragmented form with its gaps in the narrative symbolizes how in North America trans identity is in some ways still unspeakable because of the presence of transphobia at every turn. In this way, *Riding SideSaddle**'s form is a part of its content because, of course, its form epitomizes the queer. It completely breaks readers' assumptions about what a novel is, echoing queer calls for a radically new society. Its form, which is akin to a miniature filing cabinet with each card acting as a file documenting an element of trans experience, makes a statement about the marginality of trans lives and the necessity of fighting transphobia in order to make trans lives more permanent. It serves as an archive for trans experience, as one way of engaging in this fight.

Riding SideSaddle*'s content is the story of a community of sexual outlaws—the narrator, Herman, Sam, Jolene, Jenny, and Mother Clap, who also goes by Molly and Margaret—many of indeterminate gender, who usually seem to be friends. Sam's suicide by hanging and its aftermath are the novel's focus, if such a sparely developed plot can be said to have a focus. But it is also just as much about documenting the characters' various sexual activities—such as sex work (#molly #sam), "kink," using pornography (#lastwords), using sex toys (#jenny #jolene), fisting (#jolene #molly), and seeking out anonymous sex (#sam)—that would traditionally be seen as transgressive. Sam's death might also have an autoerotic element considering the relatively large amount of attention (i.e., two cards, one without a hashtag and one tagged #sam) given to hir orgasm when ze hangs hirself.[31] As in *A Safe Girl to Love*, *Riding SideSaddle**'s sexual content emphasizes the characters' sexual agency without any moral condemnation.

The narrative has no clear beginning or ending if one were to try to arrange the cards chronologically, although obviously the cards when

Sam is alive take place earlier than some of the others, and the card about hir funeral (#sam) is one of the later ones. Sam's death is clearly traumatic for the narrator (#me #sam), but its ambiguity for Sam hirself is yet another example of the novel's insistence on openness. Sam's death may be read as a heart-wrenching reminder of transphobia's effects because ze kills hirself because ze cannot take it anymore. Or it may be read as a liberating act of claiming hir sexual pleasure as ze fights against the violences of transphobia, sexism, capitalism, and perhaps racism (none of the characters' ethnicity is mentioned) that oppress hir by exiting the system altogether in one last intense orgasm.

The novel's title, a phrase not actually included in the text, highlights gender as a central issue in the novel. In horseback riding, riding sidesaddle is a gendered practice because only people wearing dresses or skirts do it. One card makes a subtle reference to this definition, asking "Who came up with" gendered clothing (#me)? According to *Urban Dictionary*, "riding sidesaddle" is also slang for men who have just had a vasectomy.[32] Both definitions highlight sexist practices: denying people (usually women) the option of wearing pants even when it is more practical to do so and framing a proactive decision about men's reproductive health as a negative feminization of their manhood (which is of course a problematic concept in the first place). But the asterisk at the end of the title queers these definitions, making the term new. The asterisk references the term "trans*," which is sometimes used to indicate the wide range of the gender-queer spectrum. The asterisk might signify transgender, or transsexual, or cross-dressing, or any number of nonbinary identities.[33] The open-endedness that the * indicates shows that *Riding SideSaddle** is interested in new conceptions of and attitudes toward gender.

These new attitudes are exemplified in Sam's, the narrator's, and Herman's unclear genders, an ambiguity parallel to that of the nature of Sam's death. The narrator refers to Sam with a female pronoun when discussing the death of Sam's goldfish and Sam's filming of hirself but also refers to Sam as "a hanged man" after hir death (all three cards are tagged #sam). The narrator has "breast[s]" (#herman #me) but also has a penis (#me #sam). The narrator refers to Herman with a male pronoun at one point (#herman #sam) and with a female pronoun at three others (#herman, #herman #sam, #herman #me). One might even read Herman as the narrator speaking of hirself in the third person rather than as a separate character.

The ambiguous gendering of these characters can be read in different ways. The switches in gender may indicate time passing, with some scenes taking place before a character's transition and some taking place afterward. Or they may indicate that while a character already identifies as trans, they have not yet had bottom surgery. There are hints that at least some of the characters are trans. For instance, the narrator says at one point, "I'm a boy again, maybe" (#me), indicating that they have switched genders for a while, and one of the sayings from *Margaret Clap's Book of Last Words* is "We are only what we are, and rarely even that" (#lastwords), which acknowledges that even the most seemingly basic fact about oneself, one's gender, is, in fact, always up for negotiation. However, none of the characters explicitly state that they are trans, so they may identify at any number of points along the spectrum of gender fluidity. As one card asks, "What do you know for sure, without any doubts at all?" (#lastwords). Regarding the novel, the answer is a few characters' names and that Sam is dead. That is it; the rest is just conjecture. Indeed, I admit that I read the novel assuming that at least some of the characters were trans because Suzanne is trans, and this is a faulty assumption on my part even though it might be accurate. *Riding SideSaddle**'s narrative ambiguity is not meant to confuse readers, however. Instead, it makes the argument that we are not supposed to figure out the gender of each character because it should not matter. We should treat people equally no matter what gender identity they choose to inhabit at the time. The characters' gender fluidity emphasizes the queer openness the novel espouses. Readers have space to make the story their own in terms of how to interpret its content as well as how to order its form.

Riding SideSaddle*'s overall ambiguity is a political move that acknowledges the importance of trans models (in this case, trans textual models) for rethinking gender. Halberstam writes that "new dynamics of resistance" are present in depictions of trans people in the arts.[34] Suzanne's novel especially fits this assertion in part because of its nontraditional form and in part because it includes eleven cards of collage drawings by Suzanne interspersed throughout it. These drawings feel random because it is unclear how they relate to the cards with text. Some look like blueprints or genetic charts, some have pictures of plants, some have one or two words alongside their drawings, some have empty brackets, some have snippets of math equations, one is a drawing of a house, and one is a drawing of a car. Four of them are drawings of people who may be characters in the novel, but there is no way to know because they do not have captions. Nearly all of them have a mix of at least two of these aspects. Their element of collage breaks boundaries, symbolizing the essence of queerness. It is important that these artworks are included in *Riding SideSaddle** because the novel's mixing of genres, what one might call its genre bending, echoes the openness toward gender identity that Suzanne's work calls for.

What's the Story?

Despite the physical difficulties of reading discussed above, the novel is worth reading, and its attempt to enter into dialogue with readers is heightened by its existence in several formats. The entire novel is available online, and this format gives the book an order that does not change, so one might argue that this is the "correct" order and that if one is reading the print version, one should organize the cards according to the online chronology.[35] But the print version of the novel explicitly claims on one of the #frontmatter cards that "there is no order," so in a sense the online edition is antithetical to Riding SideSaddle*'s mission.

There is also the question of which version is the authoritative version, a question individual readers must answer for themselves. I am someone who much prefers print versions of novels to electronic ones, and thus I cite and discuss the print version. Suzanne writes in an artist's statement on her website, "I'm not interested in making objects—only the experiences they manifest for real people. [. . .] I like narratives that are full of holes and misdirection. Bits borrowed from here and there, fragments and remixes [. . .] inviting you into an experience—the start of a conversation [. . .] accidents, contradictions, and broken expectations. Grasping at stability and form, but always coming up short."[36] It is important that Suzanne acknowledges the possibility of art having an effect on people's lives in the real world because it shows that her work is explicitly activist. Her emphasis on dialogue and the recognition that it cannot happen if one party believes they have the entire story, that they have all the answers, espouses queer values, and the community that dialogue creates is a Mennonite ideal as well. It is therefore easy to see why Suzanne chose Riding SideSaddle*'s particular form: it makes space for this "conversation." The desire for such a conversation to happen as often as possible provides the motivation to put the novel's text online for free and also implies that the important element of the novel is its message rather than one's choice of edition.

I appreciate this perspective because Suzanne's work is valuable as an archive of queer experience in general and queer Mennonite experience specifically, but I worry about its ephemeral nature. Riding SideSaddle*'s print version is already fragile because it is unbound and published by a small press, so it will gain less attention from potential readers and archiving

125

Trans Mennonite Literature

institutions such as libraries. Its online version is even more transitory and could theoretically disappear without a trace at any moment because of its lack of physical presence. Therefore, aside from my preference for print texts, I also privilege the novel's print version because it offers the best hope of preserving Suzanne's work for future readers.

There is also another version of *Riding SideSaddle**: a play, *10 Myths on the Proper Application of Beauty Products*, cowritten by Suzanne, Teacup Gorilla, Diana Dresser, and Michael Morgan.[37] In some ways, the play advocates for the novel's philosophy of openness. For instance, the narrator's first lines in the play repeat the blurb from the novel's box—"It's hard to say what happened first"—and they also say, "Memory's a chaotic jerk," indicating the haphazard nature of memory the novel's print version tries to replicate. Similarly, at one point Sam tells Jolene a story about human sacrifice that ends with a priest walking around in the sacrificed person's skin, and ze tells Jolene when Jolene is upset by the story, "That's what happens when you want to hear the end." In other words, bad things happen when we are not open-minded. The play has the hashtag #frontmatter at its conclusion, tying it to the novel and in a sense placing it as a prelude to the novel as another piece of explanatory material, like the six #frontmatter cards.

But *10 Myths on the Proper Application of Beauty Products* reads very differently than *Riding SideSaddle**. The play is often funny because much of it takes place inside the characters' shared bathroom, and they discuss issues such as whether soap ever goes bad and the best ways to appease the bathroom gods. While Sam dies in the play, hir death does not feel central as it does in the novel. The characters are more clearly trans, though the gender identities they inhabit at any given time are still not revealed. Although community is one of *Riding SideSaddle**'s main themes, the novel has a sense of alienation caused by the text's sparseness. But the play's relative linguistic lushness, which results from the characters' witty repartee with each other, conveys the importance of supportive trans community in a powerful way, echoing its communal authorship.

This authorship is significant because it epitomizes the ideal of dialogue that Suzanne mentions in her online artist's statement. The espousing of this ideal is what makes *Riding SideSaddle** a Mennonite text philosophically, not just by virtue of Suzanne's ethnicity, even though its bare-bones plot makes no mention of its characters' religious or ethnic affiliations.[38] One of the #frontmatter cards from the novel thanks Suzanne's "community of queer/trans* friends and artists" in the acknowledgments along with a few Mennonites (Jacob and Aaron Leichty and Sondra Eby) who helped influence her as a writer. She also notes that the novel includes some contributions by them as well as some other writers (#frontmatter). Although the novel does not make specific references to the Mennonite literary tradition like *A Safe Girl to Love* does, its act of bringing a number of writers into dialogue with one another epitomizes Mennonite communal values. Halberstam asserts that "it is important to study queer life models that offer alternatives to family time and family life."[39] *Riding SideSaddle** does this just as *A Safe Girl to Love* does both through its authorship and by focusing on a community of friends rather than biological family.

Serano documents how trans characters in cis literature often have their preferred genders erased, thus delegitimizing their trans identities.[40] Plett's and Suzanne's trans fiction provides a corrective to this practice that is important for literature in general, not just Mennonite literature. Their different approaches to archiving trans experience, with Plett using concrete narratives based in everyday trans life and Suzanne using a sparse style that does not even name her characters as trans in order to make space for revolutionary openness, complement each other to create a visible base for future trans Mennonite work. Their books show that a trans Mennonite identity is not an oxymoron, claiming space for trans Mennonites within Mennonite discourse.

Epilogue

The Future of Queer Mennonite Literature

Queering Mennonite Literature: Archives, Activism, and the Search for Community
contends that queer Mennonite literature creates an intersectional outlook
from these two streams of thought that defines being Mennonite as embodying queer activism: being out of step with mainstream society in radical ways
that advocate for those on the margins, including those inhabiting LGBT
identities. This ethic may or may not be within a framework of faith. The
books' act of defining asserts that homophobic institutional Mennonitism
does not have sole ownership of the term *Mennonite*. The characters in queer
Mennonite literature assert their right to use the term for themselves as
they claim their queer Mennonite identities. They do so by finding ways to
create healthy communities that employ both queer and Mennonite principles, which often overlap. In some cases these communities are Mennonite
ones, and in some they are not, but they all offer principles for how readers
can change our communities for the better.

The books make their activism visible by archiving queer lives. They build
a history of queer Mennonite experiences that insists that queer Mennonites
have been a part of the Mennonite community for as long as it has existed
and that the community must acknowledge and embrace our presence. Some
of the books even illustrate the existence of queer Mennonites by drawing
on the lives of the authors themselves. Wes Funk's fiction and Jan Guenther
Braun's *Somewhere Else* are fictionalized retellings of their lives, and Stephen
Beachy himself is a character in *boneyard*. Jessica Penner's *Shaken in the Water*
and Casey Plett's *A Safe Girl to Love* use the places their authors have lived
as locations for their narratives. The authors testify that the identity "queer
Mennonite" exists because it is one that many of them live out.

However, despite its archiving efforts, the question of ephemerality is
one that queer Mennonite literature must continue to wrestle with. Aside

from its tenuous existence in the literary marketplace, there is also the question of where scholarship that is relevant to it resides. Observe the web-based nature of many of the sources I cite, a trend that is especially evident in the second part of this epilogue, which discusses the work of Sofia Samatar. While web-based publishing has unquestionably been a boon for Mennonite literature, whether in terms of electronic texts or on-demand print publishing, the question of how to preserve all this digital work is one that historians, archivists, and librarians continue to struggle with on a societal level, not just in the case of Mennonite literature. While the books' archiving makes queer Mennonites visible, further critical efforts to illuminate the books themselves are necessary. *Queering Mennonite Literature* is not the last word.

While the book's title highlights the queer working on Mennonite literature, there is also the question of what Mennonite literature can offer queer thought. The texts studied here reveal at least three related areas where queer theorists would benefit from paying attention to Mennonite ideas. First, queer theory is sometimes too insular. Note, for instance, how almost all of it that I cite is published by either Duke University Press or New York University Press. The field's discourse sometimes struggles to move outside of its established institutional academic boundaries. As a result, it can feel disconnected from lived experience because, as Christopher Castiglia and Christopher Reed assert, it has lost some of its "revolution[ary]" purpose.[1] It is thus necessary for queer theorists to refocus on tying their work to social activism. Queer Mennonite literature shows that the religious realm is one area in need of this activism and offers models for how to do it. Laurel C. Schneider argues that such activism is required according to queer ideals: even though religious repression in large part created the need for queer theory, queer theory needs more interaction with religion because, if such theory claims to want to revolutionize all aspects of society, not just the sexual, it cannot afford to ignore the religious.[2] Mennonite literature's secular inflections and its odd in-between and open nature can be a bridge between queer theory and religion from a literary rather than a theological standpoint, which might be more palatable for many queer theorists. Observing how queer Mennonite literature as a form of literature as theory can help repair the connection between these two traditions is one example of how further efforts to apply queer theory to literature in general will make it more accessible to the public.

Second, queer thinking has always included a desire for social change. Mennonite thinking can offer expertise in two strategies necessary for this change: pacifism and thinking globally. The traditional Mennonite disavowal of violence in favor of seeking nonviolent strategies for social activism is the kind of radical, mainstream-defying thought required to keep queer theory fresh and relevant. *boneyard*'s and *Husk*'s investigations of violence and their advocacy of pacifist ethics exemplify literature as theory in this area. Similarly, Mennonite literature's valuing of global perspectives can work as a corrective to one of queer theory's insular aspects, its obsession with "the U.S. 1990s" that Kadji Amin laments.[3] This emphasis is evident in *A Safe Girl to Love*'s multinational contexts, *Somewhere Else*'s discussions of Anabaptist history, and Samatar's explicitly postcolonial work, discussed below.

Third, the queer and Mennonite traditions each stem from traumatic histories. While queer theory has often dealt with its trauma pessimistically, leading to its much-discussed "antisocial thesis," queer Mennonite literature shows how to respond to and rehabilitate a traumatic tradition in hopeful ways.[4] *Widows of Hamilton House*, *Somewhere Else*, *Shaken in the Water*, *bone-yard*, and the work of Samatar and Wes Funk all acknowledge the trauma caused by homophobia (and in some cases the traumas of sexism, racism, and physical violence) but refuse to acquiesce to it, remaining insistent that better, queerer futures are possible. As both traditions work toward these futures, they can continue to draw strength from one another, looking to build upon their commonalities.

Taken together, the queer Mennonite literary texts studied here embody what José Esteban Muñoz calls "the hopes of a collective," offering a vision of a welcoming, inclusive Mennonite community and world through their social activism.[5] Such hope is also found in other queer Mennonite texts. André Swartley's *The Wretched Afterlife of Odetta Koop* and Greg Bechtel's *Boundary Problems* are queer narratives by second-generation Mennonite writers. Casey Plett's novel *Little Fish*, which is an explicitly Mennonite narrative that shares characters with *A Safe Girl to Love*, came out as this book was in press, and Andrew Harnish's *Plain Love* is in gestation.[6] So the tradition of queer Mennonite literature will continue to grow. It is the second generation's primary concern, one that meshes with the generation's broader socially activist outlook.[7] Therefore, it is fair to expect that it will have a significant influence on the development of Mennonite literature as a whole in the coming decades. It is my hope that *Queering Mennonite Literature* helps reinforce the momentum that queer Mennonite literature already possesses. As an illustration of the new paths this writing will continue to explore, I offer one last close reading of recent work by another second-generation writer with a queer oeuvre as an example of how queer Mennonite literature promises to keep questioning in productive ways.

Sofia Samatar's Postcolonial Queer Mennonite Writing

While the previous work examined in *Queering Mennonite Literature* focuses on the intersection between Mennonite and queer, Samatar's writing takes queer Mennonite literature and Mennonite literature in general a step further by also examining the issue of race. Samatar, who sometimes identifies as a "'Somali-American Mennonite Writer'" (her father is Somali and her mother is a white Swiss Mennonite from the United States),[8] responds in her 2017 essay "The Scope of This Project" to Braun's assertion that there must be unrecognized Mennonite writers of color outside of North America and that perhaps "the queering of Mennonite literature needs to start by recognizing the[se] voices."[9] Braun's reminder that the queer is about more than sexual orientation is useful for considering Samatar's work because Samatar's work epitomizes political queerness even when it does not focus on LGBT relationships.[10] Samatar acknowledges calls such as Braun's early in her essay, documenting that sometimes a desire to globalize the field of Mennonite literature has been expressed, though no steps have actually been taken to do so.[11] She spends the rest of the essay starting this work.

Samatar offers a framework for investigating what she calls "postcolonial Mennonite writing."[12] I cite her definition of this term at length because "The Scope of This Project" is one of the most important pieces of Mennonite literary theory ever published, and I believe Mennonite literary critics must heed its call if Mennonite literature is to sustain itself as a field for another thirty years and beyond. Postcolonial Mennonite writing includes

> Mennonite writers of the postcolony. It means work by writers from Asia, Africa, and Latin America. It means the literary production of those regions where the Mennonite church is largest. It means the writing of the majority. It also means the work of minority writers in North America, of black, Latinx, and indigenous Mennonites, whom I include in the postcolony, not only because they are marginalized members of settler states but because, historically, they came to the Mennonite community through a process of missionary outreach. Only a constellation of all of these writers would allow us to speak of global Mennonite literature, of world Mennonite literature.[13]

Samatar here insists on hybrid Mennonite identities that offer space to different ethnicities, nationalities, cultures, theologies, geographies, and implicitly, sexualities. Her concept epitomizes intersectional ideals, and it is significant for queer literature in general, not just queer Mennonite literature, because, as Sharon Patricia Holland asserts, queer theory has had problems figuring out how to actually do intersectionality.[14] "The Scope of This Project" offers a corrective to this issue. It describes a possibility for Mennonite literary intersectionality by suggesting studying hymns across Mennonite communities as one way "to look at world Mennonite literature."[15] This suggestion to investigate theological texts as literature, to study the hymns for how they are written rather than for just what they proclaim, is important. It does not insist that being Mennonite must include a theological element or that talking about Mennonite literature must insist on focusing on theological issues, and so it is a workable suggestion for the field as already constituted because it leaves room to discuss Mennonite ethnicity. In fact, it implies that the concept of Mennonite ethnicity can and should be broadened to include Mennonites outside of North America; after all, there are already two established Mennonite ethnicities—Swiss and Russian—so there is room for multiplicity within the concept.

Samatar posits that the prospect of conceiving new ways of defining *Mennonite*, something *Queering Mennonite Literature* does, "is exciting" and that this is why it is too early to stop talking about "identity."[16] Whether in Mennonite literature or elsewhere, there are still Mennonite identities to be named and theorized. The essay goes on to give one example by discussing the work of "the Somali-Canadian poet" Mohamud Siad Togane, who says he identifies as a "Moslem-Mennonite" because of his time as a student at Eastern Mennonite College.[17] Significantly, Togane says that he appreciates Mennonites because of their pacifist ethic, offering another example of how Mennonite ethics are revolutionarily queer even if institutional Mennonitism is not.

As Togane claims a Mennonite identity because of his experiences with Mennonites, "The Scope of This Project" insists on intersectionality because the essay is an example of the best kind of theorizing, that which stems from lived experience. Samatar says in an interview with Alicia Cole, which is again worth quoting at length, that she is interested in hybridity because binaries, which insist on fixed categories and are thus the antithesis of intersectionality, are

> trying to kill me [. . . .] I'm always trying to merge things, rather
> than balance them. I want to create new things that are mixtures

of genres or categories I've been told are incompatible. I hate separations and borders—I'm always trying to break them down. This has a lot to do with race, of course, with being a person of mixed race, and a person of two different cultures. In my position, you have to believe that boundaries can be broken down, that so-called opposites can merge. Otherwise, you can't exist.[18]

Samatar's "hat[red]" of "borders" epitomizes queer theory's view of the world and also shows the necessary nature of this approach. The work of queering Mennonite literature that she does in "The Scope of This Project" is, as the language of her interview indicates, a matter of life and death.[19] It is the kind of answer that the characters in queer Mennonite literature, who often feel despair as a result of their marginalization, are looking for. Queer Mennonites and Mennonites of color have frequently been told that they are "incompatible" with the Mennonite community, but Samatar's essay works to destroy such oppression.[20]

Samatar's speculative fiction embodies the ideal of "The Scope of This Project" of using intersectionality to fight marginalization.[21] It does so in part by embodying some of the conventions of a genre that is itself marginal in literary studies and uses the freedom of this position to investigate new visions of society, much as queer theory does. Samatar tells Tobias Carroll in an interview that one thing she appreciates about speculative fiction is "the way it keeps you a stranger."[22] Readers have an extra layer of difficulty to work through when they read speculative fiction, and this work becomes a learning opportunity. I have written here that one reason I love queer Mennonite literature is because I see myself in it, but the above quotation illustrates the opposite, and just as necessary, experience. Samatar's fiction makes readers Other because we are not a part of the worlds she depicts. When I read her 2017 short story collection *Tender*, I was on edge with anticipation at the beginning of each story because I knew that at some point I would have to readjust the mental landscape that each story built in my head. This temporary placement of ourselves as Other is an essential experience for building empathy for those who are Othered by society. Samatar recognizes this in her assertion elsewhere that "speculative fiction [. . . is] writing queerly."[23] The genre in general and her fiction specifically queer reality, calling for new ways of being.

To illustrate this queering, I do not offer a full reading of Samatar's fiction but instead highlight a few passages that illustrate the theoretical concepts she advocates for in her literary theory and interviews as a way of opening up space for the conversation begun in *Queering Mennonite Literature* to continue elsewhere. The aggregate effect of these passages, which are scattered throughout *Tender* and the 2016 novel *The Winged Histories*, is to show that Samatar's fiction explores ideas of intersectionality and hybridity as strategies of succor for the marginalized throughout, putting her theoretical ideals into practice.

The marginal plays a prominent role in *Tender*'s second story, "Ogres of East Africa." The story is told by a servant, Alibhai, who writes it "in the margins" of his employer's account book.[24] It consists of stories about the ogres in the title told to Alibhai by a townsperson, Mary, whom he has hired for the purpose. Hence readers get the descriptions of the ogres at least thirdhand: the ogres do not speak for themselves, but Mary tells their stories to Alibhai, who then writes them down. Who knows what sort of editing has happened to them in this process? Indeed, Alibhai acknowledges that Mary herself might be editing what she tells him, that even her marginal stories have their own "margins" (15). This layering, combined with the asides Alibhai addresses to readers as he transcribes each ogre narrative, makes the story an example of how, according to Ellah Wakatama Allfrey, Samatar's fiction includes the "cadence of an African oral tradition" that beckons each reader "to become a *listener*" as it "tell[s] stories within stories."[25] Such geographical specificity is important because despite its status as speculative fiction, the story roots itself in history and place. It is dated "1907," Alibhai states that he is from "Mombasa," and as the title states, he is studying the ogres of East Africa (10). The specter of colonialism thereby casts its shadow over the story, as its characters are black British subjects. But the story offers hope in the face of this marginalization because of the local narratives it shares. Mary's stories and Alibhai's transcription of them show that the marginalized have desirable knowledge even though that knowledge seems itself to be marginalized.

The following story, "Walkdog," advocates for an ethic of relating to the Other in the form of a school report by its semiautobiographical narrator, Yolanda, who is "African and German and Spanish and God knows what else" (23). Her multiple ethnic identities and their open-endedness ("God knows what else") symbolize the hybridity Samatar discusses with Cole. Yolanda tells the story of a classmate, Andy, a persecuted "dork" whom she is friends with despite worrying about being "contaminated by his nerd gas," which causes her to try to hide the friendship (22–23). However, after he is beaten up and disappears at the end of the story, she realizes she should have done a better job of relating to him (28–30). Andy's disappearance may be liberating for him because he asks for his grandmother's conjure mat before he disappears, so it is possible that he uses the mat to take him to a better place. However, it is crushing for Yolanda and, by extension, readers. She realizes she has failed him as a friend because she participated in his marginalization by refusing to accept his nerdiness. Her discovery of this fact leaves readers with the powerful message that simply recognizing the humanity of others and treating them with kindness are necessary steps in ending oppression.

Another story, "A Brief History of Nonduality Studies" (125–34), employs the idea of rejecting binaries that Samatar names in her interview with Cole. In the best queer fashion, Samatar gives Cole a list of binaries that she wants readers to work on breaking down, including "the borders between male and female."[26] Although the story title claims to give a history of an academic field and the story itself mentions important figures in the field, the story never actually defines what "nonduality studies" is, so the history it relates is rendered nonsensical because there is no referent to tie it to. But this lacuna is actually the story's essential idea. The story leaves readers to fill the gap by imagining what we would like the field to be. One may imagine that it examines how to break down dichotomous thinking and how to conceive of the world intersectionally instead. It thus embodies the queering that Samatar advocates in the interview through its open-endedness.

The openness in "A Brief History of Nonduality Studies" is also present in "Meet Me in Iram," whose narrator says that they "would like to build an entire philosophy out of Iram, the absent city" (172). What does it mean to create a way of life from something that is "absent," that does not exist? The narrator tells readers, "You can help me" to figure out how to live in a way that does not worry about the standards of "normal" (172). Again, the story uses the gap it creates to make space for the imagining of a better society. The radical openness it creates envisions the destruction of borders and the marginalization that goes along with them.

The Winged Histories offers a concrete example of the intersectional visions explored in these four stories. One thread of the novel's tapestry of narratives portrays a relationship between two women, Tav and Seren.[27] The novel implies that all the characters in its world are of color and explicitly notes that Tav has "the Faluidhen coloring, [. . .] that dazzling dark skin that makes [Faluidhen women] glow like lamps in the middle of the day."[28] Here, *The Winged Histories* offers a vision of a society that celebrates dark skin rather than discriminating against it, as Faluidhen coloring is associated with nobility. Aside from being black and queer, Tav is also a revolutionary, a characteristic that works to symbolize the radical nature of the other elements of her identity. Although Tav and Seren's society views same-sex relationships as immature, their relationship persists through the years, playing a recurring role in the extended meditation on their lives narrated by Seren.[29] The women's insistence on maintaining their relationship despite societal disapproval reminds readers that fighting injustice always encounters resistance but is necessary anyway. The women's willingness to persevere argues that the identity "black queer" is one worth fighting for.

Tender's longest story, "Fallow," Samatar's one explicitly Mennonite story, also examines LGBT relationships.[30] In it, a group of Mennonites have left a dying Earth and founded a community, Fallow, on a distant planet. Unfortunately, their potential utopia sours and becomes a theocracy. Rebellions against the regime are quickly snuffed out, but records of them are illicitly kept by two archivists, Brother Lookout and the narrator herself through her retelling of Brother Lookout's story. Like Ruth in *Widows of Hamilton House*, these characters realize that keeping records of marginalized stories is important both to preserve their histories and to keep them available for future readers who might need those stories to save them by teaching them how to live. Although it takes place in the future, "Fallow" participates in the archiving of queer Mennonite experience like other pieces of queer Mennonite literature in its mention of Brother Lookout's enjoyment of bondage and in its narrator's hope for a new society (243).

Despite the restrictive nature of Fallow—in many ways, it is no freer than Wapiti in Rudy Wiebe's *Peace Shall Destroy Many* (the template-setter of oppressive fictional Mennonite communities), and it causes the narrator's sister, Temar, to enact the usual Mennonite literary trope of leaving the community because of its restrictions—there is one way it represents ideal community. One character, Sister Wheel, was in a long-term "covenant[ed]" relationship with another woman, Rahel, before Rahel died (233, 239). This fact is mentioned in passing in a discussion of Sister Wheel's widowhood. The lack of commentary on the women's relationship indicates that Fallow accepts same-sex relationships as a part of the community's life. The story therefore depicts a context where the identity "queer Mennonite" has become an established, unremarkable one. Fallow's LGBT inclusiveness shows that there is hope even for the most broken communities. This is a hope that all queer Mennonite literature shares.

Notes

Introduction

1. Braun, *Somewhere Else*, 137.

2. That is, criticism of texts that may be considered "Mennonite literature," or work by writers with some form of Mennonite background, whether these texts involve Mennonite subject matter or not. This criticism is not necessarily written by critics with Mennonite connections, although much of it has been. Mennonites are the theological descendants of the Anabaptist strain of the sixteenth-century Protestant Reformation. For a history of Mennonites in North America, see Loewen and Nolt, *Seeking Places of Peace*.

3. Attempts to address this problem by examining queer theory's intersections with other critical approaches include Juana María Rodríguez's *Queer Latinidad*, E. Patrick Johnson and Mae G. Henderson's edited essay collection *Black Queer Studies*, Johnson's edited essay collection *No Tea, No Shade*, and Janet Halley and Andrew Parker's edited essay collection *After Sex?*

4. Hinojosa, "From Goshen to Delano," 206.

5. Plett, "Other Women," in *A Safe Girl to Love*, 1–32.

6. Hinojosa, "From Goshen to Delano," 211. Alicia Dueck-Read makes a similar point specifically regarding queer theory in "Breaking the Binary," 118.

7. Grosz, "Experimental Desire," 196.

8. de Lauretis, "Queer Theory," i, v.

9. I use the acronym LGBT throughout *Queering Mennonite Literature* rather than the more comprehensive LGBTQ2IA+ (lesbian, gay, bisexual, trans, queer, two-spirit, intersex, asexual, other) because the characters I examine only inhabit the first four categories and, as I explain earlier, I use the term *queer* in a broader sense than it is usually used in LGBTQ, so in order to avoid confusion, I do not use this acronym. My use of LGBT is certainly not meant to exclude other sexual identities. For example, I would love for there to be a Mennonite novel about an openly intersex protagonist, but this is a narrative that has yet to be written.

10. For instance, Cohen, "Punks, Bulldaggers, and Welfare Queens," 91; Ford, "What's Queer About Race?," 123.

11. Nelson, *Argonauts*, 29.

12. Clare, *Exile and Pride*, 113; Kafer, *Feminist, Queer, Crip*, 16; Cvetkovich, *Depression*, 3; Ford, "What's Queer About Race?," 122; Hennessy, "Material of Sex," 135.

13. Halley and Parker, "Introduction," 1.

14. Ibid., 2.

15. Ibid., 7.

16. Significant early texts include Gordon Friesen's *Flamethrowers*, Rudy Wiebe's *Peace Shall Destroy Many* and *The Blue Mountains of China*, Warren Kliewer's *The Violators*, and Dallas Wiebe's *Skyblue the Badass*. While all these texts are by men, since the 1980s there has been just as much, if not more, Mennonite literature written by women as men.

17. Later anthologies of note include Steven Yutzy's *Greeting the Dawn*, Ann Hostetler's *A Cappella*, Elsie K. Neufeld's *Half in the Sun*, and *Rhubarb*'s 2017 trilogy of issues (numbers 40–42) that were published simultaneously in book form: David Bergen's *9 Mennonite Stories*, Clarise Foster's *29 Mennonite Poets*, and Hildi Froese Tiessen's *11 Encounters with Mennonite Fiction*.

18. For a brief history of this emphasis, see Zacharias, *Rewriting the Break Event*, 34–36.

19. Conferences were held at the University of Waterloo in 1990, at Goshen College in 1997 and 2002, at Bluffton University in 2006, at the University of Winnipeg in 2009 and 2017, at Eastern Mennonite University in 2012, and at Fresno Pacific University in 2015. There are also plans to hold a conference at Goshen College in 2020. For more on the conferences, see Cruz, "Bibliography."

20. See, for instance, Hostetler, "Introduction: Mennonite Voices in Poetry," xix; and Kasdorf, "Making," 14–16. Kasdorf's essay both introduced U.S. Mennonites to the Canadian Mennonite literary scene and had some effect on Kasdorf, an important poet and critic in the field, in her thinking about the writer as "transgressor" in her own work, which in turn helped this model influence younger writers and critics in the field (including myself: I learned how to write transgressively as I do here from reading Kasdorf's work). Kasdorf, "Sunday Morning Confession," 7–8.

21. Unlike the other journals in this list, the *Journal of Mennonite Studies* is not owned by a Mennonite institution (it is published by the University of Winnipeg), but it is edited by Mennonites.

22. Much work from later conferences has also been published and has also helped sustain the field. For a list of special issues of various journals containing this work, see Cruz, "Bibliography," 103–5. *Acts of Concealment* and *Migrant Muses* have played an especially significant role, however, because they are the earliest (and largest) collections of conference work and thus helped establish important subjects in the field while also modeling what Mennonite literary discourse might look like.

23. Ruth calls for "the imaginative courage for the literary artist to become involved in the very soul-drama of his [*sic*] covenant-community." Ruth, *Mennonite Identity*, 70. While Mennonite literary criticism now discusses Mennonite writing as an ethnic literature rather than as a spiritual discipline, Ruth's insistence that Mennonite literature has relevance for theological Mennonitism continues to influence some discourse in the field. Gundy's *Songs from an Empty Cage* is a prominent example. It should be noted that Ruth has distanced himself from his original stance. He tells Julia Spicher Kasdorf "that he would not write the lectures that became *Mennonite Identity* in quite the same way now" and that he appreciates how Mennonite literature has developed. Kasdorf, "Dreams of the Written Character," 32.

24. Elmer Suderman offers an early (so early that it cites Reimer's 1991 lectures that later became *Mennonite Literary Voices* rather than the book itself) summary of this debate that is still one of the clearest and most useful available in "Mennonites, the Mennonite Community, and Mennonite Writers." Other examinations of the Ruth-Reimer debate include Tiessen, "Beyond the Binary," 13–15; Loewen, "Mennonite Literature," 566–70; Gundy, *Walker*, 102–4; and Zacharias, "Introduction," 9–10.

25. For instance, I know from personal conversations that about half of the writers whose work I examine here are estranged from Mennonite theology to some extent, as am I.

26. Castiglia and Reed, *If Memory Serves*, 5.

27. Cheng, *Radical Love*, 60; Pellegrini, "Queer Structures," 240–41.

28. Story, "On the Cusp of Deviance," 363.

29. Kafer, *Feminist, Queer, Crip*, 17–18.

30. Nelson, *Argonauts*, 74.

31. While the treatment of U.S. Mennonite literature as an ethnic literature developed partly as an echoing of treating Canadian Mennonite literature as an ethnic literature, non-Mennonite literary critics have viewed U.S. Mennonite literature as ethnic since at least Sanford Pinsker's 1975 interview of Merle Good, "The Mennonite as Ethnic Writer."

32. Doerksen, *Take and Read*, 66.

33. Beck, *MennoFolk*, 36–37. On Mennonite ethnicity in Mennonite literature, see also Zacharias, "Introduction," 6–7.

34. Wiebe, "For the Mennonite Churches," 26; Goossen, "From Aryanism to Anabaptism," 162.

35. For instance, with the exception of Neufeld's *Half in the Sun* and Bergen's *9 Mennonite Stories*, all the later anthologies cited above in note 17 include work from multiple countries. All the Mennonite/s Writing conferences since 1997 have included an international roster of presenters even when the conferences themselves have been focused on literature from a single country, as was the case in 1997 (United States) and 2009 (Canada).

36. Kafer, *Feminist, Queer, Crip*, 19; Halberstam, *Queer Art of Failure*, 11.

37. Gundy, *Walker*, 264–68.

38. Reimer, *Surplus at the Border*, 199.

39. Harnish, "LGBT Mennonite Fiction" and "Excerpt from *Plain Love*"; Braun, "Complicated Becoming"; Cruz, "Reading My Life in the Text"; Plett, "Natural Links." Plett also read part of a story from *A Safe Girl to Love* at the panel.

40. Tiessen, "Beyond 'What We by Habit or Custom Already Know,'" 26; Zacharias, "'A Garden of Spears,'" 43.

41. Gundy, "Mennonite/s Writing." Gundy did not attend the 2015 Fresno conference because he was teaching abroad, thus it is especially significant that he discussed queer Mennonite literature in his lectures because this attention was paid independent of the Fresno panel, showing that queer Mennonite literature is finally beginning to gain traction among critics.

42. It is significant that the conference had a queer keynote speaker, Julie Rak, although she is not a Mennonite and her address did not focus on explicitly queer issues.

43. I also guest-edited a special issue of the *Journal of Mennonite Writing* on "Queer Mennonite Literature" that was published in 2018 as this book was in press. One of the coeditors of the *Journal*, Ann Hostetler, asked me to edit the issue after finding out that I was writing *Queering Mennonite Literature* when I presented part of chapter 3 at the Crossing the Line: Women of Anabaptist Traditions Encounter Borders and Boundaries conference at Eastern Mennonite University in Harrisonburg, Virginia, on 23 June 2017. This invitation signifies that others in the broader field of Mennonite literature recognize that it is time to pay close attention to queer Mennonite literature.

44. Thompson, "Queer People." I thank Julia Spicher Kasdorf for bringing this article to my attention.

45. Walter Klaassen's *Anabaptism: Neither Catholic nor Protestant* played a major role in the dissemination of the "third way" concept, and this concept is now so essential in Mennonite thought that it is the title of the outreach website for Mennonite Church USA and Mennonite Canada: http://thirdway.com/. The term *upside-down kingdom* was popularized among Mennonites by Donald B. Kraybill's *The Upside-Down Kingdom*, and its argument that Jesus is on the side of the poor and the oppressed is now a generally accepted theological precept in mainstream North American Mennonitism.

46. For instance, Halberstam, *In a Queer Time and Place*, 1; Cvetkovich, *Archive of Feelings*, 120.

47. Ervin Beck examines some of the most canonical of these texts in "Mennonite Transgressive Literature."

48. Braun, "Complicated Becoming," 294–95.

49. Beck writes about the 2001 Mennonite literature course that first sparked my interest in the subject in "Mennonite Literature at Goshen College." For the record, I never had Hostetler as a professor, but I knew her during college, and her work's influence on my thinking began then. For another example of this kind of queer academic lineage building, see Castiglia, *Practices of Hope*, 150.

50. I do not discuss Swartley's work at length here, but note that his work offers another example of a younger Mennonite writer explicitly citing Mennonite literature. See Swartley, *The Wretched Afterlife of Odetta Koop*, 28, where a character reads fiction by Janet Kauffman.

51. Piontek, *Queering*, 2.

52. Reimer, *Surplus at the Border*, 3–4, 23–24, 130.

53. Wiebe has been published by McClelland and Stewart and Knopf Canada, Toews has been published by Knopf Canada, Bergen has been published by HarperCollins and McClelland and Stewart, and Janzen has been published by Henry Holt.

54. Schrock-Shenk, "Foreword," 16.

55. The *D* in this term is capitalized and the *s* is lowercase to signify the power relationship between the Dominant and their submissive.

56. Taormino, "'S Is For . . . ,'" 11.

57. Ben Power Alwin, the director of the Sexual Minorities Archives in Holyoke, Massachusetts, advocates for the acronym LGBTQISM (lesbian, gay, bisexual, trans, queer, intersex, sadist, masochist) as one way of acknowledging that being kinky is a queer, nonnormative sexual identity that thus has affinities with LGBT orientations in "Archival Justice," 182. While one positive aspect of the term *queer* as I use it is that it encompasses all these identities without an unwieldy acronym, terms such as Alwin's or the aforementioned LGBTQ2IA+ can be helpful for making each particular identity visible.

58. Califia, *Public Sex*, 166. Similarly, Piontek writes that BDSM "demonstrates that it is possible to have *bodies without orientations* and bodily pleasures that are not predicated on clear-cut sexual identities." *Queering*, 94, his emphasis.

59. Quoted in Sullivan, *A Critical Introduction*, 156.

60. Young, "Submissive," 298.

61. Ibid., 302–3.

62. Brandt, "Pornography," 54. Aside from the books discussed here, Lynnette D'anna offers fictional representations of BDSM throughout *Belly Fruit, fool's bells* [sic], and *vixen* [sic].

63. Call, *BDSM*, 11. I can attest from my personal experiences in the BDSM community that the emphasis on safety that Call describes is lived out in practice.

64. This institutional homophobia is slowly beginning to erode. For instance, the Central District Conference (CDC) of Mennonite Church USA now credentials ministers in same-sex relationships. See Mast and Mast, *Human Sexuality in a Biblical Perspective*, which documents the reasons for the CDC's position.

65. Sullivan, *A Critical Introduction*, 148.

66. Castiglia and Reed, *If Memory Serves*, 36–37.

67. Muñoz, *Cruising Utopia*, 11.

68. Adler, *Cruising the Library*, 163–64.

69. The violent ending of Wiebe's *Peace Shall Destroy Many* and Nomi's experience in Miriam Toews's *A Complicated Kindness* are two well-known examples.

70. Although the Mennonite communities in the texts at hand have much to learn from the queer concept of community, there are some historical similarities between the Mennonite community and the queer community that I examine further in chapter 1. Kay Stoner offers an early examination of these commonalities and how they have led to rituals that are surprisingly alike in "How the Peace Church Helped Make a Lesbian Out of Me." Plett gives a more recent comparison that is explicitly tied to Mennonite literature in "Natural Links of Queer and Mennonite Literature." Although my primary focus here is Mennonite literature rather than theological Mennonitism, it is important to note that the contentiousness in the queer concept of community is also present in the North American Mennonite theological community via organizations such as Pink Menno, the Brethren Mennonite Council for LGBT Interests, and Theatre of the Beat that advocate for LGBT rights within the church. However, these organizations are still refused official recognition and are denied space at denominational conventions.

71. Kopec, "Digital Humanities, Inc.," 324–25, 329; Reed, "Whiter the Bread," 61, her emphasis. See Anker and Felski, *Critique and Postcritique*, for one example of the continuing trend of the questioning of theory's role in literary studies highlighted by Kopec.

72. Prominent Mennonite examples include Gundy's *Walker in the Fog* and *Songs from an Empty Cage* and Kasdorf's *The Body and the Book*. There are numerous queer examples. Three of my favorites are "In Praise of Brigitte Fassbaender (A Musical Emanation)," in Castle's *The Apparitional Lesbian*, 200–238; Cvetkovich, "White Boots and Combat Boots"; and Delany, *Times Square Red, Times Square Blue*.

73. Cvetkovich, "Photographing Objects," 283.

74. Gundy, "Mennonite/s Writing."

75. Braun, "From Policy to the Personal," 70.

76. Plett, "Natural Links," 287.

77. Cvetkovich, *Archive of Feelings*, 8, 243.

78. Halberstam, *In a Queer Time and Place*, 159.

79. Hinojosa, "From Goshen to Delano," 207.

80. Cvetkovich, *Archive of Feelings*, 253.

81. Braun, email message to author, 3 October 2012.

82. Poetry has played an essential role in Mennonite literature's history, in part because poets such as Di Brandt, Patrick Friesen, and Julia Spicher Kasdorf were some of the earliest Mennonite writers to achieve success in the broader literary world and in part because poets such as Kasdorf, Jeff Gundy, and Ann Hostetler have been some of the most influential Mennonite literary critics. However, this book does not examine any poetry because there is very little explicitly queer Mennonite poetry, even though one could argue that because of its experiments with language and its strong activist traditions, the entire genre is queer in the political sense. *Rhubarb*, the journal of the Mennonite Literary Society, has been the primary repository for the bit of queer Mennonite poetry in print. See, for instance, Braun, "Slam"; Cruz, "New York"; and Funk, "Daddy." To the best of my knowledge, there is only one queer Mennonite play aside from Miriam Suzanne's discussed in chapter 6, Johnny Wideman's *This Will Lead to Dancing*.

83. The first generation, who mostly began publishing in the 1980s and 1990s, includes authors such as David Bergen, Sandra Birdsell, Di Brandt, Patrick Friesen, Sarah Klassen, David Waltner-Toews, and Armin Wiebe in Canada and Anna Ruth Ediger Baehr, Merle Good, Jeff Gundy, Ann Hostetler, Jean Janzen, Julia Spicher Kasdorf, and Janet Kauffman in the United States. Part of what I mean by "generation" is writers not only working as contemporaries but also working with knowledge of each other and being influenced by each other to some extent. Therefore, I would consider Rudy Wiebe as his own zero generation that gave inspiration to the first generation, because when he began writing, there was no sense of a Mennonite literary tradition in English; he had to construct it. Wiebe did not know about Friesen's *Flamethrowers* when he wrote *Peace Shall Destroy Many*.

Quoted in Giesbrecht, "O Life," 50–51. Much as Wiebe has influenced the first generation as well as the second generation, the first generation influences the second generation, who have broadened the field by making queer Mennonite literature visible.

84. *The Whistling Song*, *Distortion*, and *Some Phantom/No Time Flat* are Beachy's non-Anabaptist-themed books. *Shelf Monkey*, Corey Redekop's first novel, was published in 2007.

85. For instance, André Swartley's *The Wretched Afterlife of Odetta Koop* repeats themes from Christina Penner's *Widows of Hamilton House*, as does Emily Hedrick's *True Confessions of a God Killer*. The way Beachy's *Zeke Yoder vs. the Singularity* plays with the Anabaptist tradition shares similarities with how his *boneyard* does. Casey Plett's *Little Fish* shares characters and subjects with her *A Safe Girl to Love*.

86. Jordan, "In Search of Queer Theology Lost," 298–99; Freeman, "Afterword," 318. Similar to Jordan, I argue that Delany's novel *The Mad Man* is a secular "Anabaptist" text because of its revolutionary depiction of homeless queer characters in "Learning to Listen," 221n9.

87. For introductions to these fields, see, for queer theology, Cheng, *Radical Love*; for narrative theology, Hauerwas and Jones, *Why Narrative?*; and for theopoetics, Keefe-Perry, *Way to Water*.

88. Braun, "From Policy to the Personal," 71.

Chapter 1

1. Arondekar, Cvetkovich, Hanhardt, Kunzel, Nyong'o, Rodríguez, and Stryker, "Queer Archives," 219–20. I cite a number of examples of this turn throughout *Queering Mennonite Literature*, especially in this chapter. Three recent special issues are noteworthy: Marshall, Murphy, and Tortorici, "Queering Archives: Historical Unravelings"; Marshall, Murphy, and Tortorici, "Queering Archives: Intimate Tracings"; and Rawson and Devor, "Archives and Archiving."

2. Eichhorn, *Archival Turn*, 23.

3. In "Queer Mennonite Literature," the special issue of the *Journal of Mennonite Writing* published in summer 2018 as this book was in press, Kandis Friesen and I have a work that begins to address this lack. There are numerous Mennonite archives in North America. A partial list would include those held by historical libraries at Mennonite colleges such as Bethel College, Bluffton University, Conrad Grebel University College, Eastern Mennonite University, and Goshen College. There are also various regional archives maintained by Mennonite denominations, conferences, and private groups. Mennonite literary critic Paul Tiessen's recent work on Rudy Wiebe's archives has been helpful for my thinking about the subject. See Tiessen, "Archival Returns," "Double Identity," "Re-framing the Reaction," and his reflections on interacting with archives in "'I Want My Story Told,'" 264–65.

4. Examples of activist Mennonite work include Di Brandt's and Julia Spicher Kasdorf's feminist poetry, Todd Davis's ecocritical poetry, and Rudy Wiebe's wrestling with issues of peace throughout his explicitly Mennonite fiction.

5. Clare, *Exile and Pride*, 31, 35.

6. This necessity is often discussed in scholarship on queer archiving. See, for instance, Sheffield, "Bedside Table Archives," 114. Sheffield's essay highlights the importance of personal queer archives such as Ruth's book collection, which I discuss later in the chapter.

7. Cvetkovich, "White Boots and Combat Boots," 321.

8. For instance, Elspeth Probyn writes about the anxiety caused by the thought of working on her book, which leads to "retch[ing]" every morning, a "routine my body had set up," to which "my body insisted I pay attention" in "Writing Shame," 71. While I thankfully have not experienced retching while trying to write, I certainly relate to Probyn's description of writing uneasiness as a physical malady. For another queer account of writing anxiety, see Cvetkovich, *Depression*, 29–73.

9. Penner, *Widows of Hamilton House*, 145. Further citations of this novel are given in the text.

10. Plett, "Natural Links," 287.

11. As I discuss in chapter 3, Nora from Jessica Penner's *Shaken in the Water* is one example. This paucity extends to literature in general.

12. This is a common violence experienced by bisexuals. It remains constant enough that Fritz Klein documented it more than twenty years ago in *The Bisexual Option*, 4–5, and Shiri Eisner still feels it is necessary to discuss it in *Bi*, 209–10.

13. *New Oxford Annotated Bible*, 335n9.

14. Robert Zacharias's *Rewriting the Break Event* documents this frequency.

15. Smucker, *Henry's Red Sea*.

16. I discuss my Latinx ethnicity in Cruz, "On Postcolonial Mennonite Writing."

17. Nelson, *Argonauts*, 3.

18. Coverley, *Psychogeography*, 14.

19. Doug Lunney gives some basic information about the house and its history, much of which is included in *Widows of Hamilton House*, in "Winnipeg Home Once Hosted Seances."

20. For instance, as I discuss later in this chapter, Sam in Wes Funk's *Baggage* moves from rural Saskatchewan to Saskatoon because he is estranged from his Mennonite family; as I discuss in chapter 2, Jess in Jan Guenther Braun's *Somewhere Else* goes into exile from her Mennonite community; and as I discuss in chapter 5, Sheldon in Corey Redekop's *Husk* renounces Mennonitism because it condemns him for being gay.

21. The fact that the theme of the 2017 Mennonite/s Writing conference at the University of Winnipeg was "Personal Narratives of Place and Displacement" shows that issues of space continue to play a major role in both Mennonite literature and Mennonite thinking in general.

22. Other queer writers also investigate séances as a queer practice. See, for example, Paula Martinac's novel *Out of Time*, which also has archiving as a primary theme, and Sarah Waters's novel *Affinity*.

23. Penner, *Shaken in the Water*, 71, 84–86; Swartley, *Wretched Afterlife of Odetta Koop*; Funk, *Wes Side Story*, 94–98.

24. Cvetkovich, *Archive of Feelings*, 245.

25. For instance, I wrote a chapter of my dissertation on Delany's novel *The Tides of Lust*, which went out of print almost immediately after it was published in 1973, and mine is the only scholarly article on

Toews's first novel, *Summer of My Amazing Luck*. See Cruz, "Narrative Ethics." This paucity extends to Toews's second and fourth novels, *A Boy of Good Breeding* and *The Flying Troutmans*, as well. Her explicitly Mennonite third and fifth novels, *A Complicated Kindness* and *Irma Voth*, are the ones that receive critical attention.

26. Wiebe, *Our Asian Journey*; Suzanne, *Riding SideSaddle**. Another rarity narrative: I remember that at the end of Ann Hostetler's presentation at the 2002 Mennonite/s Writing conference at Goshen College, she had some of the few remaining copies of Anna Ruth Ediger Baehr's poetry collection *Moonflowers at Dusk* to hand out to the audience, which Baehr's daughter had given to Hostetler when she found out Hostetler was researching Baehr. There was a mad rush to the front for them. I still have mine. Hostetler's presentation was published as "Three Women Poets." Hostetler confirms that she still has "3 or 4" copies left to give away to interested scholars. Hostetler, Facebook message to author, 5 July 2017.

27. Cvetkovich, *Archive of Feelings*, 7.

28. Adler, *Cruising the Library*, 105.

29. Hamilton, *Intention and Survival*. A PDF of the book is available at https://umanitoba.ca/libraries/units/archives/media/Hamilton_Intention_and_Survival.pdf.

30. Cvetkovich, *Archive of Feelings*, 48. One early example of this archiving is chapter 4 of Juana María Rodríguez's *Queer Latinidad*, which documents queer chatrooms online.

31. Interestingly, Ruth includes sibling incest in her list of odd subjects, an event that does not occur in *Widows of Hamilton House* but plays a major role in Jessica Penner's *Shaken in the Water*, as I discuss in chapter 3.

32. This notion has permeated North American Mennonitism in official and unofficial ways. Many Mennonite martyrdom stories include an element of call. See, for instance, the story of Clayton Kratz, who was asked to be a relief worker in Russia on a Tuesday and was on the ship headed there that Friday, in Bauman, *Coals of Fire*, 111–18. There are also stories of influential churchmen, such as Harold S. Bender, who frequently called people to serve the church in various capacities. See Gundy, *Walker*,

145; and Keim, *Harold S. Bender*. I recall the eminent Mennonite historian Theron Schlabach telling me in conversation when I was his student that the reason he got a PhD in history was because Guy F. Hershberger, Bender's contemporary, told him to because there was a dearth of historians suitable for employment by Mennonite colleges. Swiss Mennonites traditionally called their pastors and other church leaders by the lot, although this practice has disappeared among all but the most conservative congregations. For a recent discussion of the theological aspects of call from a Mennonite perspective, see Miller, *Living Faith*.

33. Funk, *Wes Side Story*, 84. Further citations of this work are given in the text. Despite its subtitle, Funk specifically names the book as "autobiography" rather than memoir on the copyright page and pledges his attempt to make it "truthful." This choice to write about his entire life rather than just his writing career (which is why it is improper to call it a memoir) is significant because, as I argue later in this chapter, he attempts to offer the narrative of a queer life for use as a model for others.

34. Lewis, "I Am 64," 27.

35. Stoner, "How the Peace Church Helped Make a Lesbian Out of Me," 10–11. The spiritual and geographical journey toward worldliness that Stoner names is so archetypal that it was already being satirized in the 1980s. See Lesher, *Muppie Manual*.

36. Plett, "Natural Links," 287.

37. On the practice of barebacking and how it can function as a liberating, antihomophobic practice, see Dean, *Unlimited Intimacy*. Marlon M. Bailey offers an important expansion of Dean's ideas in "Black Gay (Raw) Sex."

38. Lee, *Biography*, 21.

39. Along with *Dead Rock Stars*, see Funk, *Humble Beginnings, Baggage*, and *Cherry Blossoms*.

40. Although, as I argue here, Funk's title works in liberating ways, it is also necessary to acknowledge that he chooses to riff off of the title of a work that is racist. Unlike its inspiration *Romeo and Juliet*, where the Montagues and Capulets are social equals who happen to hate each other, in *West Side Story*, Puerto Ricans are portrayed as dangerous racial Others who

143

must be subdued at all costs. This discriminatory stance is evident in the names of the gangs: the whites are the Jets, symbols of technological progress and emblems of the future, and the Puerto Ricans are the Sharks, animalistic and bloodthirsty. See Shakespeare and Laurents, *Romeo and Juliet & West Side Story*. As a Puerto Rican, I wish that Funk had chosen a different title and that he did not have the racial blind spot that his title reveals. But as a queer, I find much that is valuable in *Wes Side Story* despite its titular flaw.

41. Frank, *Letting Stories Breathe*, 75.

42. Arondekar, Cvetkovich, Hanhardt, Kunzel, Nyong'o, Rodríguez, and Stryker, "Queer Archives," 213.

43. Halberstam, *Queer Art of Failure*, v.

44. Ibid., 3, 7, 88.

45. Cvetkovich, *Archive of Feelings*, 7. I first encountered a citation of Cvetkovich's book in Leung, "Archiving Queer Feelings in Hong Kong," 400–401, and I acknowledge the importance of Leung's essay for my thinking about Funk's work. It may seem odd to cite an essay on queer experience in Hong Kong when discussing queer experience in Saskatchewan, but I do so because Leung's focus on the regional is a useful model for thinking about Funk's work, which is proudly rooted in both rural and urban Saskatechewan. This citation also emphasizes the point that queers are marginal everywhere.

46. See Workplay Publishing's website (http://www.workplaypublishing.com/default.html).

47. Regarding a related activist movement, Eichhorn notes the importance of self-publishing for the feminist movement since the 1970s in *The Archival Turn*, 169n37.

48. Beachy, *Zeke Yoder vs. the Singularity*. See https://www.kickstarter.com/projects/1541842544/zeke-yoder-vs-the-singularity-an-amish-sci-fi-nove, which as of 3 July 2017 was still up even though the campaign was over.

49. Stryker and Currah, "Introduction," 10.

50. Trembath, "Local Author." See also Friesen, "In Memory."

51. Funk, *Baggage*, 167. Funk's third novel, *Cherry Blossoms*, about a heterosexual woman, is the least autobiographical of his books (and thus I do not examine it here), but even it includes some autobiographical elements, such as vacation destinations and Funk's usual country-to-city migration story.

52. Rohy, "In the Queer Archive," 343.

53. To cite a Mennonite example, the writing voice in Rudy Wiebe's *Of This Earth* is very different from the voice in, say, *The Blue Mountains of China*.

54. Funk explicitly advocates this principle in his choice to have *Humble Beginnings* contain multiple genres.

55. Funk, *Dead Rock Stars*, 20.

56. Halberstam, *In a Queer Time and Place*, 42. Unfortunately, queer rural fiction is still rather rare overall, though many queer Mennonite texts include rural settings like *Dead Rock Stars* does.

57. Lee, *Biography*, 14.

58. Robert Zacharias's *After Identity* wrestles with this issue, as does Hildi Froese Tiessen's "Beyond 'What We by Habit or Custom Already Know.'"

59. Funk, *Baggage*, 5, emphasis in the original.

60. Wiebe, *Blue Mountains of China*, 188–215.

61. Funk, *Baggage*, 65, 103.

62. Friesen, "From the Editor's Desk."

63. Bannon, *Odd Girl Out, I Am a Woman, Women in the Shadows, Journey to a Woman*, and *Beebo Brinker*.

64. These traditional condemnatory endings include characters suffering not only from breakups but also from "illness," mental breakdowns, and "suicide" as punishment for their queer relationships. Stryker, *Queer Pulp*, 51–52, 57. Likewise, Cvetkovich notes that in 1950s fiction, lesbians usually end up "sad, lonely, or dead" in *Archive of Feelings*, 253. Kristen Hogan documents how the availability of lesbian fiction such as Bannon's "with *good* endings" felt "life-changing" for lesbians in *The Feminist Bookstore Movement*, 2, emphasis in the original.

Chapter 2

1. Braun, "From Policy to the Personal," 76.

2. Ahmed, *Living a Feminist Life*, 213–14.

3. Muñoz, *Cruising Utopia*, 3, 30, 6.

4. Braun, "From Policy to the Personal," 70. The General Conference Mennonite Church merged with the "Old" Mennonite Church, both of which were binational, to form the affiliated-yet-separate Mennonite Church Canada and Mennonite Church USA in 2001. The General Conference had split from the Mennonite Church in 1860. For a history of Mennonite denominational schisms, see Kniss, *Disquiet in the Land*.

5. Braun, "From Policy to the Personal," 72.

6. Ibid., 71.

7. Ibid., 78.

8. Braun, "Queer Sex at Bible College," 13.

9. Braun, "From Policy to the Personal," 73–74.

10. Braun, "Queer Sex at Bible College," 13.

11. Ibid., 14.

12. Ibid., 15.

13. Ibid.

14. Braun, "Complicated Becoming," 292.

15. Ibid., 294.

16. Ibid., 295.

17. Braun, "From Policy to the Personal," 70.

18. Andrew Harnish recounts some of this process in "LGBT Mennonite Fiction," 279.

19. Braun, *Somewhere Else*, 11–13. Further citations of this novel are given in the text.

20. Brandt, "In Praise of Hybridity," 127.

21. As noted in chapter 1, Barbara Smucker's *Henry's Red Sea* fictionalizes the efforts of Russian Mennonites who were refugees in Germany after World War II to get to Paraguay before they were repatriated to the Soviet Union. Janice Dick's *Out of the Storm*, which according to its blurb is "historical fiction with a touch of romance" and is marketed to Mennonite lay readers, is one fictional retelling of Russian Mennonites' attempts to flee to Canada in the 1920s to escape Soviet communism. Such books teach that their stories are heroic narratives of faithfulness and martyrdom, and while I recognize the importance of these values, I think it might be possible to teach them to the community in less disturbing, less propagandistic ways. Perhaps these stories are used less today (I do not know because I

do not have children), but when Braun (and by extension, Jess) and I were growing up in the 1980s, they were the norm.

22. Braun, "From Policy to the Personal," 75.

23. The novel's cover will itself act as an archiving of this genre of ephemera once the switch to electronic tickets that gains momentum every day is complete. On tickets as epitomizing the ephemeral because of their indispensable nature, which disappears as soon as they are used, see Rickards, *This Is Ephemera*, 7, 10–11.

24. For recent work on rural queer identities, see Gray, Johnson, and Gilley, *Queering the Countryside*.

25. Rodríguez, *Sexual Futures*, 137.

26. My reminiscing is inspired by Rodríguez's accounts of her own illicit, informal attempts at self-sex education as a young person in *Sexual Futures*, 103–6, 146–47. Other queer narratives about living in community include Delany, *Heavenly Breakfast*; and Peterson, *Next Year, for Sure*.

27. For a story of successfully becoming a queer Mennonite theologian, see Zimmerman, "Teaching Ethics While Queer and Mennonite."

28. Braun, "From Policy to the Personal," 74.

29. A partial list of foundational pieces of creative writing in this tradition includes Birdsell, *Agassiz: A Novel in Stories*; Brandt, *questions i asked my mother* [*sic*]; Kasdorf, *Eve's Striptease*; and Kauffman, *Collaborators*. Critical/theoretical pieces include Birky, "When Flesh Becomes Word"; Brandt, *Dancing Naked*; Hostetler, "Three Women Poets"; and Kasdorf, *Body and the Book*.

30. Summers, "Introduction," ix. Other early print attempts to catalogue queer literature include Drake, *The Gay Canon*; and Stryker, *Queer Pulp*. For an ongoing digital example, see *Casey the Canadian Lesbrarian*.

31. Ahmed, *Living a Feminist Life*, 240.

32. Castle, *Apparitional Lesbian*, 2–4. One of Castle's endnotes mentions an instance of queer persecution that may be especially relevant to Mennonites. It tells of "Bets Wiebes, accused in Amsterdam in 1792 of lying with another woman," who spent time in jail as a result (240n4). Could this woman have had Mennonite connections?

It is possible, since "Wiebes" is a known variation of "Wiebe," which is a common Mennonite name "of Dutch origin." Krahn, "Wiebe," 943. It may be an unanswerable question, but the reason for engaging in such speculation is to show that as long as there have been Mennonites, there have been queer Mennonites. We just do not know about specific individuals because the community has suppressed their stories.

33. Ahmed, *Living a Feminist Life*, 216. I have heard similar stories from friends. Therefore, the need for narratives that claim lesbian existence remains.

34. Ibid., 230.

35. Ibid., 255.

36. For accounts of how pornography can be educational, see Hartley, "Porn"; Dewhurst, "*Gay Sunshine*," 216–19; Dean, "Stumped," 432–35; and Rodríguez, *Sexual Futures*, 146–47.

37. Aside from Brandt's aforementioned text, see Wiebe, *Peace Shall Destroy Many*; Friesen, *The Shunning*; and Kasdorf, *Sleeping Preacher*.

38. As I explain elsewhere, it is impossible to get away from one's Mennonite identity no matter how hard one tries, and thus it is best to accept it and learn how to make it a healthy part of oneself. See Cruz, "Reading My Life in the Text," 281–82.

39. Stoner, "How the Peace Church Helped Make a Lesbian Out of Me," 10.

40. Gundy, *Walker*, 133–41, especially 140–41.

41. Muñoz, *Cruising Utopia*, 172.

Chapter 3

1. Penner, *Shaken in the Water*, 15. Further citations of this novel, which are from the 2013 Foxhead Books edition rather than the 2017 Workplay Publishing edition (see the discussion of these two editions in chapter 1), are given in the text.

2. Schweighofer, "Rethinking the Closet," 230.

3. Menno S. Harder explains that Harder "is a common Mennonite name" in "Harder," 658. "Peter Harder" is therefore a legitimately realistic name for a Mennonite character despite its pornographic resonances.

4. Cvetkovich, "Photographing Objects," 281.

5. Lynnette D'anna's *sing me no more* [*sic*] is the earliest piece of queer Mennonite literature I am aware of, though, as I note in chapter 4, this honor might actually go to the *Martyrs Mirror*.

6. Sedgwick, *Between Men*, 21.

7. Castle, *Apparitional Lesbian*, 72–73.

8. Schweighofer, "Rethinking the Closet," 229–30.

9. Cvetkovich, *Archive of Feelings*, 88–89.

10. Ibid., 100–106. On BDSM as a form of therapy, see Avenatti and Jones, "Kinks and Shrinks," 90–91.

11. Arana, "Sibling Incest Stories," 45–50.

12. Clare, *Exile and Pride*, 130–31.

13. Ibid., 136–37.

14. Arana, "Sibling Incest Stories," 44.

15. Kafer, *Feminist, Queer, Crip*, 31.

16. For what it is worth, Penner tells Julia Spicher Kasdorf in an interview, "A Mosaic of Broken Dishes," that, along with Agnes, she likes Johan the most of all her characters, thus indicating that readers should give their sexual subversion a fair hearing.

17. Ervin Beck's "Mennonite Transgressive Literature" provides a history of significant Mennonite texts, including Wiebe's, that have caused the kind of reaction my students worried Penner's novel might have.

18. Friesen, *Flamethrowers*, 11–33, 15, 73. Robert Zacharias's *Rewriting the Break Event* provides an overview of the numerous examples of the first theme. The most famous example of the second theme is in Rudy Wiebe's *The Blue Mountains of China*, 271–72. On the third theme, see, for instance, the well-known example of Di Brandt's poem "nonresistance, or love Mennonite style" from *Agnes in the Sky*, 38–39.

19. Tiessen, "Literary Refractions," 66; Wiebe, *Skyblue the Badass*. Skyblue appears in three stories in *The Transparent Eye-Ball and Other Stories*, in five stories in *Going to the Mountain*, in five stories in *The Vox Populi Street Stories*, and throughout all of *Skyblue's Essays*, which is fiction despite its title.

20. While *Flamethrowers* got some good reviews in important venues such as the *New York Times*, the novel sold poorly

and was soon forgotten. See Teichroew, "Gordon Friesen," 12–13.

21. Wiebe became friends with the *Review*'s longtime celebrity editor George Plimpton, and some of his memories are included in Nelson W. Aldrich Jr.'s oral history, *George, Being George*, 278–79.

22. For instance, see Barth, *Lost in the Funhouse*, and Barthelme, *City Life*.

23. Penner, "Mosaic."

24. Hostetler, "Introduction."

25. It is, however, important to note that both authors apparently appreciated the attention Mennonite literary critics have given their work. We see this in Friesen's willingness to give Allan Teichroew an interview for Teichroew's "Gordon Friesen" and in Wiebe's choice to publish some of his later works in Mennonite venues. See, for instance, Wiebe, "Can a Mennonite Be an Atheist?," "Love in Old Age," and *On the Cross*. Jeff Gundy briefly discusses Wiebe's Mennonite return in *Walker in the Fog*, 137.

26. Friesen, *Flamethrowers*, 156; Wiebe, *Skyblue the Badass*, 124, 132.

27. Penner, "Research Notes."

Chapter 4

1. Roth, "Complex Legacy," 279.

2. The Amish split off from Mennonites in 1693, and an affinity remains between the two groups as a result of their shared Anabaptist heritage. Beachy was raised Mennonite but has Amish ancestry. For more on the Amish/Mennonite schism, see Roth, *Letters of the Amish Division*.

3. My use of this language is influenced by Theodor Adorno's well-known assertion that "to write poetry after Auschwitz is barbaric" in *Prisms*, 34.

4. Van Braght, *Martyrs Mirror*, 831, 1058, and 1094. David Luthy notes that these illustrations were first included in the 1685 Dutch edition, which had 104 etchings, in *A History*, 11. For more on the illustrations excluded from the Herald Press edition, see Weaver-Zercher, "Research Note."

5. Beachy, *boneyard*, 14. Further citations of this novel are given in the text.

6. Luyken's etchings have not been included in any of the North American German editions of the *Martyrs Mirror*,

thus Jake is using an English edition. This is plausible even though the Amish tend not to use English in the home because Amish bookstores frequently stock English editions of the book. See Luthy, *A History*, 70. I thank Joe Springer of the Mennonite Historical Library in Goshen, Indiana, for his help in clarifying this issue.

7. Julia Spicher Kasdorf gives a thoroughly researched account of the shooting in "To Pasture," 328–30.

8. Ibid., 331.

9. Roth's "Complex" is a recent example of advocacy in favor of telling martyr stories.

10. Kasdorf, "To Pasture," 329. *boneyard* repeats this story in a footnote (193n49).

11. Acker, *I Dreamt I Was a Nymphomaniac Imagining*, 101–9; Acker, *Don Quixote, which was a dream*, 166–71. In *boneyard*, Jake's random references to himself as a "pirate" (284–85, 296), which, unlike his time as a rock musician, go unexplained, may also be read as references to Acker's *Pussy, King of the Pirates*. Beachy's novel *Glory Hole*, the writing of which gets mentioned in *boneyard* (e.g., 9), also includes this repetitive trope by repeating narrative aspects from *boneyard*. For instance, there is another Amish teenager, Amos Yoder, who, like Jake, writes disturbing short stories and throws them into the fire, where they are saved by the "Beachy" character, Philip Yoder, and have the same burn marks as Jake's manuscript. Beachy, *Glory Hole*, 182–83. A post on the Jake Yoder Facebook page from 19 September 2017 notes that Amos is a "'fictionalized'" version of Jake and asks whether "I [Jake] can sue him [Beachy] for libel" because Jake finds the portrayal of himself as Amos "exploit[ative]." See https://www.facebook.com/jake.yoder.585.

12. Kasdorf, "To Pasture," 330.

13. Van Braght, *Martyrs Mirror*, 592–610, 992, 1002.

14. For example, Kasdorf writes that she used to think she "knew what the book was about" because she was familiar with its illustrations. "Mightier," 45.

15. Beachy is not the first novelist to write about a gay Amishman. In *Thrill of the Chaste*, Valerie Weaver-Zercher notes that there are some Amish romance novels (written

by non-Amish, non-Mennonite writers, and thus not examined here) about LGBT relationships (4, 6, 254n10).

16. David L. Weaver-Zercher notes that Luyken was a poet as well as a visual artist and continued to write poetry throughout his life in *"Martyrs Mirror,"* 96–97. If the oral tradition that Friesen mentions is true, then Luyken may have been the first queer Mennonite writer.

17. Beachy, "Editor's Preface," 17.

18. Krehbiel, "Staying Alive," 141.

19. One early example of this gender studies maxim is found in Thomas Waugh's "Men's Pornography."

20. Martens and Cramer, "By What Criteria."

21. Gundy, *Songs from an Empty Cage*, 43.

22. As Kasdorf notes, another kind of gender bending is also present in the *Martyrs Mirror*, as several female martyrs are described as "manly" in their resistance to persecution. "Mightier," 56–57. While this description draws on what twenty-first-century readers would call oppressive gender stereotypes, as it is possible for any gender to be strong in spirit like the martyrs, it is nevertheless interesting that van Braght is willing to acknowledge that crossing gendered boundaries can be a powerful political act. He does not condemn the "manly" women for straying outside "biblical" gender roles, recognizing that it is sometimes necessary to transgress. This is yet another instance of his book's queerness.

23. Another example that is also reprinted in *boneyard* is the illustration of Andrew the apostle being crucified on what is now known as a "St. Andrew's cross" (205). These crosses are often used in BDSM scenes. Staci Newmahr describes this use in *Playing on the Edge*, 81–82.

24. Patrick S. Cheng notes that queer theologians have written about "the homoerotic elements" of Pelagius's story in *Radical Love*, 117. In light of this writing, perhaps Jake's use of the *Martyrs Mirror* is not so surprising after all.

25. Zacharias, *Rewriting the Break Event*, 177.

26. Ward, "Queer Feminist Pigs," 132.

27. For an analysis of the types of scenes in Luyken's illustrations, see Weaver-Zercher, *"Martyrs Mirror,"* 99–118.

28. Kasdorf, "Mightier," 68.

29. Newmahr explains the connection between pain and pleasure in *Playing on the Edge*, 134–37. She also offers helpful discussions of the concept of "play" throughout. For instance, see 8–9, 83–84, 108, 128.

30. For example, Ann Hostetler writes that when she was taught about martyrs as a child, she knew that if it had been her, she would have refused martyrdom: "I wanted to be the girl who lived." "The Self in Mennonite Garb," 37. For a similar sentiment, see Gundy, "Ancient Themes #1: The Martyrs & the Child," in *Rhapsody with Dark Matter*, 55–56. Roth also lists some recent reasons for skepticism toward the veneration of martyrs in "Complex," 280.

31. David Weaver-Zercher asserts that van Braght titled his book *The Bloody Theater* because "there was something theatrical about the martyr's experiences, and especially their executions" in *"Martyrs Mirror,"* 58. So even the book's author agreed that part of its appeal for readers is its titillating, vivid nature rather than just its spiritual lessons.

32. Indeed, as Krehbiel contends, "we're at the point where the way we repeat these stories says far more about who we are than do the histories themselves." "Staying Alive," 140. Referencing the *Martyrs Mirror* has seemingly become a kind of shibboleth to show belonging in certain Anabaptist circles rather than a way of teaching nonresistant ethics. The most well-known example of this fetishizing is the story of Dirk Willems. David Luthy's *Dirk Willems* provides a helpful overview of recent examples, as does Kasdorf, who also offers commentary on why it is problematic in "Mightier," 59–64. See also Weaver-Zercher, *"Martyrs Mirror,"* 103–4, 264–91.

33. This argument spills over into a YouTube video from 29 September 2011, "Who Is Jake Yoder?," which includes interviews of Beachy and Brown alongside professor "Jurgen Kraybill" from "Bergholtz Mennonite College in Ohio" as an investigative news crew attempts to discern whether Jake really exists. Neither Kraybill nor Bergholtz actually exists, but Mennonite viewers will find their names funny because of their stereotypically

Mennonite nature. The video is available at https://www.youtube.com/watch?v= 3D7st2wA7kw.

34. Quoted in Burke, "Amish Searching for Healing."

35. Roth, "Complex Legacy," 280 and throughout. The term *right remembering* was previously, and perhaps first, used in a Mennonite context in Dave and Neta Jackson's *On Fire for Christ: Stories of Anabaptist Martyrs Retold from "Martyrs Mirror,"* as quoted in Kasdorf, "Right Remembering," 13. My thanks to Kasdorf for bringing this citation to my attention.

Chapter 5

1. Frank, *Letting Stories Breathe*, 75.

2. Redekop, *Husk*, 177, 244. Further citations of this novel are given in the text.

3. My thinking here is influenced by Eli Clare's discussion of the problematic assumption held by many people without disabilities that the only way people with disabilities can have fulfilling lives is if their disabilities are cured. See Clare, *Exile and Pride*, 122–23. Clare further examines the issue of cure in *Brilliant Imperfection*.

4. Frank, *Letting Stories Breathe*, 117.

5. Indeed, in a short YouTube clip uploaded by Winnipeg Free Press, Redekop calls *Husk* "the great Canadian gay Mennonite zombie novel" and asserts, "I defy you to prove me different!" His statement is humorous, of course, because *Husk* is the only contender for the label. "*Husk*: The Great Canadian Gay Mennonite Zombie Novel."

6. Redekop himself acknowledges that family awkwardness might result from the publication of *Husk*, as the last line of the dedication reads, "Grandma, please close the book now" (vi). Redekop knows that some people will find the book scandalous, but scandalousness in the queer tradition can lead to liberation, and so again, the novel is queer not just because of its sexual matter but in a broader political sense as well.

7. Di Brandt's "Pornography and Silence and Mennonites and Women" in *Dancing Naked*, 50–56, and Julia Spicher Kasdorf's

"Writing like a Mennonite" in *The Body and the Book*, 167–89, are two classic essays discussing how these attitudes are harmful, including how they can lead to sexual abuse within and outside of the Mennonite community. For perspectives on queer sex work, see Laing, Pilcher, and Smith, *Queer Sex Work*.

8. Berlant and Warner, "Sex in Public," 171.

9. Clare, *Exile and Pride*, 129.

10. Harris, "Zombies," 64.

11. Jeff Gundy writes in "Mennonite/s Writing" that some scenes are "repellent, even disgusting, even for one who prides himself on being pretty hard to shock," and I concur. I am barely able to skim the description of the bus restroom where Sheldon has his heart attack (42–45).

12. For writing on disability from a Mennonite perspective, see the "Dis/Ability" special issue of *Rhubarb*.

13. Kafer, *Feminist, Queer, Crip*, 11. Kafer calls for an intersectional approach to ending ableism, much like *Husk* uses Sheldon as an intersectional metaphor for thinking about oppression. She notes that her "crip theory" approach, which is explicitly "politic[al]," shares much with queer theory's approach to strategies for social change (15–16).

14. For a discussion of the history of people with disabilities in freak shows, see Clare, *Exile and Pride*, 85–103.

15. Redekop identifies himself as a "vegetarian" in "Mennonites Do Not Write," 48. Therefore, while it is not a topic I will pursue here, one might claim that the nauseating scenes of Sheldon eating human flesh throughout the novel argue against eating meat in general.

16. Clare, *Exile and Pride*, 97.

17. Obviously, I read Doctor Frankenstein's creature sympathetically. To quote a Facebook meme I saw once, "Knowledge is knowing that Frankenstein is not the monster / Wisdom is knowing that Frankenstein is the monster." For an example of a nonsympathetic perspective, see Lipking, "*Frankenstein*, the True Story." For a classic queer reclaiming of the creature, see Stryker, "My Words to Victor Frankenstein above the Village of Chamounix."

18. Kafer, *Feminist, Queer, Crip*, 25–26.

19. There is also a 1975 film called *Night of the Walking Dead* directed by León Klimovsky, but it is about vampires. Sheldon is clearly making a zombie film reference because after calling the dementia patients "the walking dead," he calls their floor "the ward of the tattered ambulatory cadaver" (90), which describes a stereotypical zombie, not a vampire.

20. Klassen, "Zombie Anabaptapocolypse."

21. The *Mennonot* was a zine "For Mennos on the Margins" published between 1993 and 2003. It often discussed Mennonite literature as one area of resistance to Mennonite theological orthodoxy and was queer-friendly from its beginning, which was a rarity for Mennonite-related publications at the time. One could easily imagine an interview with Sheldon Funk being published there. Its thirteen issues are available at http://www.keybridgeltd.com/mennonot/downloads.htm.

22. Redekop, "Mennonites," 48–49.

23. According to John C. Wenger, the last name "Funk," while being "Swiss Mennonite" in origin, is also commonly found among Russian Mennonites. "Funk," 420. Such a crossover is a rarity in Mennonite names, and it makes Sheldon a kind of everyMennonite, not just an everyzombie.

24. Nonqueer examples of this character type include Mastie Stoltzfus in Kenneth Reed's *Mennonite Soldier*, Nikolai Fast in Al Reimer's *My Harp Is Turned to Mourning*, and Nomi Nickel in Miriam Toews's *A Complicated Kindness*.

25. Gundy, "Mennonite/s Writing."

26. Klassen, "Zombie Anabaptapocolypse."

27. Harris, "Zombies," 71–73. In "The Zombie Anabaptapocolypse," Klassen contends that at the end of the novel when Sheldon releases the zombies that Dixon has been keeping prisoner in his compound, he is "probably unleashing a zombie apocalypse on the world," but I disagree. The zombies are in the middle of the desert with no humans to feed on, and many of them are already in an advanced state of decay (244). The few that might be able to walk far enough to actually get somewhere inhabited by humans will be slow enough for humans

to destroy. Humans will be able to recognize the zombies as such because, as a result of Sheldon's celebrity, they know that zombies are real.

28. The classic discussion of this belief is in Bender, *Anabaptist Vision*, 4, 33–34.

29. Aside from the *Martyrs Mirror*, many Mennonite children have also grown up with stories from Elizabeth Hershberger Bauman's *Coals of Fire* (still in print), which retells stories from the *Martyrs Mirror* along with more contemporary martyr narratives. I could also cite numerous other children's books about martyrdom published by Herald Press. For more on *Coals of Fire* and some of these other books, see Reimer, "Passing on the Faith."

30. Gundy, "Mennonite/s Writing." I read Gundy as using "nonresistance" to be interchangeable with "peace," and he does agree that Sheldon "ha[s] a moral sense." However, it is important to note that for many Mennonites, "nonresistance" used to mean not just pacifism but a complete submissiveness to authority that precluded any kind of social protest against violence, whether perpetrated by governments or individuals. The title and content of Guy Franklin Hershberger's *War, Peace, and Nonresistance* is one example of this usage.

31. While thriftiness is not solely a Mennonite trait, it is, indeed, a Mennonite trait. Craig Haas and Steve Nolt offer some stereotypical, satirical, yet accurate examples of how this trait manifests itself, such as in saving "plastic bread bags," old manila "folders [. . . ,] wrapping paper [. . . , and t]ea bags" in *The Mennonite Starter Kit*, 37, 40.

32. I do not mean to imply here that only Mennonite books deal with issues of violence and peace but that the treatment of these issues in *Husk* is influenced by its Mennonite context.

Chapter 6

1. Halberstam, *In a Queer Time and Place*, 77.

2. Plett, *A Safe Girl to Love*, 141. Further citations of this book are given in the text.

3. Cvetkovich, *Archive of Feelings*, 253.

4. While coming out for LGB persons is often a liberating gesture, this is not necessarily the case for trans persons because it unfairly leads to their body becoming "contested." Seid, "Reveal," 176.

5. Halberstam, *In a Queer Time and Place*, 44.

6. I draw on my own experiences in the BDSM community here and throughout this section. Staci Newmahr documents this appreciation of pain and its markings in *Playing on the Edge*, 94. The character Tootles in Sassafras Lowrey's *Lost Boi* is one well-developed fictional example of this appreciation. Regarding BDSM, Lowrey's novel is an excellent example of the "literature as theory" concept discussed in the introduction.

7. For the record, members of the BDSM community generally hate James's novel because the kinky elements of Ana and Christian's sexual encounters are not nearly as consensual as they should be. If someone reads *Fifty Shades of Grey* as a BDSM how-to manual, they will be dangerously misinformed. I do not read Carla (or, especially, Plett) as advocating for James's novel; rather, I read the reference to it as simply drawing on the novel's societally ubiquitous nature (at least among non-Mennonites) to use it as shorthand to indicate kinkiness.

8. Indeed, some authors argue that BDSM includes a clear spiritual dimension. See, for instance, Flowers and Flowers, *Carnal Alchemy*, and Harrington, *Sacred Kink*. Patrick S. Cheng explains that some queer theologians use the metaphor of BDSM tops and bottoms to investigate the relationship between God and humans in *Radical Love*, 52–53.

9. The thinking here is that if your new top turns out to be a psychopath rather than a legitimate BDSM practitioner, it is a lot less convenient for them to kill you at their place, where they then have to dispose of the body, than at your place, where they can just leave you to rot.

10. For a trans autoethnographic account of how engaging in BDSM builds community, see Stryker, "Dungeon Intimacies."

11. This story was first published as a chapbook with illustrations. See Plett, *Lizzy & Annie*. The rarity of this chapbook is a prime example of the ephemerality of queer material culture discussed in chapter 1.

12. *A Safe Girl to Love*'s multiple portrayals of nipple torture are akin to the way the prolific queer author Samuel R. Delany gives many of his characters a fetish for men with dirty fingernails, one that Delany himself shares. See Delany, "Aversion/Perversion/Diversion," 129.

13. Hoang, *A View from the Bottom*, 2–3.

14. Ibid., 12.

15. Serano, *Whipping Girl*, 30. See also Rodríguez, *Sexual Futures*, 55.

16. While, as Rachel Schreiber shows in "'Someone You Know Is a Sex Worker,'" 257–60, not all sex workers dislike their work, and some actively choose it as a career, the portrayals of sex work in *A Safe Girl to Love* make it clear that the characters do not enjoy it.

17. Serano, *Whipping Girl*, 261. For an examination of Canadian trans sex work that remains relevant to the characters' experiences in *A Safe Girl to Love* even though it is about such work in the 1970s and 1980s, see Ross, "Outdoor Brothel Culture."

18. This implication is confirmed in Plett's novel *Little Fish*, 108.

19. Rodríguez, *Sexual Futures*, 16. See also Holt, "Being Paid to Be in Pain," 82.

20. Plett, "Coke."

21. "manifesto, n." *Oxford English Dictionary*.

22. Suzanne, *Riding SideSaddle*: A Novel*, Version 1.0. See my discussion below of the citation difficulties *Riding SideSaddle** presents. The quotation cited here is from one of the #me cards.

23. Stockton, *Beautiful Bottom, Beautiful Shame*, 42–46.

24. See Sara Stambaugh's *I Hear the Reaper's Song* for an example of Mennonite literature that examines the issue of plain dress in a historically accurate way.

25. These conversations took place during a family reunion in August 2016.

26. Robert Zacharias calls this image of a generic conservative Mennonite who has never actually existed historically because of the mishmash of Anabaptist traditions that they represent "the Mennonite Thing," in "The Mennonite Thing," which examines its frequent appearance throughout (nonqueer) Mennonite literature.

151

27. See the Bluestockings bookstore website (http://bluestockings.com/) and the Museum of Sex website (http://www.museumofsex.com/) for more on these venues. Queering the Map (http://www.queeringthemap.com/) is an online project that allows users to map queer spaces in order to make them visible. For a well-known non-Mennonite example of this kind of transformative encounter with queer texts, see Alison Bechdel's memoir *Fun Home*, 74–76.

28. Serano, *Whipping Girl*, 316. The manifestos are found on pages 11–20 and 315–17.

29. Since *Queering Mennonite Literature* is rooted in queer theory, it is necessary to note that Serano questions queer theory by arguing that it often silences actual trans experience because it insists on breaking down the gender binary, whereas claiming one's gender can be a powerful act for trans people. Serano, *Whipping Girl*, 208–9, 357. While I feel that the definition of queer theory Serano uses to make her point is too simplistic, as I explain in the introduction, the queer is something that must continue to be queered, so I acknowledge that critiques such as Serano's have an important place in queer discourse.

30. The novel's promotional website (which is different from the online version of the novel discussed below) claims that there are "250 interchangeable index cards," but my copy of the story only has 246 plus the 6 front matter cards. It is possible my copy was shortchanged a few story cards, but the 252 total that it has barely fit into the box, so my assumption is the "250" figure is simply meant as an approximation. http://www.ridingsidesaddle.com/.

31. Some readers may be unaware of gender-neutral pronouns such as those used here, which are common in queer writing. They are one example of the queer emphasis on transforming all of society in more inclusive ways. While the narrator uses traditional gendered pronouns to refer to the other characters, I use gender-neutral pronouns because, as I discuss, a number of the characters' genders may be read as fluid throughout the novel. On the fetish of autoerotic asphyxiation, see

Love, *Encyclopedia of Unusual Sex Practices*, 21–22.

32. "Riding sidesaddle," *Urban Dictionary*.

33. For more on the fluidity and openness of these terms, see Stryker and Currah, "Introduction," 1, 4–6.

34. Halberstam, *In a Queer Time and Place*, 104.

35. Suzanne, *Riding SideSaddle**, 2016. This version of the novel includes the illustrations from the print version as well as several embedded songs.

36. Suzanne, "Some Kind of Manifesto."

37. Suzanne, Teacup Gorilla, Dresser, and Morgan, 10 *Myths on the Proper Application of Beauty Products*. Note that this title is similar to Plett's "Twenty Hot Tips to Shopping Success" and that the trope of offering makeup tips appears elsewhere in trans fiction in Imogen Binnie's *Nevada*, 30–32. Binnie's makeup tips are written in the same how-to style as Plett's story, and Binnie is the author of one of the blurbs on *A Safe Girl to Love*'s back cover. The trans community building advocated for in Plett's and Suzanne's work is already happening in the real-life trans literary community. For Plett's thoughts on *Nevada*, see "Notes."

38. Two cards reference Bible verses: "My body is a temple, the temple of the lord" (#me) is reminiscent of 1 Corinthians 6:19 ("What? know ye not that your body is the temple of the Holy Ghost which is in you"), and the card about Sam's hanging beginning "The ejaculate of a hanged man, dripped on the ground, is rumored to sprout the mandrake plant" (#sam) references the mandrakes in Genesis 30:14–16.

39. Halberstam, *In a Queer Time and Place*, 153.

40. Serano, *Whipping Girl*, 199–204.

Epilogue

1. Castiglia and Reed, *If Memory Serves*, 172.

2. Schneider, "More Than a Feeling," 259–60.

3. Amin, *Disturbing Attachments*, 177.

4. For a discussion of the major works that embody this thesis, see Muñoz, *Cruising Utopia*, 10–11, 91–94.

5. Ibid., 3.

6. Aside from the above-mentioned books, see Harnish, "Excerpt from *Plain Love*." On the queer aspects in three stories from Bechtel's book, see Cruz, "Learning to Listen."

7. See, for example, Dominique Chew's *The Meaning of Grace*, a memoir in poems about race and Mennonite identity, and Abigail Carl-Klassen's *Shelter Management*, a poetry collection about U.S./Mexico border issues.

8. Quoted in Beck, "Sofia Samatar." Beck's essay provides a helpful brief biography of Samatar.

9. Samatar, "Scope of This Project."

10. Indeed, some scholars argue that being a person of color is a form of queerness, much as I argue that Mennonite ideals are queer. See, for instance, Cruz, *Color of Kink*, 3; Rodríguez, *Sexual Futures*, 2; Scott, *Extravagant Abjection*, 10; and the entirety of Stockton, *Beautiful Bottom, Beautiful Shame*.

11. The one exception, which Samatar mentions at the end of her essay, is the attention that has been given to Yorifumi Yaguchi's work. His poetry is included in Phyllis Pellman Good's germinal *Three Mennonite Poets* and is the subject of two critical essays by Wilbur Birky, "Yorifumi Yaguchi" and "Staring Down the Muzzle from Yamoto to Baghdad." Yaguchi used to be considered canonical in that he was included in Ervin Beck's 2001 Mennonite Literature course (and perhaps during other years as well) at Goshen College, in which I was a student. But he has fallen off of the critical radar over the past decade.

12. Samatar, "Scope of This Project." In an early attempt to bring Mennonite literature into dialogue with postcolonial theory, in "Introduction: Mennonite Writing and the Post-colonial Condition," Hildi Froese Tiessen explores how the Canadian Mennonite experience is a postcolonial one. While Tiessen's essay is not necessarily antithetical to Samatar's, its emphasis is much different in that it only examines one geographical setting.

13. Samatar, "Scope of This Project."

14. Holland, *Erotic Life of Racism*, 66.

15. Samatar, "Scope of This Project."

16. Ibid.

17. Ibid. Togane writes of his experiences with Mennonites in *The Bottle and the Bushman*, 4, 5, 30, 33.

18. Samatar, "Conversation with Sofia Samatar." Samatar also discusses intersectionality in "In Search of Women's Histories." Hybridity is a major theme in Samatar and Samatar, *Monster Portraits*, which includes drawings by Samatar's brother, Del, and short stories responding to the drawings by Samatar herself.

19. Samatar also uses this kind of language, which is not meant hyperbolically, in an essay, "Skin Feeling," about the difficulties of being black in academia, explaining that working on "diversity" issues as a token person of color can feel like "a suicidal project." For a description of the difficulties inherent in academic diversity work, see Ahmed, *Living a Feminist Life*, 93–114.

20. As a Mennonite of color whom most people read as being white, I can attest that I have heard white Mennonites make racist statements because they thought it was somehow acceptable to do so around me on a number of occasions. Samatar briefly discusses Mennonite racism and its paradoxical relationship to Mennonite mission work in "Interview: Sofia Samatar."

21. This book is not the place for the extended discussion that the recent flowering of Mennonite speculative fiction deserves. However, in order to give some context for the speculative aspects of Samatar's fiction, I will note that there are numerous Mennonite texts in the genre. Casey Plett has coedited an anthology with Cat Fitzpatrick, *Meanwhile, Elsewhere*, and the stories in Bechtel's *Boundary Problems* are also speculative. Novels in the genre include Keith Miller's *The Book of Flying, The Book on Fire*, and *The Sins of Angels*; André Swartley's *Americanus Rex* and *The Wretched Afterlife of Odetta Koop*; and Stephen Beachy's *Zeke Yoder vs. the Singularity*. This is not a comprehensive list. Note that most of these writers are also writing queerly. For a description of the relatively long history of the intersection between speculative fiction and the queer, see Call, *BDSM*, 16–25.

22. Samatar, "'I'm Generally Anti-realist.'"

23. Samatar, "Writing Queerly."

24. Samatar, *Tender*, 10. Further citations of this book are given in the text.

25. Allfrey, "Chronicle of Ghosts," her emphasis.

26. Samatar, "Conversation with Sofia Samatar."

27. Jeff Gundy observes that all three of the significant romantic relationships in Samatar's first two books are "dramatically unconventional," with the other two involving supernatural beings and one being between cousins. "'There Is No Knife, but Only Flesh,'" 71. In other words, there is more queer ground to explore in Samatar's fiction than I cover here.

28. Samatar, *Winged Histories*, 171.

29. Ibid., 67, 189–225.

30. The word *Mennonite* is never used in the story. However, aside from including frequent references to traditional Mennonite activities such as shunning and hymn singing, the story reveals that some of the community's former "misguided prophets" include "Jan van Leyden [. . . and] Claas Epp," and its former migrations include "the hills of Pennsylvania replac[ing] the lost hills of Germany and the wheat fields of Saskatchewan those of Russia" (235, 260). Van Leyden was the leader of the Anabaptist Münsterite uprising in 1534–35, and Epp led Mennonites who believed Jesus's return was immanent on the "Great Trek" from Russia to Turkestan in 1880. Although Samatar's fiction is almost exclusively not explicitly Mennonite, she acknowledges the influence of first-generation Mennonite writers on her. In extemporaneous prefatory remarks to her keynote address at the Crossing the Line: Women of Anabaptist Traditions Encounter Borders and Boundaries conference at Eastern Mennonite University in Harrisonburg, Virginia, on 24 June 2017, she recounted how Julia Spicher Kasdorf, who introduced her, was the first author she met who was "neither male nor old" and who thereby helped Samatar envision the identity of "writer" for herself. The address was later published as Samatar, "In Search of Women's Histories."

154

Bibliography

Acker, Kathy. *Don Quixote, which was a dream.* New York: Grove Press, 1986.
———. *I Dreamt I Was a Nymphomaniac: Imagining.* 1980. In *Portrait of an Eye: Three Novels*, 91–184. New York: Grove Press, 1998.
———. *Pussy, King of the Pirates.* New York: Grove Press, 1996.
Adler, Melissa. *Cruising the Library: Perversities in the Organization of Knowledge.* New York: Fordham University Press, 2017.
Adorno, Theodor. *Prisms.* Translated by Samuel Weber and Shierry Weber. Cambridge: Massachusetts Institute of Technology Press, 1981.
Ahmed, Sara. *Living a Feminist Life.* Durham, NC: Duke University Press, 2017.
Aldrich, Nelson W., Jr., ed. *George, Being George: George Plimpton's Life as Told, Admired, Deplored, and Envied by 200 Friends, Relatives, Lovers, Acquaintances, Rivals—and a Few Unappreciative Observers.* New York: Random House, 2008.
Allfrey, Ellah Wakatama. "A Chronicle of Ghosts—Reading Sofia Samatar." *Journal of Mennonite Writing* 9, no. 2 (2017). http://www.mennonitewriting .org/journal/9/2/chronicle-ghosts -reading-sofia-samatar/#all.
Alwin, Ben Power. "Archival Justice: An Interview with Ben Power Alwin." By K. J. Rawson. *Radical History Review* 122 (2015): 177–87.

Amin, Kadji. *Disturbing Attachments: Genet, Modern Pederasty, and Queer History.* Durham, NC: Duke University Press, 2017.
Anker, Elizabeth S., and Rita Felski, eds. *Critique and Postcritique.* Durham, NC: Duke University Press, 2017.
Arana, R. Victoria. "Sibling Incest Stories." *Dreamworks* 4, no. 1 (1984–85): 44–51.
Arondekar, Anjali, Ann Cvetkovich, Christina B. Hanhardt, Regina Kunzel, Tavia Nyong'o, Juana María Rodríguez, and Susan Stryker. "Queer Archives: A Roundtable Discussion." *Radical History Review* 122 (2015): 211–31.
Avenatti, Cassandra, and Eliza Jones. "Kinks and Shrinks: The Therapeutic Value of Queer Sex Work." In Laing, Pilcher, and Smith, *Queer Sex Work*, 88–94.
Baehr, Anna Ruth Ediger. *Moonflowers at Dusk.* Northport, NY: Birnham Wood Graphics, 1996.
Bailey, Marlon M. "Black Gay (Raw) Sex." In Johnson, *No Tea*, 239–61.
Bannon, Ann. *Beebo Brinker.* 1962. San Francisco: Cleis Press, 2001.
———. *I Am a Woman.* 1959. San Francisco: Cleis Press, 2002.
———. *Journey to a Woman.* 1960. San Francisco: Cleis Press, 2003.
———. *Odd Girl Out.* 1957. San Francisco: Cleis Press, 2001.
———. *Women in the Shadows.* 1959. San Francisco: Cleis Press, 2002.

Barth, John. *Lost in the Funhouse: Fiction for Print, Tape, Live Voice.* Garden City, NY: Doubleday, 1968.

Barthelme, Donald. *City Life.* New York: Farrar, Straus & Giroux, 1970.

Bauman, Elizabeth Hershberger. *Coals of Fire.* Scottdale, PA: Herald Press, 1954.

Beachy, Kirsten Eve. "Editor's Preface." In Beachy, *Tongue Screws*, 15–17.

———, ed. *Tongue Screws and Testimonies: Poems, Stories, and Essays Inspired by the "Martyrs Mirror."* Scottdale, PA: Herald Press, 2010.

Beachy, Stephen. *boneyard.* Portland, OR: Verse Chorus Press, 2011.

———. *Distortion.* New York: Harrington Park Press, 2001.

———. *Glory Hole.* Tuscaloosa, AL: FC2, 2017.

———. *Some Phantom/No Time Flat: Two Novellas.* 2006. Portland, OR: Verse Chorus Press, 2013.

———. *The Whistling Song.* New York: W. W. Norton, 1991.

———. *Zeke Yoder vs. the Singularity.* Self-published, CreateSpace, 2016.

———. *"Zeke Yoder vs. the Singularity*: An Amish Sci-fi Novel." Kickstarter.com. 2016. https://www.kickstarter.com/projects/1541842544/zeke-yoder-vs-the-singularity-an-amish-sci-fi-nove.

Bechdel, Alison. *Fun Home: A Family Tragicomic.* 2006. Boston: Mariner Books, 2007.

Bechtel, Greg. *Boundary Problems: Stories.* Calgary: Freehand Books, 2014.

Beck, Ervin. *MennoFolk: Mennonite and Amish Folk Traditions.* Scottdale, PA: Herald Press, 2004.

———. "Mennonite Literature at Goshen College." *Journal of Mennonite Writing* 8, no. 1 (2016). http://www.mennonitewriting.org/journal/8/1/mennonite-literature-goshen-college/#all.

———. "Mennonite Transgressive Literature." In Zacharias, *After Identity*, 52–69.

———. "Sofia Samatar: Service for Culture." *Journal of Mennonite Writing* 9, no. 2 (2017). http://www.mennonitewriting.org/journal/9/2/sofia-samatar-service-culture/#all.

Bender, Harold S. *The Anabaptist Vision.* Scottdale, PA: Herald Press, 1944.

Bergen, David, ed. *9 Mennonite Stories.* Winnipeg: Mennonite Literary Society, 2017.

Berlant, Lauren, and Michael Warner. "Sex in Public." In Hall and Jagose, *Routledge*, 165–79.

Binnie, Imogen. *Nevada.* New York: Topside Press, 2013.

Birdsell, Sandra. *Agassiz: A Novel in Stories.* Minneapolis: Milkweed Editions, 1991.

Birky, Beth Martin. "When Flesh Becomes Word: Creating Space for the Female Body in Mennonite Women's Poetry." In Roth and Beck, *Migrant Muses*, 197–208.

Birky, Wilbur. "Staring Down the Muzzle from Yamoto to Baghdad." *Journal of Mennonite Writing* 1, no. 2 (2009). http://www.mennonitewriting.org/journal/1/2/staring-down-muzzle/#all.

———. "Yorifumi Yaguchi: International Mennonite Poet and Prophet of Peace." *Mennonite Quarterly Review* 77, no. 4 (2003): 559–77.

Bluestockings bookstore website. http://bluestockings.com/.

Brandt, Di. *Agnes in the Sky.* Winnipeg: Turnstone Press, 1990.

———. *Dancing Naked: Narrative Strategies for Writing Across Centuries.* Stratford, ON: Mercury Press, 1996.

———. "In Praise of Hybridity: Reflections from Southwestern Manitoba." In Zacharias, *After Identity*, 125–42.

———. *questions i asked my mother.* Winnipeg: Turnstone Press, 1987.

Braun, Jan Guenther. "A Complicated Becoming." *Journal of Mennonite Studies* 34 (2016): 291–97.

———. "From Policy to the Personal: One Queer Mennonite's Journey." *Journal of Mennonite Studies* 26 (2008): 69–80.

———. "Queer Sex at Bible College." *Rhubarb*, Spring 2013, 13–15.

———. "Slam." *Rhubarb*, Fall 2004, 40.

———. *Somewhere Else.* Winnipeg: Arbeiter Ring Publishing, 2008.

Brintnall, Kent L., Joseph A. Mitchell, and Stephen D. Moore, eds. *Sexual Disorientations: Queer Temporalities, Affects, Theologies.* New York: Fordham University Press, 2018.

Burke, Daniel. "Amish Searching for Healing, Forgiveness After 'The Amish 9/11.'" *Religion News Service*, 5 October 2006. http://web.archive.org/web/20061021051654/http://www.religionnews.com/ArticleofWeek100506.html.

Califia, Patrick [Pat Califia]. *Public Sex: The Culture of Radical Sex*. 2nd ed. San Francisco: Cleis Press, 2000.

Call, Lewis. *BDSM in American Science Fiction and Fantasy*. New York: Palgrave Macmillan, 2013.

Carl-Klassen, Abigail. *Shelter Management*. Chicago: Dancing Girl Press, 2017.

Casey the Canadian Lesbrarian (blog). https://caseythecanadianlesbrarian.com/.

Castiglia, Christopher. *The Practices of Hope: Literary Criticism in Disenchanted Times*. New York: New York University Press, 2017.

Castiglia, Christopher, and Christopher Reed. *If Memory Serves: Gay Men, AIDS, and the Promise of the Queer Past*. Minneapolis: University of Minnesota Press, 2012.

Castle, Terry. *The Apparitional Lesbian: Female Homosexuality and Modern Culture*. New York: Columbia University Press, 1993.

Cheng, Patrick S. *Radical Love: An Introduction to Queer Theology*. New York: Seabury Books, 2011.

Chew, Dominique. *The Meaning of Grace*. Goshen, IN: Pinchpenny Press, 2015.

Clare, Eli. *Brilliant Imperfection: Grappling with Cure*. Durham, NC: Duke University Press, 2017.

———. *Exile and Pride: Disability, Queerness, and Liberation*. Durham, NC: Duke University Press, 2015.

Cohen, Cathy J. "Punks, Bulldaggers, and Welfare Queens: The Radical Potential of Queer Politics?" In Hall and Jagose, *Routledge*, 74–95.

Coverley, Merlin. *Psychogeography*. Harpenden, UK: Pocket Essentials, 2010.

Cruz, Ariane. *The Color of Kink: Black Women, BDSM, and Pornography*. New York: New York University Press, 2016.

Cruz, Daniel Shank. "A Bibliography and Subject Index of Published Work from the Mennonite/s Writing Conferences." *Mennonite Quarterly Review* 91, no. 1 (2017): 93–130.

———. "Learning to Listen in Greg Bechtel's 'Smut Stories.'" In *Education with the Grain of the Universe: A Peaceable Vision for the Future of Mennonite Schools, Colleges, and Universities*, edited by J. Denny Weaver, 213–22. Telford, PA: Cascadia Publishing House, 2017.

———. "Narrative Ethics in Miriam Toews's *Summer of My Amazing Luck*." *Journal of Mennonite Writing* 5, no. 1 (2013). http://www.mennonitewriting.org/journal/5/1/narrative-ethics-miriam-toews-summer-my-amazing-lu/#all.

———. "New York, or What I Learned in Voluntary Service." *Rhubarb*, Spring 2008, 21–26.

———. "On Postcolonial Mennonite Writing: Theorizing a Queer Latinx Mennonite Life." *Journal of Mennonite Writing* 9, no. 4 (2017). https://mennonitewriting.org/journal/9/4/postcolonial-mennonite-writing-theorizing-queer-la/?page=5#all.

———. "Queering Mennonite Literature." In Zacharias, *After Identity*, 143–58.

———, ed. "Queer Mennonite Literature." Special issue, *Journal of Mennonite Writing* 10, no. 3 (2018). https://mennonitewriting.org/journal/10/3/.

———. "Reading My Life in the Text: Adventures of a Queer Mennonite Critic." *Journal of Mennonite Studies* 34 (2016): 280–86.

Cvetkovich, Ann. *An Archive of Feelings: Trauma, Sexuality, and Lesbian Public Cultures*. Durham, NC: Duke University Press, 2003.

———. *Depression: A Public Feeling*. Durham, NC: Duke University Press, 2012.

———. "Photographing Objects as Queer Archival Practice." In *Feeling Photography*, edited by Elspeth H. Brown and Thy Phu, 273–96. Durham, NC: Duke University Press, 2014.

———. "White Boots and Combat Boots: My Life as a Lesbian Go-Go Dancer." In *Dancing Desires: Choreographing Sexualities On and Off the Stage*, edited by Jane Desmond, 315–48. Madison: University of Wisconsin Press, 2001.

D'anna, Lynnette. *Belly Fruit*. Vancouver: New Star Books, 2000.

———. *fool's bells*. Toronto: Insomniac Press, 1999.

——— [Lynnette Dueck]. *sing me no more.* Vancouver: Press Gang, 1992.

———. *vixen.* Toronto: Insomniac Press, 2001.

Dean, Tim. "Stumped." In Dean, Ruszczycky, and Squires, *Porn Archives*, 420–40.

———. *Unlimited Intimacy: Reflections on the Subculture of Barebacking.* Chicago: University of Chicago Press, 2009.

Dean, Tim, Steven Ruszczycky, and David Squires, eds. *Porn Archives.* Durham, NC: Duke University Press, 2014.

Delany, Samuel R. "Aversion/Perversion/ Diversion." In *Longer Views: Extended Essays*, 119–43. Hanover, NH: Wesleyan University Press/University Press of New England, 1996.

———. *Heavenly Breakfast: An Essay on the Winter of Love.* New York: Bantam Books, 1979.

———. *Times Square Red, Times Square Blue.* New York: New York University Press, 1999.

de Lauretis, Teresa. "Queer Theory: Lesbian and Gay Sexualities: An Introduction." *differences: A Journal of Feminist Cultural Studies* 3, no. 2 (1991): i– xviii.

Dewhurst, Robert. "*Gay Sunshine*, Pornopoetic Collage, and Queer Archive." In Dean, Ruszczycky, and Squires, *Porn Archives*, 213–33.

Dick, Janice. *Out of the Storm.* Waterloo, ON: Herald Press, 2004.

"Dis/Ability." Special issue, *Rhubarb*, Summer 2016.

Doerksen, Paul G. *Take and Read: Reflecting Theologically on Books.* Eugene, OR: Wipf & Stock, 2016.

Drake, Robert. *The Gay Canon: Great Books Every Gay Man Should Read.* New York: Anchor Books, 1998.

Dueck-Read, Alicia. "Breaking the Binary: Queering Mennonite Identity." *Journal of Mennonite Studies* 33 (2015): 115–33.

Eichhorn, Kate. *The Archival Turn in Feminism: Outrage in Order.* Philadelphia: Temple University Press, 2013.

Eisner, Shiri. *Bi: Notes for a Bisexual Revolution.* Berkeley, CA: Seal Press, 2013.

Fitzpatrick, Cat, and Casey Plett, eds. *Meanwhile, Elsewhere: Science Fiction and Fantasy from Transgender Writers.* New York: Topside Press, 2017.

Flowers, Stephen E., and Crystal Dawn Flowers. *Carnal Alchemy: Sadomagical Techniques for Pleasure, Pain, and Self-Transformation.* Rochester, VT: Inner Traditions, 2013.

Ford, Richard Thompson. "What's Queer About Race?" In Halley and Parker, *After Sex?*, 121–29.

Foster, Clarise. *29 Mennonite Poets.* Winnipeg: Mennonite Literary Society, 2017.

Frank, Arthur W. *Letting Stories Breathe: A Socio-Narratology.* Chicago: University of Chicago Press, 2010.

Freeman, Elizabeth. Afterword to *Sexual Disorientations: Queer Temporalities, Affects, Theologies*, 315–19. Edited by Kent L. Brintnall, Joseph A. Mitchell, and Stephen D. Moore. New York: Fordham University Press, 2018.

Friesen, Bernice. "From the Editor's Desk." *Rhubarb*, Winter 2015, 2.

———. "In Memory." *Rhubarb*, Winter 2015, 63.

Friesen, Gordon. *Flamethrowers.* Caldwell, ID: Caxton Printers, 1936.

Friesen, Patrick. *The Shunning.* Winnipeg: Turnstone Press, 1980.

Funk, Wes. *Baggage.* Regina, SK: Benchmark Press, 2010.

———. *Cherry Blossoms.* Regina, SK: Your Nickel's Worth Publishing, 2012.

———. "Daddy." *Rhubarb*, Winter 2015, 62.

———. *Dead Rock Stars: Illustrated Edition.* Illustrated by Kevin Hastings. Regina, SK: Your Nickel's Worth Publishing, 2015.

———. *Humble Beginnings.* Saskatoon, SK: Self-published, 2006.

———. *Wes Side Story: A Memoir.* Regina, SK: Your Nickel's Worth Publishing, 2014.

Giesbrecht, Herbert. "O Life, How Naked and How Hard When Known!" 1963. In Keith, *A Voice in the Land*, 50–63.

Good, Merle. "The Mennonite as Ethnic Writer: A Conversation with Merle Good." By Sanford Pinsker. *Journal of Ethnic Studies* 3, no. 2 (1975): 57–64.

Good, Phyllis Pellman, ed. *Three Mennonite Poets.* Intercourse, PA: Good Books, 1986.

Goossen, Benjamin W. "From Aryanism to Anabaptism: Nazi Race Science and the Language of Mennonite Ethnicity." *Mennonite Quarterly Review* 90, no. 2 (2016): 135–63.

Gray, Mary L., Colin R. Johnson, and Brian J. Gilley, eds. *Queering the Countryside: New Frontiers in Rural Queer Studies.* New York: New York University Press, 2016.

Grosz, Elizabeth. "Experimental Desire: Rethinking Queer Subjectivity." In Hall and Jagose, *Routledge*, 194–211.

Gundy, Jeff. "Mennonite/s Writing: Explorations and Exposition." *Mennonite Life* 70 (2016). https://ml .bethelks.edu/issue/vol-70/article/ mennonites-writing-explorations -and-exposition/.

———. *Rhapsody with Dark Matter.* Huron, OH: Bottom Dog Press, 2000.

———. *Songs from an Empty Cage: Poetry, Mystery, Anabaptism, and Peace.* Telford, PA: Cascadia Publishing House, 2013.

———. "'There Is No Knife, but Only Flesh': Sofia Samatar and the Language of Other Worlds." In Tiessen, 11 *Encounters*, 69–85.

———. *Walker in the Fog: On Mennonite Writing.* Telford, PA: Cascadia Publishing House, 2005.

Gusler, Chad. "OMG!! Geleijn Cornelus Is Hott!!" In Beachy, *Tongue Screws*, 54–58.

Haas, Craig, and Steve Nolt. *The Mennonite Starter Kit: A Handy Guide for the New Mennonite (Everything They Forgot to Tell You in Church Membership Class!).* Intercourse, PA: Good Books, 1993.

Halberstam, J. Jack [Judith Halberstam]. *In a Queer Time and Place: Transgender Bodies, Subcultural Lives.* New York: New York University Press, 2005.

——— [Judith Halberstam]. *The Queer Art of Failure.* Durham, NC: Duke University Press, 2011.

Hall, Donald E., and Annamarie Jagose, eds. *The Routledge Queer Studies Reader.* London: Routledge, 2013.

Halley, Janet, and Andrew Parker, eds. *After Sex? On Writing Since Queer Theory.* Durham, NC: Duke University Press, 2011.

———. Introduction to *After Sex? On Writing Since Queer Theory*, 1–14. Edited by Janet Halley and Andrew Parker. Durham, NC: Duke University Press, 2011.

Hamilton, T. Glen. *Intention and Survival: Psychical Research Studies and the Bearing of Intentional Actions by Trance Personalities on the Problem of Human Survival.* Toronto: Macmillan, 1942.

Harder, Menno S. "Harder." In *The Mennonite Encyclopedia.* Vol. 2, 658. Scottdale, PA: Herald Press, 1956.

Harnish, Andrew. "An Excerpt from *Plain Love.*" *Journal of Mennonite Studies* 34 (2016): 297–302.

———. "LGBT Mennonite Fiction: A Panel from Mennonite/s Writing VII: An Introductory Reflection." *Journal of Mennonite Studies* 34 (2016): 279–80.

Harrington, Lee. *Sacred Kink: The Eightfold Paths of BDSM and Beyond.* 2nd ed. Anchorage, AK: Mystic Productions Press, 2016.

Harris, Daniel. "Zombies." *Salmagundi* 190/191 (2016): 62–73.

Hartley, Nina. "Porn: An Effective Vehicle for Sexual Role Modeling and Education." In Taormino, Shimizu, Penley, and Miller-Young, *Feminist Porn*, 228–36.

Hauerwas, Stanley, and L. Gregory Jones, eds. *Why Narrative? Readings in Narrative Theology.* Eugene, OR: Wipf & Stock, 1997.

Hedrick, Emily. *True Confessions of a God Killer: A Postmodern Pilgrim's Progress.* Telford, PA: DreamSeeker Books, 2014.

Hennessy, Rosemary. "The Material of Sex." In Hall and Jagose, *Routledge*, 134–49.

Hershberger, Guy Franklin. *War, Peace, and Nonresistance.* Scottdale, PA: Herald Press, 1944.

Hinojosa, Felipe. "From Goshen to Delano: Toward a Relational Approach to Mennonite Studies." *Mennonite Quarterly Review* 91, no. 2 (2017): 201–12.

Hoang, Nguyen Tan. *A View from the Bottom: Asian American Masculinity and Sexual Representation.* Durham, NC: Duke University Press, 2014.

Hogan, Kristen. *The Feminist Bookstore Movement: Lesbian Antiracism and Feminist Accountability.* Durham, NC: Duke University Press, 2016.

Holland, Sharon Patricia. *The Erotic Life of Racism.* Durham, NC: Duke University Press, 2012.

Holt, Victoria. "Being Paid to Be in Pain: The Experiences of a Professional Submissive." In Laing, Pilcher, and Smith, *Queer Sex Work*, 79–87.

Hostetler, Ann, ed. *A Cappella: Mennonite Voices in Poetry*. Iowa City: University of Iowa Press, 2003.

———. Introduction to *Journal of Mennonite Writing* 7, no. 3 (2015). http://www .mennonitewriting.org/journal/7/3/ introduction-mennonites-writing -vii/.

———. "Introduction: Mennonite Voices in Poetry." In Hostetler, *A Cappella*, xv–xx.

———. "The Self in Mennonite Garb: Where Does the Writing Come From?" *Mennonite Quarterly Review* 87, no. 1 (2013): 23–40.

———. "Three Women Poets and the Beginnings of Mennonite Poetry in the U.S.: Anna Ruth Ediger Baehr, Jane Rohrer, Jean Janzen." *Mennonite Quarterly Review* 77, no. 4 (2003): 521–45.

"*Husk*: The Great Canadian Gay Mennonite Zombie Novel." YouTube video, 21 September 2012. https://www .youtube.com/watch?v=ecu37u7T8Js.

Johnson, B. S. *The Unfortunates*. 1969. New York: New Directions, 2007.

Johnson, E. Patrick, ed. *No Tea, No Shade: New Writings in Black Queer Studies*. Durham, NC: Duke University Press, 2016.

Johnson, E. Patrick, and Mae G. Henderson, eds. *Black Queer Studies: A Critical Anthology*. Durham, NC: Duke University Press, 2005.

Jordan, Mark D. "In Search of Queer Theology Lost." In Brintnall, Mitchell, and Moore, *Sexual Disorientations*, 296–308.

July, Miranda. *The First Bad Man*. New York: Scribner, 2015.

Kafer, Alison. *Feminist, Queer, Crip*. Bloomington: Indiana University Press, 2013.

Kasdorf, Julia Spicher. *The Body and the Book: Writing from a Mennonite Life; Essays and Poems*. 2001. University Park: Pennsylvania State University Press, 2009.

———. "Dreams of the Written Character." In *The Measure of My Days: Engaging the Life and Thought of John L. Ruth*, edited by Reuben Z. Miller and Joseph S. Miller, 29–37. Telford, PA: Cascadia Publishing House, 2004.

———. *Eve's Striptease*. Pittsburgh: University of Pittsburgh Press, 1998.

———. "The Making of Canada's 'Mennonite' Writers." *Festival Quarterly*, Summer 1990, 14–16.

———. "Mightier Than the Sword: *Martyrs Mirror* in the New World." *Conrad Grebel Review* 31, no. 1 (2013): 44–70.

———. "Right Remembering the Martyr Stories." *Mennonite Historical Bulletin*, April 1991, 12–13.

———. *Sleeping Preacher*. Pittsburgh: University of Pittsburgh Press, 1992.

———. "Sunday Morning Confession." *Mennonite Quarterly Review* 87, no. 1 (2013): 7–10.

———. "To Pasture: 'Amish Forgiveness,' Silence, and the West Nickel Mines School Shooting." *CrossCurrents* 59, no. 3 (2007): 328–47.

Kauffman, Janet. *The Body in Four Parts*. St. Paul: Graywolf Press, 1993.

———. *Collaborators*. New York: Alfred A. Knopf, 1986.

Keefe-Perry, L. Callid. *Way to Water: A Theopoetics Primer*. Eugene, OR: Cascade Books, 2014.

Keim, Albert N. *Harold S. Bender, 1897–1962*. Scottdale, PA: Herald Press, 1998.

Keith, W. J., ed. *A Voice in the Land: Essays by and About Rudy Wiebe*. Edmonton: NeWest Press, 1981.

King, Michael A. *Fractured Dance: Gadamer and a Mennonite Conflict over Homosexuality*. Telford, PA: Pandora Press U.S., 2001.

Klaassen, Walter. *Anabaptism: Neither Catholic nor Protestant*. Waterloo, ON: Conrad Press, 1973.

Klassen, Sheri. "The Zombie Anabaptapocolypse." *slklassen* (blog). 26 October 2015. https://slklassen.com/2015/10/ 26/the-zombie-anabaptapocolypse/.

Klein, Fritz. *The Bisexual Option*. 2nd ed. Binghamton, NY: Harrington Park Press, 1993.

Kliewer, Warren. *The Violators*. Francestown, NH: Marshall Jones Company, 1964.

Klimovsky, León, dir. *Night of the Walking Dead*. Spain: Richard Films, 1975. Film.

Kniss, Fred. *Disquiet in the Land: Cultural Conflict in American Mennonite Communities*. New Brunswick, NJ: Rutgers University Press, 1997.

Kopec, Andrew. "The Digital Humanities, Inc.: Literary Criticism and the Fate of a Profession." *PMLA* 131, no. 2 (2016): 324–39.

Krahn, Cornelius. "Wiebe." In *The Mennonite Encyclopedia*. Vol. 4, 943–44. Scottdale, PA: Herald Press, 1959.

Kraybill, Donald B. *The Upside-Down Kingdom*. Scottdale, PA: Herald Press, 1978.

Krehbiel, Stephanie. "Staying Alive: How Martyrdom Made Me a Warrior." In Beachy, *Tongue Screws*, 133–44.

Laing, Mary, Katy Pilcher, and Nicola Smith, eds. *Queer Sex Work*. London: Routledge, 2015.

Lee, Hermione. *Biography: A Very Short Introduction*. Oxford, UK: Oxford University Press, 2009.

Lesher, Emerson L. *The Muppie Manual: The Mennonite Urban Professional's Handbook for Humility and Success or (How to be the Gentle in the City)*. Intercourse, PA: Good Books, 1985.

Leung, Helen Hok-Sze. "Archiving Queer Feelings in Hong Kong." In Hall and Jagose, *Routledge*, 398–411.

Lewis, Abram J. "'I Am 64 and Paul McCartney Doesn't Care': The Haunting of the Transgender Archive and the Challenges of Queer History." *Radical History Review* 120 (2014): 13–34.

Lipking, Lawrence. "*Frankenstein*, the True Story; or, Rousseau Judges Jean-Jacques." In Shelley, *Frankenstein*, 313–31.

Loewen, Harry. "Mennonite Literature in Canadian and American Mennonite Historiography: An Introduction." *Mennonite Quarterly Review* 73, no. 3 (1999): 557–70.

Loewen, Royden, and Steven M. Nolt. *Seeking Places of Peace: Global Mennonite History Series: North America*. Intercourse, PA: Good Books, 2012.

Love, Brenda. *The Encyclopedia of Unusual Sex Practices*. 1992. London: Greenwich Editions, 1999.

Lowrey, Sassafras. *Lost Boi*. Vancouver: Arsenal Pulp Press, 2015.

Lunney, Doug. "Winnipeg Home Once Hosted Seances." *Winnipeg Sun*, 30 October 2015. http://www.winnipegsun.com/2015/10/30/winnipeg-home-once-hosted-seances.

Luthy, David. *Dirk Willems: His Noble Deed Lives On*. Aylmer, ON: Pathway Publishers, 2011.

———. *A History of the Printings of the "Martyrs' Mirror": Dutch, German, English 1660–2012*. Aylmer, ON: Pathway Publishers, 2013.

Marshall, Daniel, Kevin P. Murphy, and Zeb Tortorici, eds. "Queering Archives: Historical Unravelings." Special issue, *Radical History Review* 120 (2014).

———, eds. "Queering Archives: Intimate Tracings." Special issue, *Radical History Review* 122 (2015).

Martens, Paul, and David Cramer. "By What Criteria Does a 'Grand, Noble Experiment' Fail? What the Case of John Howard Yoder Reveals About the Mennonite Church." *Mennonite Quarterly Review* 89, no. 1 (2015): 171–93.

Martinac, Paula. *Out of Time*. Seattle: Seal Press, 1990.

Mast, Carrie A., and Gerald J. Mast, eds. *Human Sexuality in a Biblical Perspective: A Study Guide*. Telford, PA: Cascadia Publishing House, 2016.

MennoMedia. *Third Way*. http://thirdway.com/.

"Mennonot Issues Archive." *Mennonot*. http://www.keybridgeltd.com/mennonot/downloads.htm.

Miller, Keith. *The Book of Flying*. New York: Riverhead Books, 2004.

———. *The Book on Fire*. Stafford, UK: Immanion Press, 2009.

———. *The Sins of Angels*. Hornsea, UK: PS Publishing, 2016.

Miller, Keith Graber. *Living Faith: Embracing God's Callings*. Telford, PA: Cascadia Publishing House, 2012.

Muñoz, José Esteban. *Cruising Utopia: The Then and There of Queer Futurity*. New York: New York University Press, 2009.

Museum of Sex. http://www.museumofsex.com/.

Nelson, Maggie. *The Argonauts*. Minneapolis: Graywolf Press, 2015.

161

Neufeld, Elsie K., ed. *Half in the Sun: Anthology of Mennonite Writing*. Vancouver: Ronsdale Press, 2006.

The New Oxford Annotated Bible: New Revised Standard Version. New York: Oxford University Press, 1994.

Newmahr, Staci. *Playing on the Edge: Sadomasochism, Risk, and Intimacy*. Bloomington: Indiana University Press, 2011.

OED Online, s.v. "manifesto." Accessed March 2017. http://www.oed.com/view/Entry/113499?rskey=TfUkFh&result=1&isAdvanced=false.

Pellegrini, Ann. "Queer Structures of Religious Feeling: What Time Is Now?" In Brintnall, Mitchell, and Moore, *Sexual Disorientations*, 240–57.

Penner, Christina. *Widows of Hamilton House*. Winnipeg: Enfield & Wizenty, 2008.

Penner, Jessica. "A Mosaic of Broken Dishes." By Julia Spicher Kasdorf. *Journal of Mennonite Writing* 5, no. 3 (2013). http://www.mennonitewriting.org/journal/5/3/mosaic-broken-dishes/#all.

———. "Research Notes: *Shaken in the Water*." *Necessary Fiction*, 3 May 2013. http://necessaryfiction.com/blog/ResearchNotesShakenintheWater.

———. *Shaken in the Water*. Tipp City, OH: Foxhead Books, 2013.

———. *Shaken in the Water*. 2013. Newton, KS: Workplay Publishing, 2017.

Peterson, Zoey Leigh. *Next Year, for Sure*. New York: Scribner, 2017.

Piontek, Thomas. *Queering Gay and Lesbian Studies*. Urbana: University of Illinois Press, 2006.

Plett, Casey. "Coke." *Progress Never Stops for Nostalgic Transsexuals* (blog). 17 February 2017. https://caseyplett.wordpress.com/2017/02/17/coke/.

———. *Little Fish*. Vancouver: Arsenal Pulp Press, 2018.

———. *Lizzy & Annie*. Illustrated by Annie Mok. Self-published, 2013–14.

———. "Natural Links of Queer and Mennonite Literature." *Journal of Mennonite Studies* 34 (2016): 286–90.

———. "Notes from My Talk at Drake." *Progress Never Stops for Nostalgic Transsexuals* (blog). 3 April 2018. https://caseyplett.wordpress.com/2018/04/03/notes-from-my-talk-at-drake/.

———. *A Safe Girl to Love*. New York: Topside Press, 2014.

Probyn, Elspeth. "Writing Shame." In *The Affect Theory Reader*, edited by Melissa Gregg and Gregory J. Seigworth, 71–90. Durham, NC: Duke University Press, 2010.

Queering the Map. http://www.queeringthemap.com/.

Rawson, K. J., and Aaron Devor, eds. "Archives and Archiving." Special issue, *TSQ: Transgender Studies Quarterly* 2, no. 4 (2015).

Redekop, Corey. *Husk*. Toronto: ECW Press, 2012.

———. "Mennonites Do Not Write." *Rhubarb*, Summer 2012, 48–49.

———. *Shelf Monkey*. Toronto: ECW Press, 2007.

Reed, Alison. "The Whiter the Bread, the Quicker You're Dead: Spectacular Absence and Post-racialized Blackness in (White) Queer Theory." In Johnson, *No Tea*, 48–64.

Reed, Kenneth. *Mennonite Soldier*. Scottdale, PA: Herald Press, 1974.

Reimer, Al. *Mennonite Literary Voices: Past and Present*. North Newton, KS: Bethel College, 1993.

———. *My Harp Is Turned to Mourning*. Winnipeg: Windflower Communications, 1990.

Reimer, Douglas. *Surplus at the Border: Mennonite Writing in Canada*. Winnipeg: Turnstone Press, 2002.

Reimer, Kathy Meyer. "Passing on the Faith: Mennonite Writing for Children." *Journal of Mennonite Writing* 2, no. 3 (2010). http://www.mennonitewriting.org/journal/2/3/passing-faith-mennonite-writing-children/#all.

Rickards, Maurice. *This Is Ephemera: Collecting Printed Throwaways*. Newton Abbot, UK: David & Charles, 1978.

Riding SideSaddle*. http://www.ridingsidesaddle.com/.

Rodríguez, Juana María. *Queer Latinidad: Identity Practices, Discursive Spaces*. New York: New York University Press, 2003.

———. *Sexual Futures, Queer Gestures, and Other Latina Longings*. New York: New York University Press, 2014.

Rohy, Valerie. "In the Queer Archive: *Fun Home*." *GLQ: A Journal of Lesbian and Gay Studies* 16, no. 3 (2010): 340–61.

Romero, George A., dir. *Night of the Living Dead*. United States: Image Ten, 1968. Film.

Ross, Becki L. "Outdoor Brothel Culture: The Un/Making of a Trans Stroll in Vancouver's West End, 1975–84." In Laing, Pilcher, and Smith, *Queer Sex Work*, 189–99.

Roth, John D. "The Complex Legacy of the *Martyrs Mirror* among Mennonites in North America." *Mennonite Quarterly Review* 87, no. 3 (2013): 277–316.

———, ed. *Letters of the Amish Division: A Sourcebook*. 2nd ed. Goshen, IN: Mennonite Historical Society, 2002.

Roth, John D., and Ervin Beck, eds. *Migrant Muses: Mennonite/s Writing in the U.S.* Goshen, IN: Mennonite Historical Society, 1998.

Ruth, John L. *Mennonite Identity and Literary Art*. Scottdale, PA: Herald Press, 1978.

Samatar, Del, and Sofia Samatar. *Monster Portraits*. Brookline, MA: Rose Metal Press, 2018.

Samatar, Sofia. "A Conversation with Sofia Samatar." By Alicia Cole. *Black Fox Literary Magazine*, 22 December 2014. http://www.blackfoxlitmag.com/2014/12/22/a-conversation-with-sofia-samatar/.

———. "'I'm Generally Anti-realist': An Interview with Sofia Samatar." By Tobias Carroll. *Vol. 1 Brooklyn*, 26 May 2015. http://www.vol1brooklyn.com/2015/05/26/im-generally-anti-realist-an-interview-with-sofia-samatar/.

———. "In Search of Women's Histories: Crossing Space, Crossing Communities, Crossing Time." *Journal of Mennonite Writing* 9, no. 3 (2017). https://mennonitewriting.org/journal/9/3/search-womens-histories-crossing-space-crossing-co/#all.

———. "Interview: Sofia Samatar." By Aaron Bady. *Post45*, 18 December 2014. http://post45.research.yale.edu/2014/12/interview-sofia-samatar/.

———. "The Scope of This Project." *Journal of Mennonite Writing* 9, no. 2 (2017). http://www.mennonitewriting.org/journal/9/2/scope-project/#all.

———. "Skin Feeling." *The New Inquiry*, 25 September 2015. https://thenewinquiry.com/skin-feeling/.

———. *Tender: Stories*. Easthampton, MA: Small Beer Press, 2017.

———. *The Winged Histories*. Easthampton, MA: Small Beer Press, 2016.

———. "Writing Queerly: Three Snapshots." *Uncanny: A Magazine of Science Fiction and Fantasy*, 2015. http://uncannymagazine.com/article/writing-queerly-three-snapshots/.

Schneider, Laurel C. "More Than a Feeling: A Queer Notion of Survivance." In Brintnall, Mitchell, and Moore, *Sexual Disorientations*, 258–76.

Schreiber, Rachel. "'Someone You Know Is a Sex Worker': A Media Campaign for the St James Infirmary." In Laing, Pilcher, and Smith, *Queer Sex Work*, 255–62.

Schrock-Shenk, Carolyn. Foreword to *Stumbling toward a Genuine Conversation on Homosexuality*, 13–18. Edited by Michael A. King. Telford, PA: Cascadia Publishing House, 2007.

Schweighofer, Katherine. "Rethinking the Closet: Queer Life in Rural Geographies." In Gray, Johnson, and Gilley, *Queering the Countryside*, 223–43.

Scott, Darieck. *Extravagant Abjection: Blackness, Power, and Sexuality in the African American Literary Imagination*. New York: New York University Press, 2010.

Sedgwick, Eve Kosofsky. *Between Men: English Literature and Male Homosocial Desire*. New York: Columbia University Press, 1985.

Seid, Danielle M. "Reveal." *TSQ: Transgender Studies Quarterly* 1, nos. 1–2 (2014): 176–77.

Serano, Julia. *Whipping Girl: A Transsexual Woman on Sexism and the Scapegoating of Femininity*. 2nd ed. Berkeley, CA: Seal Press, 2016.

Shakespeare, William, and Arthur Laurents. *Romeo and Juliet & West Side Story*. New York: Dell, 1965.

Sheffield, Rebecka Taves. "The Bedside Table Archives: Archive Intervention and Lesbian Intimate Domestic Culture." *Radical History Review* 120 (2014): 108–20.

Shelley, Mary. *Frankenstein; or, the Modern Prometheus*. 1818. Edited by J. Paul Hunter. New York: W. W. Norton, 1996.

Smucker, Barbara. *Henry's Red Sea*. Scottdale, PA: Herald Press, 1955.

Stambaugh, Sara. *I Hear the Reaper's Song*. Intercourse, PA: Good Books, 1984.

Stockton, Kathryn Bond. *Beautiful Bottom, Beautiful Shame: Where "Black" Meets "Queer."* Durham, NC: Duke University Press, 2006.

Stoner, Kay. "How the Peace Church Helped Make a Lesbian Out of Me." *Mennonot*, Fall 1994, 10–12. http://www.keybridgeltd.com/mennonot/Issue3.pdf.

Story, Kaila Adia. "On the Cusp of Deviance: Respectability Politics and the Cultural Marketplace of Sameness." In Johnson, *No Tea*, 362–79.

Stryker, Susan. "Dungeon Intimacies: The Poetics of Transsexual Sadomasochism." *Parallax* 14, no. 1 (2008): 36–47.

———. "My Words to Victor Frankenstein above the Village of Chamounix: Performing Transgender Rage." *GLQ: A Journal of Lesbian and Gay Studies* 1, no. 3 (1994): 237–54.

———. *Queer Pulp: Perverted Passions from the Golden Age of the Paperback*. San Francisco: Chronicle Books, 2001.

Stryker, Susan and Paisley Currah. Introduction to *TSQ: Transgender Studies Quarterly* 1, nos. 1–2 (2014): 1–18.

Suderman, Elmer. "Mennonites, the Mennonite Community, and Mennonite Writers." *Mennonite Life* 47, no. 3 (1992): 21–26.

Sullivan, Nikki. *A Critical Introduction to Queer Theory*. New York: New York University Press, 2003.

Summers, Claude J. Introduction to *The Gay and Lesbian Literary Heritage: A Reader's Companion to the Writers and Their Works, from Antiquity to the Present*, ix–xiv. Edited by Claude J. Summers. New York: Owl Books, 1995.

Suzanne, Miriam. *Riding SideSaddle**. 2016. https://oddbooksapp.com/book/ridingsidesaddle.

——— [Eric M. Suzanne]. *Riding SideSaddle*: A Novel*. Version 1.0. Denver: Spring-Gun Press, 2015.

———. "Some Kind of Manifesto." 2016. Miriam Suzanne's website. http://www.miriamsuzanne.com/why/.

Suzanne, Miriam, Teacup Gorilla, Diana Dresser, and Michael Morgan. *10 Myths on the Proper Application of Beauty Products*. 2016. OddBooks website. https://oddbooksapp.com/book/10-myths.

Swartley, André. *Americanus Rex*. Bluffton, OH: Workplay Publishing, 2009.

———. *The Wretched Afterlife of Odetta Koop*. Newton, KS: Workplay Publishing, 2015.

Taormino, Tristan. "'S Is For . . .': The Terms, Principles, and Pleasures of Kink." In Taormino, *Ultimate*, 3–32.

———, ed. *The Ultimate Guide to Kink: BDSM, Role Play and the Erotic Edge*. Berkeley, CA: Cleis Press, 2012.

Taormino, Tristan, Celine Parreñas Shimizu, Constance Penley, and Mireille Miller-Young, eds. *The Feminist Porn Book: The Politics of Producing Pleasure*. New York: Feminist Press, 2013.

Teichroew, Allan. "Gordon Friesen: Writer, Radical and Ex-Mennonite." *Mennonite Life* 38, no. 2 (1983): 4–17.

Thompson, Dorothy. "Queer People." *Ladies' Home Journal*, January 1952. http://www.swissmennonite.org/feature_archive/2005/200510.html.

Tiessen, Hildi Froese. "Beyond the Binary: Re-inscribing Cultural Identity in the Literature of Mennonites." In Roth and Beck, *Migrant Muses*, 11–21.

———. "Beyond 'What We by Habit or Custom Already Know' or, What Do We Mean When We Talk about Mennonite Writing?" *Mennonite Quarterly Review* 90, no. 1 (2016): 11–27.

———, ed. *11 Encounters with Mennonite Fiction*. Winnipeg: Mennonite Literary Society, 2017.

———. "Introduction: Mennonite Writing and the Post-colonial Condition." In Tiessen and Hinchcliffe, *Acts of Concealment*, 11–21.

———, ed. *Liars and Rascals: Mennonite Short Stories*. Waterloo, ON: University of Waterloo Press, 1989.

———. "Literary Refractions." *Conrad Grebel Review* 17, no. 3 (1999): 66.

164

———, ed. "Mennonite/s Writing in Canada." Special issue, *The New Quarterly* 10, nos. 1–2 (1990).

———, ed. "New Mennonite Writing." Special issue, *Prairie Fire* 11, no. 2 (1990).

Tiessen, Hildi Froese, and Peter Hinchcliffe, eds. *Acts of Concealment: Mennonite/s Writing in Canada*. Waterloo, ON: University of Waterloo Press, 1992.

Tiessen, Paul. "Archival Returns: Rudy Wiebe and the Coming Back of Thom Wiens." In Tiessen, *11 Encounters*, 50–68.

———. "Double Identity: Covering the *Peace Shall Destroy Many* Project." In Zacharias, *After Identity*, 70–85.

———. "'I Want My Story Told': The Sheila Watson Archive, the Reader, and the Search for Voice." In *Basements and Attics, Closets and Cyberspace: Explorations in Canadian Women's Archives*, edited by Linda Morra and Jessica Schagerl, 263–80. Waterloo, ON: Wilfrid Laurier University Press, 2012.

———. "Re-framing the Reaction to *Peace Shall Destroy Many*: Rudy Wiebe, Delbert Wiens, and the Mennonite Brethren." *Mennonite Quarterly Review* 90, no. 1 (2016): 73–102.

Toews, Miriam. *A Complicated Kindness*. New York: Counterpoint, 2005.

———. *Summer of My Amazing Luck*. Rev. ed. New York: Counterpoint, 2006.

Togane, Mohamud S. *The Bottle and the Bushman: Poems of the Prodigal Son*. Ste.-Anne de Bellevue, QC: Muses' Company, 1986.

Trembath, Sean. "Local Author Wes Funk Dead at 46." *Saskatoon StarPhoenix*, 13 October 2015. http://www.thestarphoenix.com/Local+author+Funk+dead/11432193/story.html.

Urban Dictionary, s.v. "riding sidesaddle." Last modified 4 February 2004. Accessed 2 March 2017. http://www.urbandictionary.com/define.php?term=Riding+Sidesaddle&utm_source=search-action.

van Braght, Thieleman J. *The Bloody Theater or Martyrs Mirror of the Defenseless Christians Who Baptized Only Upon Confession of Faith, and Who Suffered and Died for the Testimony of Jesus, Their Saviour, From the Time of Christ to the Year A.D. 1660*. 1660. Translated by Joseph F. Sohm. Scottdale, PA: Herald Press, 1950.

Ward, Jane. "Queer Feminist Pigs: A Spectator's Manifesta." In Taormino, Shimizu, Penley, and Miller-Young, *Feminist Porn*, 130–39.

Waters, Sarah. *Affinity*. London: Virago Press, 1999.

———. *The Night Watch*. New York: Riverhead Books, 2006.

———. *Tipping the Velvet*. London: Virago Press, 1998.

Waugh, Thomas. "Men's Pornography: Gay vs. Straight." In *Out in Culture: Gay, Lesbian, and Queer Essays on Popular Culture*, edited by Corey K. Creekmur and Alexander Doty, 305–27. Durham, NC: Duke University Press, 1995.

Weaver-Zercher, David L. *"Martyrs Mirror": A Social History*. Baltimore: Johns Hopkins University Press, 2016.

———. "Research Note: The 1938 Edition of *Martyrs Mirror*; Why Only Fifty-Five Luyken Images?" *Mennonite Quarterly Review* 91, no. 2 (2017): 247–61.

Weaver-Zercher, Valerie. *Thrill of the Chaste: The Allure of Amish Romance Novels*. Baltimore: Johns Hopkins University Press, 2013.

Wenger, John C. "Funk." In *The Mennonite Encyclopedia*. Vol. 2, 420–421. Scottdale, PA: Herald Press, 1956.

"Who Is Jake Yoder? 10 Minute Investigative Reports on *boneyard*." YouTube video, 29 September 2011. https://www.youtube.com/watch?v=3D7st2wA7kw.

Wideman, Johnny. *This Will Lead to Dancing*. Stouffville, ON: Theatre of the Beat, 2017.

Wiebe, Dallas. "Can a Mennonite Be an Atheist?" *Conrad Grebel Review* 16, no. 3 (1998): 122–32.

———. *Going to the Mountain*. Providence, RI: Burning Deck Press, 1988.

———. "Love in Old Age." *Conrad Grebel Review* 17, no. 3 (1999): 67–71.

———. *On the Cross: Devotional Poems*. Telford, PA: DreamSeeker Books, 2005.

———. *Our Asian Journey*. Waterloo, ON: MLR Editions Canada, 1997.

———. *Skyblue the Badass*. Garden City, NY: Paris Review-Doubleday, 1969.

———. *Skyblue's Essays*. Providence, RI: Burning Deck Press, 1995.

―――. *The Transparent Eye-Ball and Other Stories*. Providence, RI: Burning Deck Press, 1982.

―――. *The Vox Populi Street Stories*. Providence, RI: Burning Deck Press, 2003.

Wiebe, Rudy. *The Blue Mountains of China*. 1970. Toronto: McClelland and Stewart, 1995.

―――. "For the Mennonite Churches: A Last Chance." 1964. In Keith, *A Voice in the Land*, 25–31.

―――. *Of This Earth: A Mennonite Boyhood in the Boreal Forest*. 2006. Intercourse, PA: Good Books, 2007.

―――. *Peace Shall Destroy Many*. Toronto: McClelland and Stewart, 1962.

Workplay Publishing. http://www .workplaypublishing.com/default .html.

Young, Madison. "Submissive: A Personal Manifesto." In Taormino, *Ultimate*, 297–308.

Yutzy, Steven, ed. *Greeting the Dawn: An Anthology of New Mennonite Writing*. Goshen, IN: Pinchpenny Press, 1998.

Zacharias, Robert, ed. *After Identity: Mennonite Writing in North America*. University Park: Pennsylvania State University Press, 2015.

―――. "'A Garden of Spears': Reconsidering the Mennonite/s Writing Project." *Mennonite Quarterly Review* 90, no. 1 (2016): 29–50.

―――. "Introduction: Mennonite/s Writing in North America." In Zacharias, *After Identity*, 1–18.

―――. "The Mennonite Thing: Identity for a Post-identity Age." In Zacharias, *After Identity*, 106–22.

―――. *Rewriting the Break Event: Mennonites and Migration in Canadian Literature*. Winnipeg: University of Manitoba Press, 2013.

Zimmerman, Yvonne C. "Teaching Ethics While Queer and Mennonite." *Conrad Grebel Review* 35, no. 1 (2017): 83–94.

Index

171

Lightning Source UK Ltd.
Milton Keynes UK
UKHW010843210821
389039UK00008B/459